Excel VBA Programming
FOR
DUMMIES®

by John Walkenbach

WILEY

Wiley Publishing, Inc.

Excel VBA Programming For Dummies®

Published by
Wiley Publishing, Inc.
111 River Street
Hoboken, NJ 07030-5774

For general information on our other products and services or to obtain technical support, please contact our Customer Care Department within the U.S. at 800-762-2974, outside the U.S. at 317-572-3993, or fax 317-572-4002.

Wiley also publishes its books in a variety of electronic formats. Some content that appears in print may not be available in electronic books.

Library of Congress Control Number: 2004107892

ISBN: 0-7645-7412-4

Manufactured in the United States of America

10 9 8 7 6 5 4 3 2

1B/QV/QY/QU/IN

WILEY

About the Author

John Walkenbach is the author of more than 40 spreadsheet books and lives in southern Arizona. Visit his Web site at http://j-walk.com.

Author's Acknowledgments

Thanks to all of the talented people at Wiley Publishing for making it so easy to write these books. Special thanks to Dick Kusleika, the technical editor for this book. Dick uncovered quite a few errors and set me straight on a few things.

Publisher's Acknowledgments

We're proud of this book; please send us your comments through our online registration form located at www.dummies.com/register/.

Some of the people who helped bring this book to market include the following:

Acquisitions, Editorial, and Media Development

Project Editor: Beth Taylor

Executive Editor: Greg Croy

Copy Editor: Tonya Cupp

Technical Editor: Dick Kusleika

Editorial Manager: Leah Cameron

Media Development Specialist: Kit Malone

Media Development Manager: Laura VanWinkle

Media Development Supervisor: Richard Graves

Editorial Assistant: Amanda Foxworth

Cartoons: Rich Tennant, www.the5thwave.com

Composition

Project Coordinator: Adrienne Martinez

Layout and Graphics: Amanda Carter, Andrea Dahl, Lauren Goddard, Stephanie D. Jumper, Michael Kruzil, Lynsey Osborn, Jacque Roth

Proofreaders: Laura Albert, TECHBOOKS Production Services

Indexer: TECHBOOKS Production Services

Publishing and Editorial for Technology Dummies

Richard Swadley, Vice President and Executive Group Publisher

Andy Cummings, Vice President and Publisher

Mary Bednarek, Executive Acquisitions Director

Mary C. Corder, Editorial Director

Publishing for Consumer Dummies

Diane Graves Steele, Vice President and Publisher

Joyce Pepple, Acquisitions Director

Composition Services

Gerry Fahey, Vice President of Production Services

Debbie Stailey, Director of Composition Services

Contents at a Glance

Table of Contents

Introduction

*G*reetings, prospective Excel programmer . . .

Thanks for buying my book. I think you'll find that it offers a fast, enjoyable way to discover the ins and outs of Microsoft Excel programming. Even if you don't have the foggiest idea of what programming is all about, this book can help you make Excel jump through hoops in no time (well, it will take *some* time).

Unlike most programming books, this one is written in plain English, and even normal people can understand it. Even better, it's filled with information of the "just the facts, ma'am" variety — and not the drivel you might need once every third lifetime.

Is This the Right Book?

Go to any large bookstore and you'll find many Excel books (far too many, as far as I'm concerned). A quick overview can help you decide whether this book is really right for you. This book

- ✓ Is designed for intermediate to advanced Excel users who want to learn Visual Basic for Applications (VBA) programming.
- ✓ Requires no previous programming experience.
- ✓ Covers the most commonly used commands.
- ✓ Is appropriate for Excel 2000 through Excel 2003. Fact is, there are very few significant differences among Excel 2000, Excel 2002, and Excel 2003.
- ✓ Just might make you crack a smile occasionally — it even has cartoons.

If you are using Excel 5, Excel 95, or Excel 97, this book is not for you. Although there are many similarities between the current version of Excel and previous versions, there are also many subtle (and not-so-subtle) differences that can be perplexing and can likely confuse you. If you're still using a pre-2000 version of Excel, locate a book that is specific to that version. Or consider upgrading your copy of Excel.

This is *not* an introductory Excel book. If you're looking for a general-purpose Excel book, check out any of the following books, which are all published by Wiley:

- *Excel 2003 For Dummies,* by Greg Harvey
- *Excel 2003 Bible,* by John Walkenbach (yep, that's me)
- *Excel 2003 For Dummies Quick Reference,* by John Walkenbach (me again) and Colin Banfield

Notice that the title of this book isn't *The Complete Guide to Excel VBA Programming For Dummies.* I don't cover all aspects of Excel programming — but then again, you probably don't want to know *everything* about this topic. In the unlikely event you want a more comprehensive Excel programming book, you might try *Microsoft Excel 2003 Power Programming with VBA,* by John Walkenbach (is this guy prolific, or what?), also published by Wiley Publishing.

So You Want to Be a Programmer . . .

Besides earning money to pay my bills, my main goal in writing this book is to teach Excel users how to use the VBA language — a tool that helps you significantly enhance the power of the world's most popular spreadsheet. Using VBA, however, involves programming. (Yikes! The *p* word.)

If you're like most computer users, the word *programmer* conjures up an image of someone who looks and behaves nothing like you. Perhaps words such as *nerd, geek,* and *dweeb* come to mind.

Times have changed. Computer programming has become much easier, and even so-called normal people now engage in this activity. *Programming* simply means developing instructions that the computer automatically carries out. *Excel programming* refers to the fact that you can instruct Excel to automatically do things that you normally do manually — saving you lots of time and (you hope) reducing errors. I could go on, but I need to save some good stuff for Chapter 1.

If you've read this far, it's a safe bet that you need to become an Excel programmer. This could be something you came up with yourself or (more likely) something your boss decided. In this book, I tell you enough about Excel programming so that you won't feel like an idiot the next time you're trapped in a conference room with a group of Excel aficionados. And by the time you finish this book, you can honestly say, "Yeah, I do some Excel programming."

Why Bother?

Most Excel users never bother to learn VBA programming. Your interest in this topic definitely places you among an elite group. Welcome to the fold! If you're still not convinced that learning Excel programming is a good idea, I've come up with a few good reasons why you might want to take the time to learn VBA programming.

- **It will make you more marketable.** Like it or not, Microsoft's applications are extremely popular. You may already know that all applications in Microsoft Office support VBA. The more you know about VBA, the better your chances for advancement in your job.

- **It lets you get the most out of your software investment** (or, more likely, your *employer's* software investment). Using Excel without knowing VBA is sort of like buying a TV set and watching only the odd-numbered channels.

- **It will improve your productivity (eventually).** Learning VBA definitely takes some time, but you'll more than make up for this in the amount of time you ultimately save because you're more productive. Sort of like what they told you about going to college.

- **It's fun (well, sometimes).** Some people really enjoy making Excel do things that are otherwise impossible. By the time you finish this book, you just might be one of those people.

Now are you convinced?

What I Assume about You

People who write books usually have a target reader in mind. For this book, my target reader is a conglomerate of dozens of Excel users I've met over the years (either in person or out in cyberspace). The following points more or less describe my hypothetical target reader:

- You have access to a PC at work — and probably at home.

- You're running Excel 2000 or later.

- You've been using computers for several years.

- You use Excel frequently in your work, and you consider yourself to be more knowledgeable about Excel than the average bear.

- You need to make Excel do some things that you currently can't make it do.

- You have little or no programming experience.

- You understand that the Help system in Excel can actually be useful. Face it, this book doesn't cover everything. If you get on good speaking terms with the Help system, you'll be able to fill in some of the missing pieces.

- You need to accomplish some work, and you have a low tolerance for thick, boring computer books.

Obligatory Typographical Conventions Section

All computer books have a section like this. (I think some federal law requires it.) Read it or skip it.

Sometimes, I refer to key combinations — which means you hold down one key while you press another. For example, Ctrl+Z means you hold down the Ctrl key while you press Z.

For menu commands, I use a distinctive character to separate menu items. For example, you use the following command to open a workbook file:

File⇨Open

Excel programming involves developing *code* — that is, the instructions Excel follows. All code in this book appears in a monospace font, like this:

```
Range("A1:A12").Select
```

Some long lines of code don't fit between the margins in this book. In such cases, I use the standard VBA line continuation character sequence: a space followed by an underscore character. Here's an example:

```
Selection.PasteSpecial Paste:=xlValues, _
   Operation:=xlNone, SkipBlanks:=False, _
   Transpose:=False
```

When you enter this code, you can type it as written or place it on a single line (omitting the spaces and the underscore characters).

Check Your Security Settings

It's a cruel world out there. It seems that some scam artist is always trying to take advantage of you or cause some type of problem. The world of computing is equally cruel. You probably know about computer viruses, which can cause some nasty things to happen to your system. But did you know that computer viruses can also reside in an Excel file? It's true. In fact, it's relatively easy to write a computer virus using VBA. An unknowing user can open an Excel file and spread the virus to other Excel workbooks.

Over the years, Microsoft has become increasingly concerned about security issues. This is a good thing, but it also means that Excel users need to understand how things work. You can check Excel's security settings by using the Tools ⇨ Macro ⇨ Security command. Your options are Very High, High, Medium, and Low. Check Excel's Help system for details on these settings.

Consider this scenario: You spend a week writing a killer VBA program that will revolutionize your company. You test it thoroughly, and then send it to your boss. He calls you into his office and claims that your macro doesn't do anything at all. What's going on? Chances are, your boss's security setting does not allow macros to run. Or, maybe he chose to disable the macros when he opened the file.

Bottom line? Just because an Excel workbook contains a macro it is no guarantee that the macro will ever be executed. It all depends on the security setting and whether the user chooses to enable or disable macros for that file.

In order to work with this book, you will need to enable macros for the files you work with. My advice is to use the Medium security level. Then, when you open a file that you've created, you can simply enable the macros. If you open a file from someone you don't know, you should disable the macros and check the VBA code to ensure that it doesn't contain anything destructive or malicious.

How This Book Is Organized

I divided this book into seven major parts, each of which contains several chapters. Although I arranged the chapters in a fairly logical sequence, you can read them in any order you choose. Here's a quick preview of what's in store for you.

Part 1: Introducing VBA

Part I has but two chapters. I introduce the VBA language in the first chapter. In Chapter 2, I let you get your feet wet right away by taking you on a hands-on guided tour.

Part 11: How VBA Works with Excel

In writing this book, I assumed that you already know how to use Excel. The four chapters in Part II give you a better grasp on how VBA is implemented in Excel. These chapters are all important, so I don't recommend skipping past them, okay?

Part 111: Programming Concepts

The eight chapters in Part III get you into the nitty-gritty of what programming is all about. You may not need to know all this stuff, but you'll be glad it's there if you ever do need it.

Part 1V: Developing Custom Dialog Boxes

One of the coolest parts of programming in Excel is designing custom dialog boxes (well, at least *I* like it). The four chapters in Part IV show you how to create dialog boxes that look like they came straight from the software lab at Microsoft.

Part V: Creating Custom Toolbars and Menus

Part V has two chapters, both of which address *user interface* topics. One chapter deals with creating custom menus; the other describes how to customize toolbars.

Part V1: Putting 1t All Together

The four chapters in Part VI pull together information from the preceding chapters. You find out how to develop custom worksheet functions, create add-ins, design user-oriented applications, and even work with other Office applications.

Part VII: The Part of Tens

Traditionally, books in the *For Dummies* series contain a final part that consists of short chapters containing helpful or informative lists. Because I'm a sucker for tradition, this book has two such chapters that you can peruse at your convenience. (If you're like most readers, you'll turn to this part first.)

Marginal Icons

Somewhere along the line, a market research company must have shown that publishers can sell more copies of their computer books if they add icons to the margins of those books. *Icons* are those little pictures that supposedly draw your attention to various features, or help you decide whether something is worth reading.

I don't know if this research is valid, but I'm not taking any chances. So here are the icons you'll encounter in your travels from front cover to back cover:

When you see this icon, the code being discussed is available on the Web. Download it, and eliminate lots of typing. See "Get the Sample Files," below, for more information.

This icon flags material you might consider technical. You might find it interesting, but you can safely skip it if you're in a hurry.

Don't skip information marked with this icon. It identifies a shortcut that can save you lots of time (and maybe even allow you to leave the office at a reasonable hour).

This icon tells you when you need to store information in the deep recesses of your brain for later use.

Read anything marked with this icon. Otherwise, you may lose your data, blow up your computer, cause a nuclear meltdown — or maybe even ruin your whole day.

Get the Sample Files

This book has its very own Web site where you can download the example files discussed and view Bonus Chapters. To get these files, point your Web browser to:

`www.dummies.com/go/excelvba.`

Having the sample files will save you a lot of typing. Better yet, you can play around with them and experiment with various changes. In fact, I highly recommend playing around with these files. Experimentation is the best way to learn VBA.

Now What?

Reading this introduction was your first step. Now, it's time to move on and become a programmer (there's that *p* word again!).

If you're a programming virgin, I strongly suggest that you start with Chapter 1 and progress in chapter order until you've discovered enough. Chapter 2 gives you some immediate hands-on experience, so you'll have the illusion that you're making quick progress.

But it's a free country (at least it was when I wrote these words); I won't sic the Computer Book Police on you if you opt to thumb through randomly and read whatever strikes your fancy.

I hope you have as much fun reading this book as I did writing it.

Part I
Introducing VBA

The 5th Wave   By Rich Tennant

"We're here to clean the code."

In this part . . .

*E*very book must start somewhere. This one starts by introducing you to Visual Basic for Applications (and I'm sure you two will become very good friends over the course of a few dozen chapters). After the introductions are made, Chapter 2 walks you through a real-live Excel programming session.

Chapter 1

What Is VBA?

*T*his chapter is completely devoid of any hands-on training material. It does, however, contain some essential background information that assists you in becoming an Excel programmer. In other words, this chapter paves the way for everything else that follows and gives you a feel for how Excel programming fits into the overall scheme of the universe.

Okay, So What Is VBA?

VBA, which stands for *Visual Basic for Applications,* is a programming language developed by Microsoft — you know, the company run by the richest man in the world. Excel, along with the other members of Microsoft Office 2003, includes the VBA language (at no extra charge). In a nutshell, VBA is the tool that people like you and me use to develop programs that control Excel.

Don't confuse VBA with VB (which stands for Visual Basic). VB is a programming language that lets you create standalone executable programs (those EXE files). Although VBA and VB have a lot in common, they are different animals.

A few words about terminology

Excel programming terminology can be a bit confusing. For example, VBA is a programming language, but it also serves as a macro language. What do you call something written in VBA and executed in Excel? Is it a *macro* or is it a *program?* Excel's Help system often refers to VBA procedures as *macros,* so I use that terminology. But I also call this stuff a *program.*

I use the term *automate* throughout this book. This term means that a series of steps is completed automatically. For example, if you write a macro that adds color to some cells, prints the worksheet, and then removes the color, you have *automated* those three steps.

By the way, *macro* does not stand for Messy And Confusing Repeated Operation. Rather, it comes from the Greek *makros,* which means large — which also describes your paycheck after you become an expert macro programmer.

What Can You Do with VBA?

You're probably aware that people use Excel for thousands of different tasks. Here are just a few examples:

- Keeping lists of things such as customer names, students' grades, or holiday gift ideas
- Budgeting and forecasting
- Analyzing scientific data
- Creating invoices and other forms
- Developing charts from data
- Yadda, yadda, yadda

The list could go on and on, but I think you get the idea. My point is simply that Excel is used for a wide variety of things, and everyone reading this book has different needs and expectations regarding Excel. One thing virtually every reader has in common is the *need to automate some aspect of Excel.* That, dear reader, is what VBA is all about.

For example, you might create a VBA program to format and print your month-end sales report. After developing and testing the program, you can execute the macro with a single command, causing Excel to automatically perform many time-consuming procedures. Rather than struggle through a tedious sequence of commands, you can grab a cup of joe and let your computer do the work — which is how it's supposed to be, right?

In the following sections, I briefly describe some common uses for VBA macros. One or two of these may push your button.

Inserting a text string

If you often need to enter your company name into worksheets, you can create a macro to do the typing for you. You can extend this concept as far as you like. For example, you might develop a macro that automatically types a list of all salespeople who work for your company.

Automating a task you perform frequently

Assume you're a sales manager and need to prepare a month-end sales report to keep your boss happy. If the task is straightforward, you can develop a VBA program to do it for you. Your boss will be impressed by the consistently high quality of your reports, and you'll be promoted to a new job for which you are highly unqualified.

Automating repetitive operations

If you need to perform the same action on, say, 12 different Excel workbooks, you can record a macro while you perform the task on the first workbook and then let the macro repeat your action on the other workbooks. The nice thing about this is that Excel never complains about being bored. Excel's macro recorder is similar to recording sound on a tape recorder. But it doesn't require a microphone.

Creating a custom command

Do you often issue the same sequence of Excel menu commands? If so, save yourself a few seconds by developing a macro that combines these commands into a single custom command, which you can execute with a single keystroke or button click.

Creating a custom toolbar button

You can customize the Excel toolbars with your own buttons that execute the macros you write. Office workers tend to be very impressed by this sort of thing.

Creating a custom menu command

You can also customize Excel's menus with your own commands that execute macros you write. Office workers are even more impressed by this.

Creating a simplified front end

In almost any office, you can find lots of people who don't really understand how to use computers. (Sound familiar?) Using VBA, you can make it easy for these inexperienced users to perform some useful work. For example, you can set up a foolproof data-entry template so you don't have to waste *your* time doing mundane work.

Developing new worksheet functions

Although Excel includes numerous built-in functions (such as SUM and AVERAGE), you can create *custom* worksheet functions that can greatly simplify your formulas. I guarantee you'll be surprised by how easy this is. (I show you how to do this in Chapter 21.) Even better, the Insert Function dialog box displays your custom functions, making them appear built in. Very snazzy stuff.

Creating complete, macro-driven applications

If you're willing to spend some time, you can use VBA to create large-scale applications complete with custom dialog boxes, onscreen help, and lots of other accoutrements.

Creating custom add-ins for Excel

You're probably familiar with some of the add-ins that ship with Excel. For example, the Analysis ToolPak is a popular add-in. You can use VBA to develop your own special-purpose add-ins. I developed my Power Utility Pak add-in using only VBA.

Advantages and Disadvantages of VBA

In this section I briefly describe the good things about VBA — and I also explore its darker side.

VBA advantages

You can automate almost anything you do in Excel. To do so, you write instructions that Excel carries out. Automating a task by using VBA offers several advantages:

- Excel always executes the task in exactly the same way. (In most cases, consistency is a good thing.)

- Excel performs the task much faster than you could do it manually (unless, of course, you're Clark Kent).

- If you're a good macro programmer, Excel always performs the task without errors (which probably can't be said about you or me).

- The task can be performed by someone who doesn't know anything about Excel.

- You can do things in Excel that are otherwise impossible — which can make you a very popular person around the office.

- For long, time-consuming tasks, you don't have to sit in front of your computer and get bored. Excel does the work, while you hang out at the water cooler.

VBA disadvantages

It's only fair that I give equal time to listing the disadvantages (or *potential* disadvantages) of VBA:

- You have to learn how to write programs in VBA (but that's why you bought this book, right?). Fortunately, it's not as difficult as you might expect.

- Other people who need to use your VBA programs must have their own copies of Excel. It would be nice if you could press a button that transforms your Excel/VBA application into a stand-alone program, but that isn't possible (and probably never will be).

A personal anecdote

Excel programming has its own challenges and frustrations. One of my earlier books, *Excel 5 For Windows Power Programming Techniques,* included a disk containing the examples from the book. I compressed these files so that they would fit on a single disk. Trying to be clever, I wrote a VBA program to expand the files and copy them to the appropriate directories. I spent a lot of time writing and debugging the code, and I tested it thoroughly on three different computers.

Imagine my surprise when I started receiving e-mail from readers who could not install the files. With a bit of sleuthing, I eventually discovered that the readers who were having the problem had all upgraded to Excel 5.0c. (I developed my installation program using Excel 5.0a.) It turns out that the Excel 5.0c upgrade featured a very subtle change that caused my macro to bomb. Because I'm not privy to Microsoft's plans, I didn't anticipate this problem. Needless to say, this author suffered lots of embarrassment and had to e-mail corrections to hundreds of frustrated readers.

✔ Sometimes, things go wrong. In other words, you can't blindly assume that your VBA program will always work correctly under all circumstances. Welcome to the world of debugging.

✔ VBA is a moving target. As you know, Microsoft is continually upgrading Excel. You may discover that VBA code you've written doesn't work properly with a future version of Excel. Take it from me; I discovered this the hard way, as detailed in the "A personal anecdote" sidebar.

VBA in a Nutshell

A quick and dirty summary follows of what VBA is all about. Of course, I describe all this stuff in semiexcruciating detail later in the book.

✔ **You perform actions in VBA by writing (or recording) code in a VBA module.** You view and edit VBA modules using the Visual Basic Editor (VBE).

✔ **A VBA module consists of Sub procedures.** A Sub procedure has nothing to do with underwater vessels or tasty sandwiches. Rather, it's computer code that performs some action on or with objects (discussed in a moment). The following example shows a simple Sub procedure called Test. This amazing program displays the result of 1 plus 1.

```
Sub Test()
    Sum = 1 + 1
    MsgBox "The answer is " & Sum
End Sub
```

✔ **A VBA module can also have Function procedures.** A Function procedure returns a single value. You can call it from another VBA procedure or even use it as a function in a worksheet formula. An example of a Function procedure (named AddTwo) follows. This Function accepts two numbers (called arguments) and returns the sum of those values.

```
Function AddTwo(arg1, arg2)
    AddTwo = arg1 + arg2
End Function
```

✔ **VBA manipulates objects.** Excel provides more than 100 objects that you can manipulate. Examples of objects include a workbook, a worksheet, a cell range, a chart, and a shape. You have many, many more objects at your disposal, and you can manipulate them using VBA code.

✔ **Objects are arranged in a hierarchy.** Objects can act as *containers* for other objects. At the top of the object hierarchy is Excel. Excel itself is an object called Application, and it contains other objects such as Workbook objects and CommandBar objects. The Workbook object can contain other objects, such as Worksheet objects and Chart objects. A Worksheet object can contain objects such as Range objects and PivotTable objects. The term *object model* refers to the arrangement of these objects. (See Chapter 4 for details.)

✔ **Objects of the same type form a collection.** For example, the Worksheets collection consists of all the worksheets in a particular workbook. The Charts collection consists of all Chart objects in a workbook. Collections are themselves objects.

✔ **You refer to an object by specifying its position in the object hierarchy, using a dot as a separator.** For example, you can refer to the workbook Book1.xls as

```
Application.Workbooks("Book1.xls")
```

This refers to the workbook Book1.xls in the Workbooks collection. The Workbooks collection is contained in the Application object (that is, Excel). Extending this to another level, you can refer to Sheet1 in Book1.xls as

```
Application.Workbooks("Book1.xls").Worksheets("Sheet1")
```

As shown in the following example, you can take this to still another level and refer to a specific cell (in this case, cell A1):

```
Application.Workbooks("Book1.xls").Worksheets("Sheet1").R
        ange("A1")
```

✔ **If you omit specific references, Excel uses the *active* objects.** If Book1.xls is the active workbook, you can simplify the preceding reference as follows:

```
Worksheets("Sheet1").Range("A1")
```

If you know that Sheet1 is the active sheet, you can simplify the reference even more:

```
Range("A1")
```

✏ **Objects have properties.** You can think of a property as a *setting* for an object. For example, a Range object has such properties as Value and Address. A Chart object has such properties as HasTitle and Type. You can use VBA to determine object properties and to change properties.

✏ **You refer to a property of an object by combining the object name with the property name, separated by a period.** For example, you can refer to the value in cell A1 on Sheet1 as follows:

```
Worksheets("Sheet1").Range("A1").Value
```

✏ **You can assign values to variables.** A *variable* is a named element that stores things. You can use variables in your VBA code to store such things as values, text, or property settings. To assign the value in cell A1 on Sheet1 to a variable called *Interest,* use the following VBA statement:

```
Interest = Worksheets("Sheet1").Range("A1").Value
```

✏ **Objects have methods.** A *method* is an action Excel performs with an object. For example, one of the methods for a Range object is ClearContents. This method clears the contents of the range.

✏ **You specify a method by combining the object with the method, separated by a dot.** For example, the following statement clears the contents of cell A1:

```
Worksheets("Sheet1").Range("A1").ClearContents
```

✏ **VBA includes all the constructs of modern programming languages, including arrays and looping.**

Believe it or not, the preceding list pretty much describes VBA in a nutshell. Now you just have to find out the details. That's the purpose of the rest of this book.

An Excursion into Versions

If you plan to develop VBA macros, you should have some understanding of Excel's history. I know you weren't expecting a history lesson, but this is important stuff.

Here are all the major Excel for Windows versions that have seen the light of day, along with a few words about how they handle macros:

- ✔ **Excel 2:** The original version of Excel for Windows was called Version 2 (rather than 1) so that it would correspond to the Macintosh version. Excel 2 first appeared in 1987 and nobody uses it anymore, so you can pretty much forget that it ever existed.

- ✔ **Excel 3:** Released in late 1990, this version features the XLM macro language. A few people live in a time warp and still use this version.

- ✔ **Excel 4:** This version hit the streets in early 1992. It also uses the XLM macro language. A fair number of people still use this version. (They subscribe to the philosophy *if it ain't broke, don't fix it*.)

- ✔ **Excel 5:** This one came out in early 1994. It was the first version to use VBA (but it also supports XLM). Many people continue to use this version because they are reluctant to move up to Windows 95.

- ✔ **Excel 95:** Technically known as Excel 7 (there is no Excel 6), this version began shipping in the summer of 1995. It's a 32-bit version and requires Windows 95 or Windows NT. It has a few VBA enhancements, and it supports the XLM language. Excel 95 uses the same file format as Excel 5.

- ✔ **Excel 97:** This version (also known as Excel 8) was born in January 1997. It requires Windows 95 or Windows NT. It has *many* enhancements and features an entirely new interface for programming VBA macros. Excel 97 also uses a new file format (which previous Excel versions cannot open).

- ✔ **Excel 2000:** This version's numbering scheme jumped to four digits. Excel 2000 (also known as Excel 9) made its public debut in June 1999. It includes only a few enhancements from a programmer's perspective, with most enhancements being for users — particularly online users.

- ✔ **Excel 2002:** This version (also known as Excel 10 or Excel XP) appeared in late 2001. Perhaps this version's most significant feature is the ability to recover your work when Excel crashes. This is also the first version to use copy protection (known as *product activation*).

- ✔ **Excel 2003:** As I write this book, this is the current version and it is also known as Excel 11. Of all the Excel upgrades I've ever seen (and I've seen them all), Excel 2003 has the fewest new features. In other words, most hard-core Excel users (including yours truly) were very disappointed with Excel 2003.

So what's the point of this mini history lesson? If you plan to distribute your Excel/VBA files to other users, it's vitally important that you understand which version of Excel they use. People using an older version won't be able to take advantage of features introduced in later versions. For example, VBA's Split function was introduced in Excel 2000. If your VBA code uses this function, those running an earlier version of Excel will have problems. Specifically, they will see a "compile error" message, and nothing executes.

Chapter 2

Jumping Right In

- -

In This Chapter

▶ Developing a useful VBA macro: A hands-on, step-by-step example

▶ Recording your actions using the Excel macro recorder

▶ Examining and testing recorded code

▶ Changing recorded macro

- -

I'm not much of a swimmer, but I have learned that the best way to get into a cold body of water is to jump right in — no sense prolonging the agony. By wading through this chapter, you can get your feet wet immediately but avoid getting in over your head. By the time you reach the end of this chapter, you just might start feeling better about this whole programming business. This chapter provides a step-by-step demonstration of how to develop a simple but useful VBA macro.

What You'll Be Doing

In this example, you create an Excel macro that converts selected formulas to their current values. Sure, you can do this without a macro, but it's a multi-step procedure.

To convert a range of formulas to values, you normally complete the following steps:

1. **Select the range that contains the formulas to be converted.**

2. **Copy the range to the Clipboard.**

3. **Choose Edit⇨Paste Special.**

4. **Click the Values option button in the Paste Special dialog box, which is shown in Figure 2-1.**

5. **Click OK.**

6. **Press Esc.**

This clears the cut-copy mode indicator (the moving border) in the worksheet.

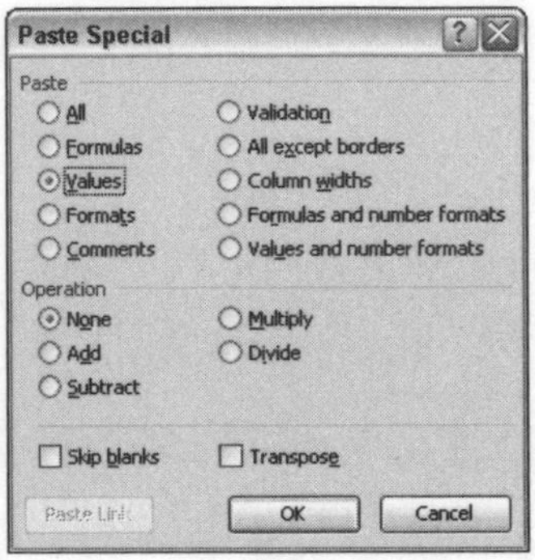

Figure 2-1:
Use the
Values
option in the
Paste
Special
dialog box
to copy
formulas as
values.

The macro you create in this chapter accomplishes all these steps in a single action. As I describe in the following sections, you start by recording your actions as you go through these steps. Then you test the macro to see whether it works. Finally, you edit the macro to add some finishing touches. Ready?

Taking the First Steps

This section describes the preparations you take prior to recording the macro. In other words, you need to take the following steps before the fun begins:

1. **Start Excel if it's not already running.**

2. **Open a new workbook.**

3. **Enter some values and formulas into the worksheet.**

   It doesn't matter what you enter. This step simply provides something to work with.

Figure 2-2 shows how my workbook looks at this point. I created this data by using the RAND function, which generates random numbers. Specifically, the cells in the range A3: D10 contain this formula:

```
=RAND()*$A$1
```

So, cell A1 contains a value and the other cells contain a formula.

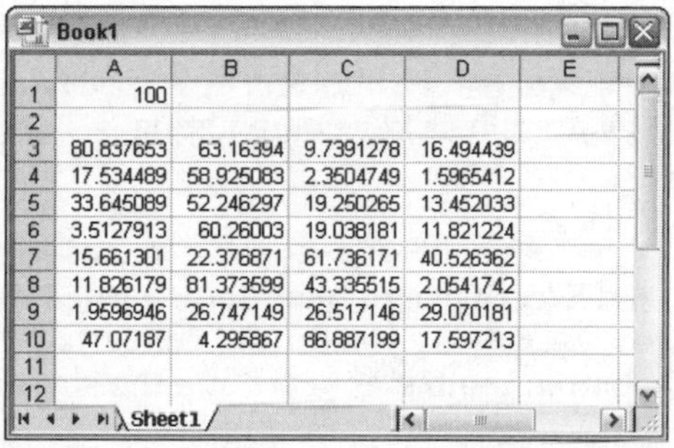

Figure 2-2:
My
worksheet's
sample
values and
formulas.

Recording the Macro

Here comes the hands-on part. Follow these instructions carefully:

1. **Select the range of cells that contains your formulas.**

   The selection can include both values and formulas. In my case, I chose the range A1:D10.

2. **Choose Tools⇨Macro⇨Record New Macro.**

   The Record Macro dialog box appears, as shown in Figure 2-3.

3. **Enter a name for the macro.**

   Excel provides a default name, but it's better to use a more descriptive name. ConvertFormulas is a good name for this one.

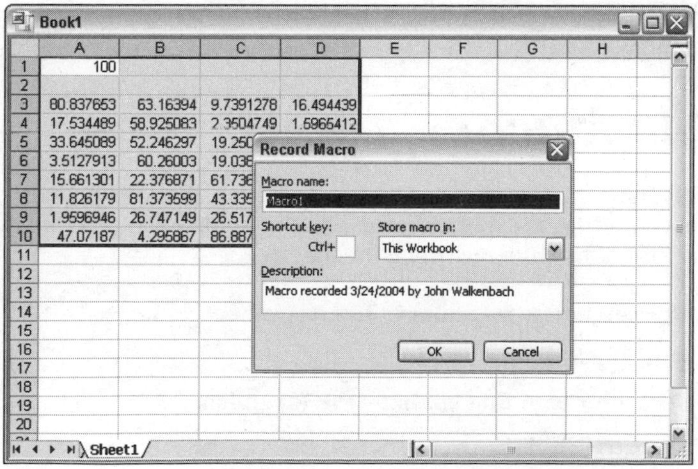

Figure 2-3:
The Record
Macro
dialog box
appears
when you're
about to
record a
macro.

4. **Enter Shift+C (for an uppercase C) as the shortcut key combo.**

   Click in the Shortcut Key box to enter a shortcut key. Specifying one lets you execute the macro by pressing a key combination — in this case, Ctrl+Shift+C.

5. **Click OK.**

   The dialog box closes and Excel's macro recorder is turned on. From this point, Excel monitors everything you do and converts it to VBA code. Notice that a two-button toolbar appears and the status bar displays *Recording*.

6. **Choose Edit⇨Copy (or press Ctrl+C).**

   This copies the selected range of cells to the Clipboard.

7. **Choose Edit⇨Paste Special.**

   Excel displays the Paste Special dialog box.

8. **Click the Values option.**

9. **Click OK to close the dialog box.**

10. **Press Esc to cancel the Excel cut-copy mode indicator.**

    The moving border (which is Excel's way of telling you that data is ready to be copied) is removed from the selection.

11. **Choose Tools⇨Macro⇨Stop Recording, or click the Stop Recording button on the mini-toolbar that's floating on your screen.**

    The macro recorder is turned off.

Congratulations! You just created your first Excel VBA macro. You might want to phone your mother and tell her the good news.

Testing the Macro

Now you can try out this macro and see whether it works properly. To test your macro, add some more formulas to the worksheet. (You wiped out the original formulas while recording the macro.)

1. **Enter some new formulas in the worksheet.**

   Again, any formulas will do.

2. **Select the range that contains the formulas.**

3. **Press Ctrl+Shift+C.**

In a flash, Excel executes the macro. The macro converts all the formulas in the selected range to their current values.

Another way to execute the macro is to choose the Tools⇨Macro⇨Macros command (or press Alt+F8) to display the Macros dialog box. Select the macro from the list (in this case, ConvertFormulas) and click Run. Make sure you select the range to be converted before executing the macro.

Examining the Macro

So far, you've recorded a macro and tested it. And if you're a curious type, you're probably wondering what this macro looks like.

Excel stores the recorded macro in the workbook, but you can't actually view the macro in Excel. To view or modify a macro, you must activate the Visual Basic Editor (VBE, for short).

Follow these steps to see the macro:

1. **Choose Tools⇨Macro⇨Visual Basic Editor (or press Alt+F11).**

    The Visual Basic Editor program window appears, as shown in Figure 2-4. This window is highly customizable, so your VBE window may look different. The VBE program window contains several other windows and is probably very intimidating. Don't fret; you'll get used to it.

2. **In the VBE window, locate the window called Project.**

    The Project window (also known as the Project Explorer window) contains a list of all workbooks that are currently open. Each project is arranged as a *tree* and can be expanded (to show more information) or contracted (to show less information).

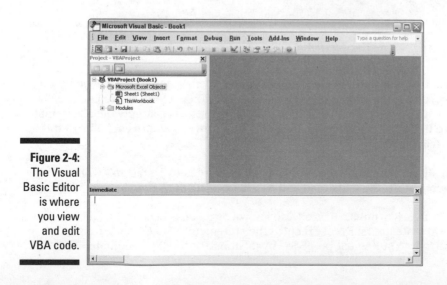

Figure 2-4:
The Visual
Basic Editor
is where
you view
and edit
VBA code.

The VBE uses quite a few different windows, any of which can be either open or closed. If a window isn't immediately visible in the VBE, you can choose an option from the View menu to display the window. For instance, if the Project window is not visible, you can choose View➪Project Explorer (or press Ctrl+R) to display it. You can display any other VBE window in a similar manner.

3. **Select the project that corresponds to the workbook in which you recorded the macro.**

    If you haven't saved the workbook, the project is probably called VBAProject (Book1).

4. **Click the plus sign (+) to the left of the folder named Modules.**

    The tree expands to show Module1, which is the only module in the project.

5. **Double-click Module1.**

    The VBA code in that module is displayed in a Code window. Figure 2-5 shows how it looks on my screen. Because the VBE program window is highly customizable, your screen may not look exactly the same.

The code in Module1 should look like this:

```
Sub ConvertFormulas()
'
' ConvertFormulas Macro
' Macro recorded 3/24/2004 by John Walkenbach
'
' Keyboard Shortcut: Ctrl+Shift+C
'
    Selection.Copy
    Selection.PasteSpecial Paste:=xlValues, _
        Operation:=xlNone, SkipBlanks:=False, _
        Transpose:=False
    Application.CutCopyMode = False
End Sub
```

Notice that this listing looks just a bit different than what you see on your screen and from what is shown in Figure 2-5. (Take a look at the lines beginning with `Selection.PasteSpecial`.) The lines have simply been reformatted to fit on the printed page. The only difference is where each line of the macro is divided.

At this point, the macro probably looks like Greek to you. Don't worry. Travel a few chapters down the road and all will be as clear as the view from Olympus.

The ConvertFormulas macro (also known as a *Sub procedure*) consists of several statements. Excel executes the statements one by one, from top to bottom. A statement preceded by an apostrophe (') is a comment.

Comments are included only for your information and are essentially ignored. In other words, Excel doesn't execute comments.

The first actual VBA statement (which begins with the word *Sub*) identifies the macro as a Sub procedure and gives its name — you provided this name before you started recording the macro. The next statement tells Excel to copy the cells in the selection. The next statement corresponds to the options you selected in the Paste Special dialog box. (This statement occupies two lines, using VBA's line continuation character — a space followed by an underscore.) The next statement cancels the Excel cut-copy mode indicator. The last statement simply signals the end of the macro subroutine.

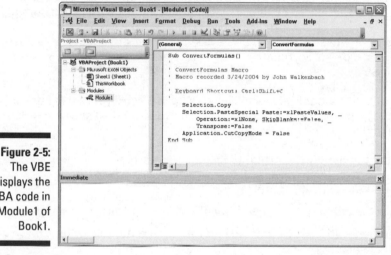

Figure 2-5:
The VBE displays the VBA code in Module1 of Book1.

Hey, I didn't record that!

I've noted that the macro recorder is like recording sound on a tape recorder. When you play back an audio tape and listen to you own voice, you invariably say "I don't sound like that." And when you look at your recorded macro, you may see some actions that you didn't think you recorded.

When you recorded the ConvertFormulas example, you didn't change the Operation, SkipBlanks, or Transpose options in the Paste Special dialog box, yet the recorder still recorded them. Don't worry, it happens all the time. When you record an action that includes a dialog box, Excel records all of the options in the dialog box, not just the ones that you change. In later chapters, you'll learn how to remove the extra stuff from a recorded macro.

Modifying the Macro

The macro you've created is fairly useful, saving you a few seconds every time you need to convert formulas to values — but it's also dangerous. After you execute this macro, you may notice that you can't choose the Edit⇨Undo command. In other words, if you execute this macro accidentally, you have no way to convert the values back to the original formulas. (Actually, you can develop macros that can be undone with the Edit⇨Undo command. That, however, is a bit beyond the scope of this book.)

In this section, you make a minor addition to the macro to prompt users to verify their intentions before the formula-to-value conversion takes place. Issuing such a warning isn't completely foolproof, but it's better than nothing.

You need to provide a pop-up message asking the user to confirm the macro by clicking Yes or No. Fortunately, a VBA statement exists that lets you do this quite easily.

Working in a VBA module is much like working in a word-processing document (except there's no word wrap). You can press Enter to start a new line and the familiar editing keys work as expected.

Here's how you modify the macro to include the warning:

1. **In the VBE, activate Module1.**

2. **Place the cursor at the beginning of the** Selection.Copy **statement.**

3. **Press Enter to insert a new line and then type the following VBA statements:**

```
Answer = MsgBox("Convert formulas to values?", vbYesNo)
If Answer <> vbYes Then Exit Sub
```

To make the new statements line up with the existing statements, press Tab before typing the new statements. Indenting text is optional but it makes your macros easier to read. Your macro should now look like the example in Figure 2-6.

These new statements cause Excel to display a message box with two buttons: Yes and No. The user's button click is stored in a variable named Answer. If the Answer is not equal to Yes, Excel exits the subroutine with no further action (<> represents *not equal to*). Figure 2-7 shows this message box in action.

Activate a worksheet and try out the revised macro to see how it works. To test your macro, you may need to add some more formulas to your worksheet.

Just as you can press Alt+F11 to display the VBE, you can again press Alt+F11 to switch back to Excel.

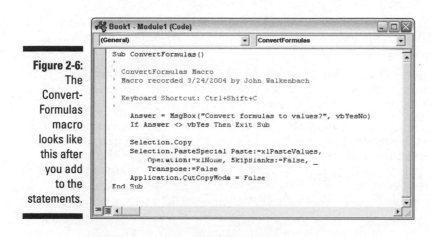

Figure 2-6:
The
Convert-
Formulas
macro
looks like
this after
you add
to the
statements.

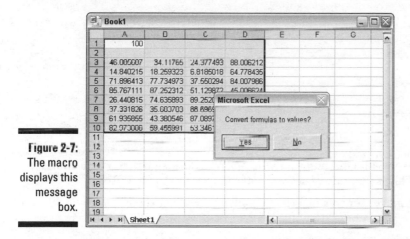

Figure 2-7:
The macro
displays this
message
box.

You'll find that clicking the No button cancels the macro, and that the formulas in the selection remain intact. When you click the No button, Excel executes the *Exit Sub* part of the statement. If you click Yes, the macro continues its normal course of action.

If you find this macro useful, save the workbook file.

More about the ConvertFormulas Macro

By the time you finish this book, you'll completely understand how the ConvertFormulas macro works — and you'll be able to develop more-sophisticated macros. For now, I wrap up the example with a few additional points about the macro:

✔ For this macro to work, its workbook must be open. If you close the workbook, the macro doesn't work (and the Ctrl+Shift+C shortcut has no effect).

✔ As long as the workbook containing the macro is open, you can run the macro while any workbook is active. In other words, the macro's own workbook doesn't have to be active.

✔ The macro isn't perfect. One of its flaws is that it generates an error if the selection isn't a range. For instance, if you select a chart and then press Ctrl+Shift+C, the macro grinds to a halt and you see the error message shown in Figure 2-8. In Chapter 14, I show you how to correct this type of problem.

Figure 2-8:
The error message is VBA's way of telling you something's wrong.

Microsoft Visual Basic

Run-time error '438':

Object doesn't support this property or method

| Continue | End | Debug | Help |

✔ Before you started recording the macro, you assigned it a new shortcut key. This is just one of several ways to execute the macro.

✔ You could enter this macro manually rather than record it. To do so, you need a good understanding of VBA. (Be patient, you'll get there.)

✔ The two statements you added after the fact are examples of VBA statements that you *cannot* record.

✔ You could store this macro in your Personal Macro Workbook. If you were to do so, the macro would be available automatically whenever you start Excel. See Chapter 6 for details about your Personal Macro Workbook.

✔ You could also convert the workbook to an add-in file. (More about this in Chapter 22.)

You've been initiated into the world of Excel programming. (Sorry, there's no secret handshake or decoder ring.) I hope this chapter helps you realize that Excel programming is something you can actually do — and even live to tell about it. Keep reading. Subsequent chapters almost certainly answer any questions you have, and you'll soon understand exactly what you did in this hands-on session.

Part II
How VBA Works with Excel

The 5th Wave   By Rich Tennant

"I hear some of the engineers from the mainframe dept. project managed the baking of this year's fruitcake."

In this part . . .

The next four chapters provide the necessary foundation for discovering the ins and outs of VBA. You find out about modules (the sheets that store your VBA code) and are introduced to the Excel object model (something you won't want to miss). You also discover the difference between subroutines and functions, and you get a crash course in the Excel macro recorder.

Chapter 3

Introducing the Visual Basic Editor

- -

In This Chapter

▶ Understanding the Visual Basic Editor

▶ Discovering the Visual Basic Editor parts

▶ Knowing what goes into a VBA module

▶ Understanding three ways to get VBA code into a module

▶ Customizing the VBA environment

- -

As an experienced Excel user, you know a good deal about workbooks, formulas, charts, and other Excel goodies. Now it's time to expand your horizons and explore an entirely new aspect of Excel: the Visual Basic Editor (VBE). In this chapter, you find out how to work with the VBE, and get down to the nitty-gritty of entering VBA code.

What Is the Visual Basic Editor?

The Visual Basic Editor is a separate application where you write and edit your Visual Basic macros. It works seamlessly with Excel. By *seamlessly,* I mean that Excel takes care of opening VBE when you need it.

You can't run the VBE separately; Excel must be running in order for the VBE to run.

Activating the VBE

The quickest way to activate the VBE is to press Alt+F11 when Excel is active. To return to Excel, press Alt+F11 again.

You can also activate the VBE by using menus within Excel. To do this, choose Tools⇨Macro⇨Visual Basic Editor.

Understanding VBE components

Figure 3-1 shows the VBE program window, with some of the key parts identified. Because so much is going on in the VBE, maximize the window to see as much as possible.

Chances are your VBE program window won't look exactly like the window shown in Figure 3-1. This window is highly customizable — you can hide, resize, dock, rearrange, and so on in the window.

Actually, the VBE has even more parts than are shown in Figure 3-1. I discuss these additional components in both Chapter 13 and in Part IV.

Menu bar

The VBE menu bar, of course, works like every other menu bar you've encountered. It contains commands that you use to do things with the various components in the VBE. You also find that many of the menu commands have shortcut keys associated with them.

The VBE also features shortcut menus. You can right-click virtually anything in the VBE and get a shortcut menu of common commands.

Toolbar   Menu bar   Code window

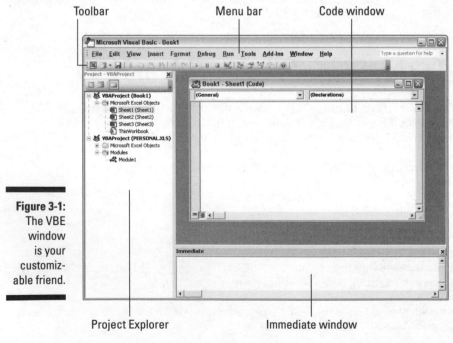

Figure 3-1:
The VBE window is your customizable friend.

Project Explorer   Immediate window

Toolbar

The Standard toolbar, which is directly under the menu bar by default (see Figure 3-1), is one of four VBE toolbars available. VBE toolbars work just like those in Excel: You can customize them, move them around, display other toolbars, and so on. Use the View⇨Toolbars command to work with VBE toolbars.

Project Explorer window

The Project Explorer window displays a tree diagram that consists of every workbook currently open in Excel (including add-ins and hidden workbooks). I discuss this window in more detail in "Working with the Project Explorer," later in this chapter.

If the Project Explorer window is not visible, press Ctrl+R or use the View⇨ Project Explorer command. To hide the Project Explorer window, click the Close button in its title bar (or right-click anywhere in the Project Explorer window and select Hide from the shortcut menu).

Code window

A Code window (sometimes known as a Module window) contains VBA code. Every object in a project has an associated Code window. To view an object's Code window, double-click the object In the Project Explorer window. For example, to view the Code window for the Sheet1 object, double-click Sheet1 in the Project Explorer window. Unless you've added some VBA code, the Code window will be empty.

You find out more about Code windows later in this chapter's "Working with a Code Window" section.

Immediate window

The Immediate window may or may not be visible. If it isn't visible, press Ctrl+G or use the View⇨Immediate Window command. To close the Immediate window, click the Close button in its title bar (or right-click anywhere in the Immediate window and select Hide from the shortcut menu).

The Immediate window is most useful for executing VBA statements directly and for debugging your code. If you're just starting out with VBA, this window won't be all that useful, so feel free to hide it and get it out of the way.

In Chapter 13, I discuss the Immediate window in detail. It may just become your good friend!

Working with the Project Explorer

When you're working in the VBE, each Excel workbook and add-in that's open is a project. You can think of a *project* as a collection of objects arranged as an outline. You can expand a project by clicking the plus sign (+) at the left of the project's name in the Project Explorer window. Contract a project by clicking the minus sign (-) to the left of a project's name. Figure 3-2 shows a Project Explorer window with three projects listed.

Figure 3-2:
This Project
Explorer
window
lists three
projects —
Book1,
investments.
xls, and
PERSONAL.
XLS.

Every project expands to show at least one *node* called Microsoft Excel Objects. This node expands to show an item for each sheet in the workbook (each sheet is considered an object), and another object called ThisWorkbook (which represents the Workbook object). If the project has any VBA modules, the project listing also shows a Modules node. And, as you see in Part IV, a project may also contain a node called Forms, which contains UserForm objects (also known as *custom dialog boxes*).

The concept of objects may be a bit fuzzy for you. However, I guarantee that things become much clearer in subsequent chapters. Don't be too concerned if you don't understand what's going on at this point.

Adding a new VBA module

Follow these steps to add a new VBA module to a project:

1. **Select the project's name in the Project Explorer window.**
2. **Choose Insert⇨Module.**

Or

1. **Right-click the project's name.**

2. **Choose Insert⇨Module from the shortcut menu.**

 When you record a macro, Excel automatically inserts a VBA module to hold the recorded code.

Removing a VBA module

Need to remove a VBA module from a project?

1. **Select the module's name in the Project Explorer window.**

2. **Choose File⇨Remove *xxx*, where *xxx* is the module name.**

Or

1. **Right-click the module's name.**

2. **Choose Remove *xxx* from the shortcut menu.**

You can remove VBA modules, but there is no way to remove the other code modules — those for the Sheet objects, or ThisWorkbook.

Exporting and importing objects

Every object in a VBA project can be saved to a separate file. Saving an individual object in a project is known as *exporting*. It stands to reason that you can also *import* objects to a project. Exporting and importing objects might be useful if you want to use a particular object (such as a VBA module or a UserForm) in a different project.

Follow these steps to export an object:

1. **Select an object in the Project Explorer window.**

2. **Choose File⇨Export File or press Ctrl+E.**

   You get a dialog box that asks for a filename. Note that the object remains in the project; only a copy of it is exported.

Importing a file to a project goes like this:

1. **Select the project's name in the Explorer window.**

2. **Choose File⇨Import File or press Ctrl+M.**

   You get a dialog box that asks for a file. You should only import a file if the file was exported using the File⇨Export File command.

Working with a Code Window

As you become proficient with VBA, you spend lots of time working in Code windows. Macros that you record are stored in a module, and you can type VBA code directly into a VBA module. Just to make sure you're straight with the concept, remember that a VBA module holds your VBA code, and a VBA module is displayed in a Code window.

Minimizing and maximizing windows

If you have several projects open, the VBE may have lots of Code windows at any given time. Figure 3-3 shows an example of what I mean.

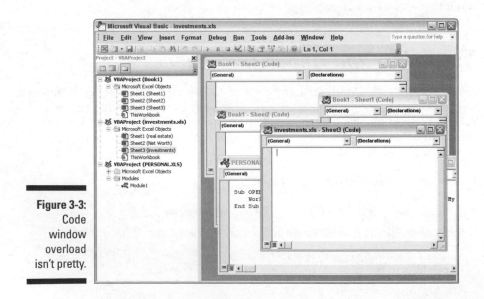

Figure 3-3:
Code
window
overload
isn't pretty.

Code windows are much like workbook windows in Excel. You can minimize them, maximize them, hide them, rearrange them, and so on. Most people find it much easier to maximize the Code window that they're working on. Doing so lets you see more code and keeps you from getting distracted.

To maximize a Code window, click the maximize button in its title bar (or just double-click its title bar). To restore a Code window to its original size, click the Restore button in its title bar.

Sometimes, you may want to have two or more Code windows visible. For example, you might want to compare the code in two modules or copy code from one module to another. You can arrange the windows manually, or use the Window⇨Tile Horizontally or Window⇨Tile Vertically command to arrange them automatically.

Minimizing a Code window gets it out of the way. You can also click the Close button in a Code window's title bar to close the window completely. To open it again, just double-click the appropriate object in the Project Explorer window.

Creating a module

In general, a VBA module can hold three types of code:

- **Sub procedures:** A set of programming instructions that performs some action.

- **Function procedures:** A set of programming instructions that returns a single value (similar in concept to a worksheet function such as SUM).

- **Declarations:** One or more information statements that you provide to VBA. For example, you can declare the data type for variables you plan to use, or set some other module-wide options.

A single VBA module can store any number of Sub procedures, Function procedures, and declarations. How you organize a VBA module is completely up to you. Some people prefer to keep all their VBA code for an application in a single VBA module; others like to split up the code into several different modules. It's a personal choice.

Getting VBA code into a module

An empty VBA module is like the fake food you see in the windows of some Chinese restaurants; it looks good but it doesn't really do much for you. Before you can do anything meaningful, you must have some VBA code in the VBA module. You can get VBA code into a VBA module in three ways:

- Entering the code directly
- Using the Excel macro recorder to record your actions and convert them to VBA code (see Chapter 6)
- Copying the code from one module and pasting it into another

Pause for a terminology break

I need to digress for a moment to discuss termi-nology. Throughout this book, I use the terms *Sub procedure, routine, procedure*, and *macro.* These terms are a bit confusing. Programming folks usually use the word *procedure* to describe an automated task. Technically, a procedure can be a Sub procedure or a Function procedure —

both of which are sometimes called *routines.* I use all these terms interchangeably. As detailed in the following chapters, however, there is an important difference between Sub and Function procedures. For now, don't worry about the ter-minology. Just try to understand the concepts.

Entering code directly

Sometimes, the best route is the most direct. Entering code directly involves . . . well, entering the code directly. In other words, you type the code via your key-board. Entering and editing text in a VBA module works as you might expect. You can select, copy, cut, paste, and do other things to the text.

Use the Tab key to indent some of the lines to make your code easier to read. This isn't necessary but it's a good habit to acquire. As you study the code I present in this book, you'll understand why indenting code lines is helpful.

A single line of VBA code can be as long as you like. However, you may want to use the line-continuation character to break up lengthy lines of code. To continue a single line of code (also known as a *statement*) from one line to the next, end the first line with a space followed by an underscore (_). Then con-tinue the statement on the next line. Here's an example of a single line of code split into three lines:

```
Selection.Sort Key1:=Range("A1"), _
    Order1:=xlAscending, Header:=xlGuess, _
    Orientation:=xlTopToBottom
```

This statement would perform exactly the same way if it were entered in a single line (with no line-continuation characters). Notice that I indented the second and third lines of this statement. Indenting makes it clear that these lines are not separate statements.

A VBA module has multiple levels of undo and redo. Therefore, if you deleted a statement that you shouldn't have, use the Undo button on the toolbar until the statement comes back. After undoing, you can use the Redo button to per-form the changes you've undone. This undo/redo business is more compli-cated to describe than it is to use. I recommend playing around with this feature until you understand how it works.

Ready to enter some real live code? Try the following steps:

1. **Create a new workbook in Excel.**

2. **Press Alt+F11 to activate the VBE.**

3. **Click the new workbook's name in the Project Explorer window.**

4. **Choose Insert⇨Module to insert a VBA module into the project.**

5. **Type the following code into the module:**

```
Sub GuessName()
    Msg = "Is your name " & Application.UserName & "?"
    Ans = MsgBox(Msg, vbYesNo)
    If Ans = vbNo Then MsgBox "Oh, never mind."
    If Ans = vbYes Then MsgBox "I must be clairvoyant!"
End Sub
```

6. **Make sure the cursor is located anywhere within the text you typed.**

7. **Press F5 to execute the procedure.**

   F5 is a shortcut for the Run⇨Run Sub/UserForm command. If you entered the code correctly, Excel executes the procedure and you can respond to the simple dialog box shown in Figure 3-4.

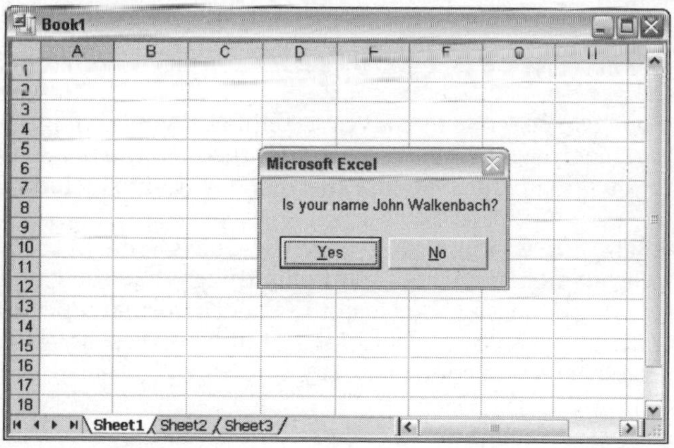

Figure 3-4: The GuessName procedure displays this message box.

When you enter the code listed in Step 5, you might notice that the VBE makes some adjustments to the text you enter. For example, after you type the Sub statement, the VBE automatically inserts the End Sub statement. And if you omit the space before or after an equal sign, the VBE inserts the space for you. Also, the VBE changes the color and capitalization of some text. This is all perfectly normal. It's just the VBE's way of keeping things neat and readable.

If you followed the previous steps, you've just written a VBA Sub procedure, also known as a *macro*. When you press F5, Excel executes the code and follows the instructions. In other words, Excel evaluates each statement and does what you told it to do. (Don't let this newfound power go to your head.) You can execute this macro any number of times — although it tends to lose its appeal after a few dozen.

For the record, this simple macro uses the following concepts, all of which are covered later in this book:

- Defining a Sub procedure (the first line)
- Assigning values to variables (Msg and Ans)
- *Concatenating* (joining) a string (using the & operator)
- Using a built-in VBA function (MsgBox)
- Using built-in VBA constants (vbYesNo, vbNo, and vbYes)
- Using an If-Then construct (twice)
- Ending a Sub procedure (the last line)

Not bad for a beginner, eh?

Using the macro recorder

Another way you can get code into a VBA module is by recording your actions using the Excel macro recorder. If you worked through the hands-on exercise in Chapter 2, you already have some experience with this technique.

There is absolutely no way you can record the GuessName procedure shown in the preceding section. You can record only things that you can do directly in Excel. Displaying a message box is not in Excel's normal repertoire. (It's a VBA thing.) The macro recorder is useful, but in many cases you'll probably have to enter at least some code manually.

Here's a step-by-step example that shows you how to record a macro that turns off the cell gridlines in a worksheet. If you want to try this example, start with a new, blank workbook and follow these steps:

1. **Activate a worksheet in the workbook.**

   Any worksheet will do.

2. **Choose Tools⇨Macro⇨Record New Macro.**

   Excel displays its Record Macro dialog box.

3. **Click OK to accept the defaults.**

   Excel automatically inserts a new VBA module into the project that corresponds to the active workbook. From this point on, Excel converts your actions into VBA code. While recording, Excel displays the word *Recording* in the status bar. Excel also displays a miniature floating toolbar that contains two toolbar buttons: Stop Recording and Relative Reference.

4. **Choose Tools⇨Options.**

   Excel displays its Options dialog box.

5. **Click the View tab.**

6. **Remove the check mark from the Gridlines option.**

   If the worksheet you're using has no gridlines, put a check mark next to the Gridlines option.

7. **Click OK to close the dialog box.**

8. **Click the Stop Recording button on the miniature toolbar.**

   Excel stops recording your actions.

To view this newly recorded macro, press Alt+F11 to activate the VBE. Locate the workbook's name in the Project Explorer window. You'll see that the project has a new module listed. The name of the module depends on whether you had any other modules in the workbook when you started recording the macro. If you didn't, the module will be named Module1. You can double-click the module to view the Code window for the module.

Here's the code generated by your actions:

```
Sub Macro1()
'
' Macro1 Macro
' Macro recorded 3/1/2004 by John Walkenbach
'
'
    ActiveWindow.DisplayGridlines = False
End Sub
```

Try out this macro:

1. **Activate a worksheet that has gridlines displayed.**

2. **Choose Tools⇨Macro⇨Macros**

   Alternatively, you can press Alt+F8. Excel displays a dialog box that lists all the available macros.

3. **Select Macro1.**

4. **Click the Run button.**

> Excel executes the macro, and the gridlines magically disappear. Are you beginning to see how this macro business can be fun?

Of course, you can execute any number of commands and perform any number of actions while the macro recorder is running. Excel dutifully translates your mouse actions and keystrokes to VBA code. It works similarly to a tape recorder, but Excel never runs out of tape.

The preceding macro isn't really all that useful. To make it useful, activate the module and change the statement to this:

```
ActiveWindow.DisplayGridlines = _
    Not ActiveWindow.DisplayGridlines
```

This modification makes the macro serve as a *toggle*. If gridlines are displayed, the macro turns them off. If gridlines are not displayed, the macro turns them on. Oops, I'm getting ahead of myself — sorry, but I couldn't resist that simple enhancement.

Copying VBA code

The final method for getting code into a VBA module is to copy it from another module. For example, a Sub or Function procedure that you write for one project might also be useful in another project. Rather than waste time reentering the code, you can activate the module and use the normal Clipboard copy-and-paste procedures. After pasting it into a VBA module, you can modify the code if necessary.

Customizing the VBA Environment

If you're serious about becoming an Excel programmer, you'll spend a lot of time with VBA modules on your screen. To help make things as comfortable as possible (no, please keep your shoes on), the VBE provides quite a few customization options.

When the VBE is active, choose Tools⇨Options. You'll see a dialog box with four tabs: Editor, Editor Format, General, and Docking. I discuss some of the most useful options in the sections that follow.

Using the Editor tab

Figure 3-5 shows the options accessed by clicking the Editor tab of the Options dialog box. Use the option in the Editor tab to control how certain things work in the VBE.

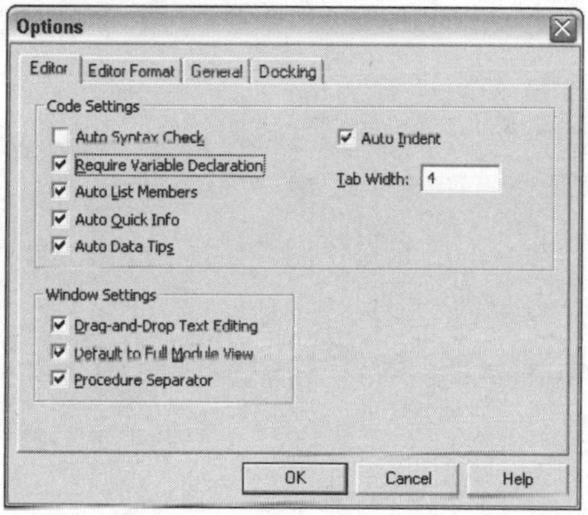

Figure 3-5:
This is the
Editor tab in
the Options
dialog box.

Auto Syntax Check option

The Auto Syntax Check setting determines whether the VBE pops up a dialog box if it discovers a syntax error while you're entering your VBA code. The dialog box tells roughly what the problem is. If you don't choose this setting, VBE flags syntax errors by displaying them in a color different from the rest of the code, and you don't have to deal with any dialog boxes popping up on your screen.

I usually keep this setting turned off because I find the dialog boxes annoying and I can usually figure out what's wrong with a statement. Before I was a VBA veteran, I found this assistance quite helpful.

Require Variable Declaration option

If the Require Variable Declaration option is set, VBE inserts the following statement at the beginning of each new VBA module you insert:

```
Option Explicit
```

Changing this setting affects only new modules, not existing modules. If this statement appears in your module, you must explicitly define each variable you use. In Chapter 7, I explain why you should develop this habit.

Auto List Members option

If the Auto List Members option is set, VBE provides some help when you're entering your VBA code. It displays a list that would logically complete the statement you're typing.

I like this option and always keep it turned on. Figure 3-6 shows an example (which will make lots more sense when you start writing VBA code).

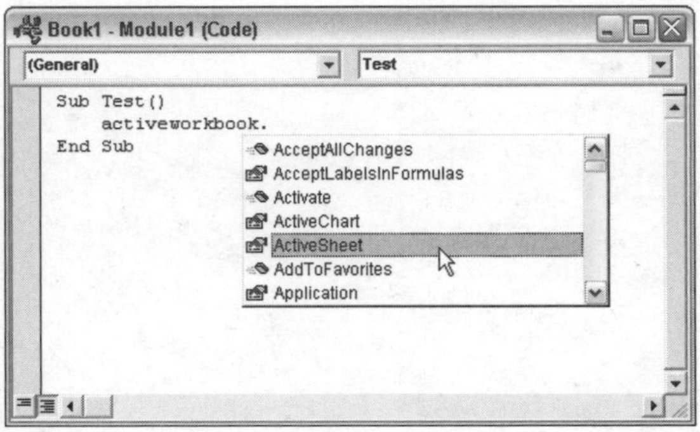

Figure 3-6:
An example
of Auto List
members.

Auto Quick Info option

If the Auto Quick Info option is set, VBE displays information about functions and their arguments as you type. This can be very helpful. Figure 3-7 shows this feature in action.

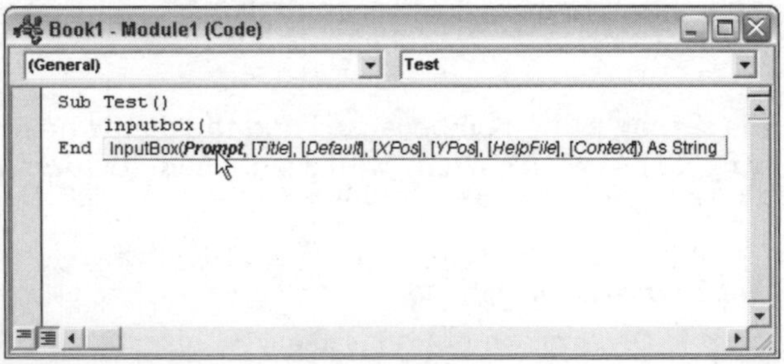

Figure 3-7:
Auto Quick
Info offers
help
about the
InputBox
function.

Auto Data Tips option

If the Auto Data Tips option is set, VBE displays the value of the variable over which your cursor is placed when you're debugging code. When you enter the wonderful world of debugging (as described in Chapter 13), you'll appreciate this option.

Auto Indent setting

The Auto Indent setting determines whether VBE automatically indents each new line of code the same as the previous line. I'm big on using indentations in my code, so I keep this option on.

Use the Tab key to indent your code, not the spacebar. Also, you can use Shift+Tab to "unindent" a line of code.

The VBE's Edit toolbar (which is hidden by default) contains two useful buttons: Indent and Outdent. These buttons let you quickly indent or "unindent" a block of code. Select the code and click one of these buttons to change the block's indenting.

Drag-and-Drop Text Editing option

The Drag-and-Drop Text Editing option, when enabled, lets you copy and move text by dragging and dropping. I keep this option on, but I hardly ever remember to use it.

Default to Full Module View option

The Default to Full Module View option sets the default state for new modules. (It doesn't affect existing modules.) If set, procedures in the Code window appear as a single scrollable list. If this option is turned off, you can see only one procedure at a time. I keep this option turned on.

Procedure Separator option

When the Procedure Separator option is turned on, separator bars appear at the end of each procedure in a Code window. I like the idea of separator bars, so I keep this option turned on.

Using the Editor Format tab

Figure 3-8 shows the Editor Format tab of the Options dialog box. With this tab you can customize the way the VBE looks.

Code Colors option

The Code Colors option lets you set the text color and background color displayed for various elements of VBA code. This is largely a matter of personal preference. Personally, I find the default colors to be just fine. But for a change of scenery, I occasionally play around with these settings.

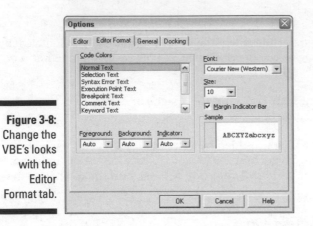

Figure 3-8:
Change the
VBE's looks
with the
Editor
Format tab.

Font option

The Font option lets you select the font that's used in your VBA modules. For best results, stick with a fixed-width font such as Courier New. In a *fixed-width font*, all characters are exactly the same width. This makes your code more readable because the characters are nicely aligned vertically and you can easily distinguish multiple spaces.

Size setting

The Size setting specifies the point size of the font in the VBA modules. This setting is a matter of personal preference determined by your video display resolution and your eyesight.

Margin Indicator Bar option

This option controls the display of the vertical margin indicator bar in your modules. You should keep this turned on; otherwise, you won't be able to see the helpful graphical indicators when you're debugging your code.

Using the General tab

Figure 3-9 shows the options available under the General tab in the Options dialog box. In almost every case, the default settings are just fine. If you're really interested in these options, consult the Help system for details.

Using the Docking tab

Figure 3-10 shows the Docking tab. These options determine how the various windows in the VBE behave. When a window is *docked,* it is fixed in place along one of the edges of the VBE program window. This makes it much easier to identify and locate a particular window. If you turn off all docking, you have a big, confusing mess of windows. Generally, the default settings work fine.

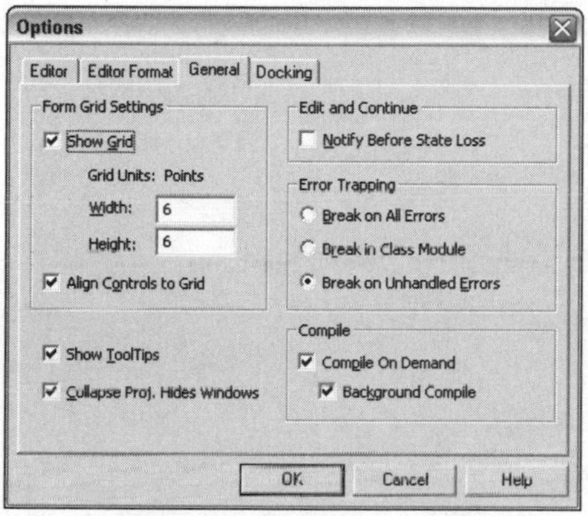

Figure 3-9:
The General
tab of the
Options
dialog box.

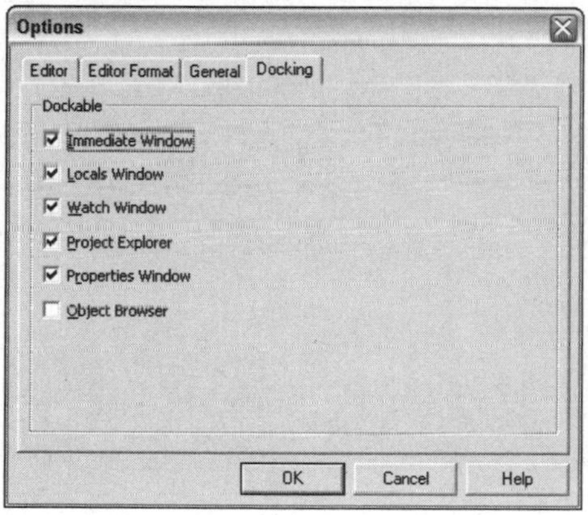

Figure 3-10:
The Docking
tab of the
Options
dialog box.

Chapter 4

Introducing the Excel Object Model

*E*veryone is familiar with the word *object*. Well, folks, forget the definition you think you know. In the world of programming, the word *object* has a different meaning. You often see it used as part of the expression *object-oriented programming*, or *OOP* for short. OOP is based on the idea that software consists of distinct objects that have attributes (or properties) and can be manipulated. These objects are not material things. Rather, they exist in the form of bits and bytes.

In this chapter, I introduce you to the Excel object model, which is a hierarchy of objects contained in Excel. By the time you finish this chapter, you'll have a reasonably good understanding of what OOP is all about — and why you need to understand this concept to become a VBA programmer. After all, Excel programming really boils down to manipulating Excel objects. It's as simple as that.

The material in this chapter may be a bit overwhelming. But please take my advice and plow through it, even if you don't fully grasp it. The important concepts presented here will make lots more sense as you progress through the book.

Excel Is an Object?

You've used Excel for quite a while, but you probably never thought of it as an object. The more you work with VBA, the more you view Excel in those terms. You'll understand that Excel is an object and that it contains other objects. Those objects, in turn, contain still more objects. In other words, VBA programming involves working with an object hierarchy.

At the top of this hierarchy is the Application object — in this case, Excel itself (the mother of all objects).

Climbing the Object Hierarchy

The Application object contains other objects. Following is a list of some of the more useful objects contained in the Excel Application:

- Addin
- CommandBar
- Window
- Workbook
- WorksheetFunction

Each object contained in the Application object can contain other objects. For example, the following is a list of objects that can be contained in a Workbook object:

- Chart
- Name
- VBProject
- Window
- Worksheet

In turn, each of these objects can contain still other objects. Consider a Worksheet object (which is contained in a Workbook object, which is contained in the Application object). Some of the objects that can be contained in a Worksheet object follow:

- Comment
- Hyperlink

> ✔ Name
> ✔ Outline
> ✔ PageSetup
> ✔ PivotTable
> ✔ Range

Put another way, if you want to do something with a range on a particular worksheet, you may find it helpful to visualize that range in the following manner:

> Range⇨contained in Worksheet⇨contained in Workbook⇨ contained in Excel

Is this beginning to make sense?

Before you come down with a bad case of object overload, it's important to understand that you never need to use most of the objects available to you. In fact, most VBA work involves only a few objects. Even better, you can almost always find the relevant object by recording a macro while doing something with that object.

Wrapping Your Mind around Collections

Collections are another key concept in VBA programming. A *collection* is a group of objects of the same type. And to add to the confusion, a collection is itself an object.

Here are a few examples of commonly used collections:

> ✔ **Workbooks:** A collection of all currently open Workbook objects
>
> ✔ **Worksheets:** A collection of all Worksheet objects contained in a particular Workbook object
>
> ✔ **Charts:** A collection of all Chart objects (chart sheets) contained in a particular Workbook object
>
> ✔ **Sheets:** A collection of all sheets (regardless of their type) contained in a particular Workbook object

You may notice that collection names are all plural, which makes sense (at least I hope).

Visualizing objects

Excel's Help system displays the complete Excel object model graphically. Locating this diagram varies, depending on the version of Excel you have. For Excel 2003, follow these steps:

1. Activate the VBE.

2. Type `Object Model` in the Help box (located to the right of the menu bar).

    The Search Results appear in the task pane.

3. Click Microsoft Excel Object model.

You see the diagram shown here.

Referring to Objects

I presented the information in the previous sections to prepare you for the next concept: referring to objects in your VBA code. Referring to an object is important because you must identify the object that you want to work with. After all, VBA can't read your mind — that feature is slated for Excel 2012.

You can work with an entire collection of objects in one fell swoop. More often, however, you need to work with a specific object in a collection (such as a particular worksheet in a workbook). To reference a single object from a collection, you put the object's name or index number in parentheses after the name of the collection, like this:

```
Worksheets("Sheet1")
```

Notice that the sheet's name is in quotation marks. If you omit the quotation marks, Excel won't be able to identify the object.

If Sheet1 is the first (or only) worksheet in the collection, you can also use the following reference:

```
Worksheets(1)
```

In this case, the number is *not* in quotation marks. Bottom line? If you refer to an object by using its name, use quotation marks. If you refer to an object by using its index number, use a plain number without quotation marks.

Another collection, called Sheets, contains all the sheets (worksheets and Chart sheets) in a workbook. If Sheet1 is the first sheet in the workbook, you can reference it as

```
Sheets(1)
```

Navigating through the hierarchy

If you want to work with the Application object, it's easy: you start by typing Application. Every other object in Excel's object model is under the Application object. You get to these objects by moving down the hierarchy and connecting each object on your way with the dot ( ) operator. To get to the Workbook object named "Book1.xls", start with the Application object and navigate down to the Workbooks collection object.

```
Application.Workbooks("Book1.xls")
```

To navigate further to a specific worksheet, add a dot operator and access the Worksheets collection object.

```
Application.Workbooks("Book1.xls").Worksheets(1)
```

Not far enough yet? If you really wanted to get the value from cell A1 on the first Worksheet of the Workbook named "Book1.xls", you need to navigate one more level to the Range object.

```
Application.Workbooks("Book1.xls").Worksheets(1).Range("A1").
          Value
```

When you refer to a Range object in this way, it's called a fully qualified reference. You've told Excel exactly which range you wanted, on which worksheet and in which workbook, and have left nothing to the imagination. And that's a good thing. Imagination is good in people, but not so good in computer programs.

Simplifying object references

If you had to fully qualify every object reference you make, your code would get quite long, and may be more difficult to read. Fortunately, Excel provides you with some shortcuts that can improve the readability (and save you some typing). For starters, the Application object is always assumed. There are only a few cases when it makes sense to type it. Omitting the Application object reference shortens the example from the previous section to

```
Workbooks("Book1.xls").Worksheets(1).Range("A1").Value
```

That's a pretty good improvement. But wait, there's more. If Book1.xls is the active workbook, you can omit that reference too. Now we're down to

```
Worksheets(1).Range("A1").Value
```

Now we're getting somewhere. Have you guessed the next shortcut? That's right, if the first worksheet is the currently active worksheet, then Excel will assume that reference and allow us to just type

```
Range("A1").Value
```

Contrary to what some people may think, Excel does not have a Cell object. A *cell* is simply a Range object that consists of just one element.

The shortcuts described here are great, but they can also be dangerous. What if you only *think* Book1.xls is the active workbook? You could get an error, or worse, get the wrong value and not even realize it's wrong. For that reason, it's best to fully qualify your object references.

In Chapter 14, I discuss the With-End With structure which helps you fully qualify your references but also helps to make the code more readable and cuts down on the typing. The best of both worlds!

Diving into Object Properties and Methods

Although knowing how to refer to objects is important, you can't do anything useful by simply referring to an object (as in the examples in the preceding sections). To accomplish anything meaningful, you must do one of two things:

- Read or modify an object's *properties*
- Specify a *method* of action to be used with an object

Another slant on McObjects, McProperties, and McMethods

Here's an analogy that may help you understand the relationships between objects, properties, and methods in VBA. In this analogy, I compare Excel with a fast-food restaurant chain.

The basic unit of Excel is a Workbook object. In a fast-food chain, the basic unit is an individual restaurant. With Excel, you can add workbooks and close workbooks, and all the open workbooks are known as Workbooks (a collection of Workbook objects). Similarly, the management of a fast-food chain can add restaurants and close restaurants, and all the restaurants in the chain can be viewed as the Restaurants collection (a collection of Restaurant objects).

An Excel workbook is an object, but it also contains other objects such as worksheets, charts, VBA modules, and so on. Furthermore, each object in a workbook can contain its own objects. For example, a Worksheet object can contain Range objects, PivotTable objects, Shape objects, and so on.

Continuing with the analogy, a fast-food restaurant (like a workbook) contains objects such as the Kitchen, DiningArea, and Tables (a collection). Furthermore, management can add or remove objects from the Restaurant object. For example, management may add more tables to the Tables collection. Each of these objects can contain other objects. For example, the Kitchen object has a Stove object, VentilationFan object, Chef object, Sink object, and so on.

So far, so good. This analogy seems to work. Let me see if I can take it further.

Excel's objects have properties. For example, a Range object has properties such as Value and Name, and a Shape object has properties such as Width, Height, and so on. Not surprisingly, objects in a fast-food restaurant also have properties. The Stove object, for example, has properties such as Temperature and NumberofBurners. The VentilationFan has its own set of properties (TurnedOn, RPM, and so forth).

Besides properties, Excel's objects also have methods, which perform an operation on an object. For example, the ClearContents method erases the contents of a Range object. An object in a fast-food restaurant also has methods. You can easily envision a ChangeThermostat method for a Stove object, or a SwitchOn method for a VentilationFan object.

In Excel, methods sometimes change an object's properties. The ClearContents method for a Range changes the Range's Value property. Similarly, the ChangeThermostat method on a Stove object affects its Temperature property. With VBA, you can write procedures to manipulate Excel's objects. In a fast-food restaurant, the management can give orders to manipulate the objects in the restaurants. ("Turn the stove on and switch the ventilation fan to high.")

The next time you visit your favorite fast-food joint, just say, "I'll have a Burger object with the Onion property set to False."

With literally thousands of properties and methods available, you can easily be overwhelmed. I've been working with this stuff for years and I'm *still* overwhelmed. But as I've said before and I say again: You'll never need to use most of the available properties and methods.

Object properties

Every object has properties. You can think of *properties* as attributes that describe the object. An object's properties determine how it looks, how it behaves, and even whether it is visible. Using VBA, you can do two things with an object's properties:

- ✔ Examine the current setting for a property
- ✔ Change the property's setting

For example, a single-cell Range object has a property called Value. The Value property stores the value contained in the cell. You can write VBA code to display the Value property, or you may write VBA code to set the Value property to a specific value. The following macro uses the VBA built-in MsgBox function to bring up a box that displays the value in cell A1 on Sheet1. See Figure 4-1.

```
Sub ShowValue()
    Contents = Worksheets("Sheet1").Range("A1").Value
    MsgBox Contents
End Sub
```

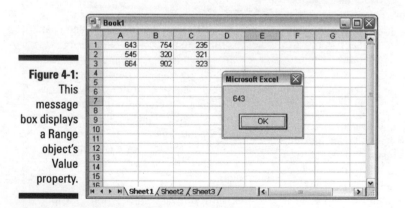

Figure 4-1: This message box displays a Range object's Value property.

MsgBox is a useful function; you often use it to display results while Excel executes your VBA code. I tell you more about this function in Chapter 15. The code in the preceding example displays the current setting of a cell's Value property. What if you want to change the setting for that property? The following macro changes the value displayed in cell A1 by changing the cell's Value property:

```
Sub ChangeValue()
    Worksheets("Sheet1").Range("A1").Value = 934
End Sub
```

After Excel executes this procedure, cell A1 on Sheet1 of the active workbook contains the value 934. (By the way, if the active workbook does not have a sheet named Sheet1, executing that macro will display an error message.)

Each object has its own set of properties, although some properties are common to many objects. For example, many (but not all) objects have a Visible property. Most objects also have a Name property.

Some object properties are read-only, which means that you can see the property's value, but you can't change it.

As I mention earlier in this chapter, a collection is also an object. This means that a collection also has properties. For example, you can determine how many workbooks are open by accessing the Worksheets collection's Count property. The following VBA procedure displays a message box that tells you how many workbooks are open:

```
Sub CountBooks()
    MsgBox Workbooks.Count
End Sub
```

Object methods

In addition to properties, objects have methods. A *method* is an action you perform with an object. A method can change an object's properties or make the object do something.

This simple example uses the Calculate method on a Range object to calculate the formula in cell A1 on Sheet1:

```
Sub CalcCell()
    Worksheets("Sheet1").Range("A1").Calculate
End Sub
```

Most methods also take one or more arguments. An *argument* is a value that further specifies the action to perform. You place the arguments for a method after the method, separated by a space. Multiple arguments are separated by a comma.

The following example activates Sheet1 (in the active workbook) and then copies the contents of cell A1 to cell B1 using the Range object's Copy method. In this example, the Copy method has one argument — the destination range for the copy operation:

```
Sub CopyOne()
    Worksheets("Sheet1").Activate
    Range("A1").Copy Range("B1")
End Sub
```

Notice that I omit the worksheet reference when I refer to the Range objects. I could do this safely because I used a statement to activate Sheet1 (using the Activate method).

Because a collection is also an object, collections have methods. The following macro uses the Add method for the Workbooks collection:

```
Sub AddAWorkbook()
    Workbooks.Add
End Sub
```

As you may expect, this statement creates a new workbook. In other words, it adds a new workbook to the Workbooks collection.

Object events

In this section, I briefly touch on one more topic that you need to know about: events. Objects respond to various *events* that occur. For example, when you're working in Excel and you activate a different workbook, an Activate event occurs. You could, for example, have a VBA macro that is designed to execute whenever an Activate event occurs.

Excel supports many events, but not all objects can respond to all events. And some objects don't respond to any events. The concept of an event becomes clear in Chapter 11 and also in Part IV.

Finding Out More

You find out more about objects, properties, and methods in the chapters that follow this one. You may also be interested in three other excellent tools:

- ✔ VBA's Help system
- ✔ The Object Browser
- ✔ Auto List Members

Using VBA's Help system

The VBA Help system describes every object, property, and method available to you. This is an excellent resource for finding out about VBA and is more comprehensive than any book on the market.

If you're working in a VBA module and want information about a particular object, method, or property, move the cursor to the word you're interested in and press F1. In a few seconds you see the appropriate help topic, complete with cross-references and perhaps even an example or two.

Figure 4-2 shows a screen from the online Help system — in this case, for a Worksheet object.

✔ Click Properties to get a complete list of this object's properties.

✔ Click Methods to get a listing of its methods.

✔ Click Events to get a listing of the events it responds to.

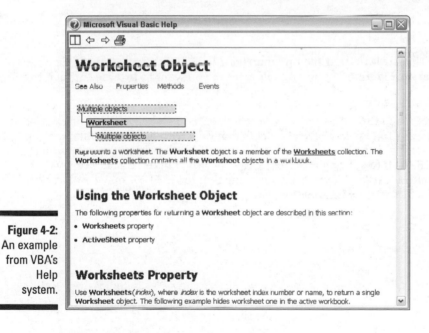

Figure 4-2: An example from VBA's Help system.

Using the Object Browser

The VBE includes another tool, known as the Object Browser. As the name implies, this tool lets you browse through the objects available to you. To access the Object Browser, press F2 when the VBE is active (or choose View⇨Object Browser). You see a window like the one shown in Figure 4-3.

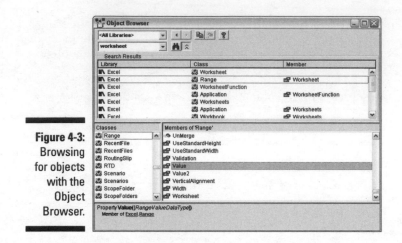

Figure 4-3:
Browsing
for objects
with the
Object
Browser.

The drop-down list at the top contains a list of all currently available object libraries. Figure 4-3 shows All Libraries. If you want to browse through Excel's objects, select Excel from the drop-down list.

The second drop-down list is where you enter a search string. For example, if you want to look at all Excel objects that deal with links, type link into the second field and click the Search button. (It has a pair of binoculars on it.) The Search Results window displays everything in the object library that contains the text *link*. If you see something that looks like it may be of interest, press F1 for more information.

Chapter 5

VBA Sub and Function Procedures

S everal times in preceding chapters I mention *Sub procedures* and allude
to the fact that *Function procedures* also play a role in VBA. In this chapter, I clear up confusion about these concepts.

Subs versus Functions

The VBA code that you write in the Visual Basic Editor is known as a *procedure.* The two most common types of procedures are Sub and Function.

- ✔ A Sub procedure is a group of VBA statements that performs an action
  (or actions) with Excel.

- ✔ A Function procedure is a group of VBA statements that performs a calculation and returns a single value.

Most of the macros you write in VBA are Sub procedures. You can think of a
Sub as being like a command: Execute the Sub procedure and something happens. (Of course, exactly *what* happens depends on the Sub procedure's VBA
code.)

A Function is also a procedure, but it's quite different from a Sub. You're
already familiar with the concept of a function. Excel includes many worksheet functions that you use every day (well, at least every weekday).
Examples include SUM, PMT, and VLOOKUP. You use these worksheet functions in formulas. Each function takes one or more arguments (although a
few functions don't use any arguments). The function does some behind-the-
scenes calculations and returns a single value. The same goes for Function
procedures that you develop with VBA.

Looking at Sub procedures

Every Sub procedure starts with the keyword Sub and ends with an End Sub statement. Here's an example:

```
Sub ShowMessage()
    MsgBox "That's all folks!"
End Sub
```

This example shows a procedure named ShowMessage. A set of parentheses follows the procedure's name. In most cases, these parentheses are empty. However, you may pass arguments to Sub procedures from other procedures. If your Sub uses arguments, list them between the parentheses.

When you record a macro with the Excel macro recorder, the result is always a Sub procedure.

As you see later in this chapter, Excel provides quite a few ways to execute a VBA Sub procedure.

Looking at Function procedures

Every Function procedure starts with the keyword Function and ends with an End Function statement. Here's a simple example:

```
Function CubeRoot(number)
    CubeRoot = number ^ (1 / 3)
End Function
```

This function, named CubeRoot, takes one argument (named *number*), which is enclosed in parentheses. Functions can have any number of arguments or none at all. When you execute the function, it returns a single value — the cube root of the argument passed to the function.

VBA allows you to specify what type of information is returned by a Function procedure. Chapter 7 contains more information on specifying data types.

You can execute a Function procedure in only two ways. You can execute it from another procedure (a Sub or another Function procedure) or use it in a worksheet formula.

You can't use the Excel macro recorder to record a Function procedure. You must manually enter every Function procedure that you create.

Naming Subs and Functions

Like humans, pets, and hurricanes, every Sub and Function procedure must have a name. Although it is perfectly acceptable to name your dog Hairball Harris, it's usually not a good idea to use such a freewheeling attitude when naming procedures. When naming procedures, you must follow a few rules:

- You can use letters, numbers, and some punctuation characters, but the first character must be a letter.
- You can't use any spaces or periods in the name.
- VBA does not distinguish between uppercase and lowercase letters.
- You can't embed any of the following characters in a name: #, $, %, &, @, ^, *, or !.
- If you write a Function procedure for use in a formula, make sure the name does not look like a cell address (for example, AC12).
- Names can be no longer than 255 characters. (Of course, you would never make a procedure name this long.)

Ideally, a procedure's name should describe the routine's purpose. A good practice is to create a name by combining a verb and a noun — for example, ProcessData, PrintReport, Sort_Array, or CheckFilename.

Some programmers prefer using sentencelike names that provide a complete description of the procedure. Some examples include WriteReportToTextFile and Get_Print_Options_and_Print_Report. The use of such lengthy names has its pros and cons. On the one hand, such names are descriptive and unambiguous. On the other hand, they take longer to type. Everyone develops a naming style, but the main objectives should be to make the names descriptive and to avoid meaningless names such as DoIt, Update, and Fix.

Executing Sub Procedures

Although you may not know much about developing Sub procedures at this point, I'm going to jump ahead a bit and discuss how to execute these procedures. This is important because a Sub procedure is worthless unless you know how to execute it.

By the way, *executing* a Sub procedure means the same thing as *running* or *calling* a Sub procedure. You can use whatever terminology you like.

You can execute a VBA Sub in many ways — that's one reason you can do so many useful things with Sub procedures. Here's an exhaustive list of the ways (well, at least all the ways I could think of) to execute a Sub procedure:

✔ With the Run➪Run Sub/UserForm command (in the VBE). Excel executes the Sub procedure at the cursor position. This menu command has two alternatives: The F5 key, and the Run Sub/UserForm button on the Standard toolbar in the VBE. These methods don't work if the procedure requires one or more arguments.

✔ From Excel's Macro dialog box (which you open by choosing Tools➪Macro➪Macros). Or you can press the Alt+F8 shortcut key. When the Macro dialog box appears, select the Sub procedure you want and click Run. This dialog box lists only the procedures that don't require an argument.

✔ Using the Ctrl+key shortcut assigned to the Sub procedure (assuming you assigned one).

✔ Clicking a button or a shape on a worksheet. The button or shape must have a Sub procedure assigned to it.

✔ From another Sub procedure that you write.

✔ From a Toolbar button. (See Chapter 19.)

✔ From a custom menu you develop. (See Chapter 20.)

✔ Automatically, when you open or close a workbook. (See Chapter 11.)

✔ When an event occurs. As I explain in Chapter 11, these events include saving the workbook, making a change to a cell, activating a sheet, and other things.

✔ From the Immediate window in the VBE. Just type the name of the Sub procedure and press Enter.

I demonstrate some of these techniques in the following sections. Before I can do that, you need to enter a Sub procedure into a VBA module.

1. **Start with a new workbook.**

2. **Press Alt+F11 to activate the VBE.**

3. **Select the workbook in the Project window.**

4. **Choose Insert➪Module to insert a new module.**

5. **Enter the following into the module:**

```
Sub CubeRoot()
    Num = InputBox("Enter a positive number")
    MsgBox Num ^ (1 /3) & " is the cube root."
End Sub
```

This simple procedure asks the user for a number and then displays that number's cube root in a message box. Figures 5-1 and 5-2 show what happens when you execute this procedure.

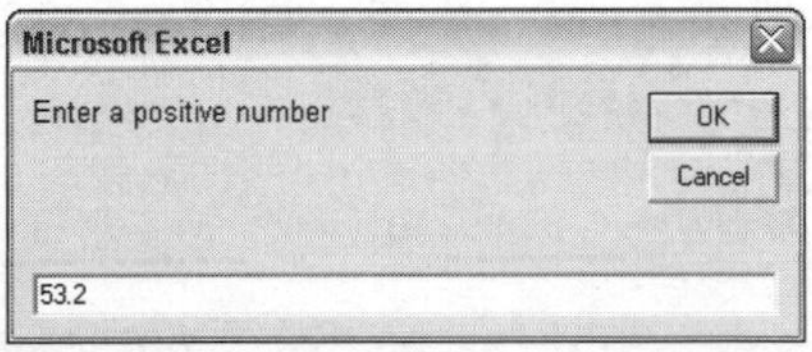

Figure 5-1:
Using the built-in VBA InputBox function to get a number.

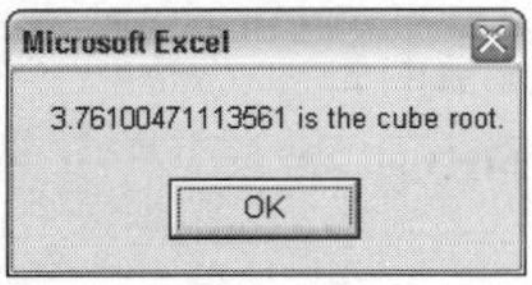

Figure 5-2:
Displaying the cube root of a number via the MsgBox function.

By the way, CubeRoot is not an example of a *good* macro. It doesn't check for errors, so it fails easily. To see what I mean, try clicking the Cancel button in the input box or entering a negative number.

Executing the Sub procedure directly

The quickest way to execute this procedure is by doing so directly from the VBA module in which you defined it. Follow these steps:

1. **Activate the VBE and select the VBA module that contains the procedure.**

2. **Move the cursor anywhere in the procedure's code**

3. **Press F5 (or choose Run⇨Run Sub/UserForm).**

4. **Respond to the input box and click OK.**

   The procedure displays the cube root of the number you entered.

You can't use the Run⇨Run Sub/UserForm command to execute a Sub procedure that uses arguments because you have no way to pass the arguments to the procedure. If the procedure contains one or more arguments, the only way to execute it is to call it from another procedure — which must supply the argument(s).

Executing the procedure from the Macro dialog box

Most of the time, you execute Sub procedures from Excel, not from the VBE. The steps below describe how to execute a macro using Excel's Macro dialog box.

1. **Activate Excel.**

   Alt+F11 is the express route.

2. **Choose Tools⇨Macro⇨Macros (or press Alt+F8).**

   Excel displays the dialog box shown in Figure 5-3.

3. **Select the macro.**

4. **Click Run (or double-click the macro's name in the list box).**

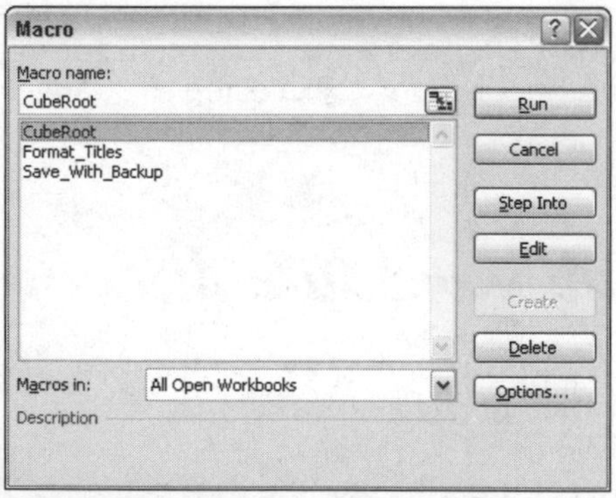

Figure 5-3:
The Macro dialog box lists all available Sub procedures.

Macro	? X
Macro name:	
CubeRoot	**Run**
CubeRoot	Cancel
Format_Titles	
Save_With_Backup	Step Into
	Edit
	Create
	Delete
Macros in: All Open Workbooks	Options...
Description	

Executing a macro using a shortcut key

Another way to execute a macro is to press its shortcut key. But before you can use this method, you have to set things up. Specifically, you must assign a shortcut key to the macro.

You have the opportunity to assign a shortcut key in the Record Macro dialog box when you begin recording a macro. If you create the procedure without using the macro recorder, you can assign a shortcut key (or change an existing shortcut key) using the following procedure:

1. **Choose Tools⇨Macro⇨Macros.**

2. **Select the Sub procedure name from the list box.**

   In this example, the procedure is named CubeRoot.

3. **Click the Options button.**

   Excel displays the dialog box shown in Figure 5-4.

4. **Click the Shortcut Key option and enter a letter in the box labeled Ctrl.**

   The letter you enter corresponds to the key combination you want to use for executing the macro. For example, if you enter the letter *c*, you can then execute the macro by pressing Ctrl+C. If you enter an upper-case letter, you need to add the Shift key to the key combination. For example, if you enter *C*, you can execute the macro by pressing Ctrl+Shift+C.

5. **Click OK or Cancel to close the Macro Options dialog box.**

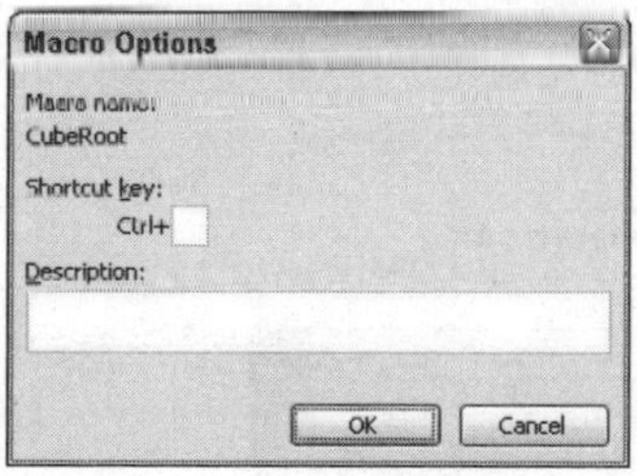

Figure 5-4:
The Macro Options dialog box lets you set options for your macros.

Macro Options

Macro name:
CubeRoot

Shortcut key:
Ctrl+

Description:

[OK]   [Cancel]

After you've assigned a shortcut key, you can press that key combination to execute the macro.

The shortcut keys you assign to macros override Excel's built-in shortcut keys. For example, if you assign Ctrl+C to a macro, you can't use this shortcut key to copy data in your workbook. This is usually not a big deal because Excel always provides other ways to execute commands.

Executing the procedure from a button or shape

You can create still another means for executing the macro by assigning the macro to a button (or any other shape) on a worksheet. To assign the macro to a button, follow these steps:

1. **Activate a worksheet.**

2. **Add a button from the Forms toolbar.**

   To display the Forms toolbar, right-click any toolbar and choose Forms from the shortcut menu.

3. **Click the Button tool on the Forms toolbar.**

4. **Drag in the worksheet to create the button.**

   After you add the button to your worksheet, Excel jumps right in and displays the Assign Macro dialog box shown in Figure 5-5.

5. **Select the macro you want to assign to the button.**

6. **Click OK.**

Clicking the button will execute the macro.

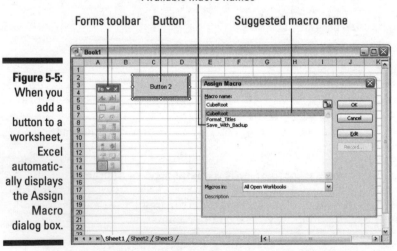

Figure 5-5: When you add a button to a worksheet, Excel automatically displays the Assign Macro dialog box.

You can also assign a macro to any other shape or object. For example, assume you'd like to execute a macro when the user clicks a Rectangle object.

1. **Add the Rectangle to the worksheet.**

   Use the Rectangle button on the Drawing toolbar.

2. **Right-click the rectangle.**

3. **Choose Assign Macro from its shortcut menu.**

4. **Select the macro from the Assign Macro dialog box.**

5. **Click OK.**

After performing these steps, clicking the rectangle will execute the macro.

Executing the procedure from another procedure

You can also execute a procedure from another procedure. Follow these steps if you want to give this a try:

1. **Activate the VBA module that holds the CubeRoot routine.**

2. **Enter this new procedure (either above or below CubeRoot code — it makes no difference):**

```
Sub NewSub()
    Call CubeRoot
End Sub
```

3. **Execute the NewSub macro.**

   The easiest way to do this is to move the cursor anywhere within the NewSub code and press F5. Notice that this NewSub procedure simply executes the CubeRoot procedure.

By the way, the keyword Call is optional. The statement can consist of only the Sub procedure's name. I find, however, that using the Call keyword makes it perfectly clear that a procedure is being called.

Executing Function Procedures

Functions, unlike Sub procedures, can be executed in only two ways:

- ✔ By calling the function from another Sub procedure or Function procedure
- ✔ By using the function in a worksheet formula

Try this simple function. Enter it into a VBA module:

```
Function CubeRoot(number)
    CubeRoot = number ^ (1/3)
End Function
```

This function is pretty wimpy — it merely calculates the cube root of the number passed to it as its argument. It does, however, provide a starting point for understanding functions. It also illustrates an important concept about functions: how to return the value that makes functions so important. (You remember that functions return values, right?)

Notice that the single line of code that makes up this Function procedure is a formula. The result of the math (number to the power of 1/3) is assigned to the variable CubeRoot. Notice that Squared CubeRoot is the function name, as well. To tell the function what value to return, you assign that value to the name of the function.

Calling the function from a Sub procedure

Because you can't execute this function directly, you must call it from another procedure. Enter the following simple procedure in the same VBA module that contains the CubeRoot function:

```
Sub CallerSub()
    Ans = CubeRoot(125)
    MsgBox Ans
End Sub
```

When you execute the CallerSub procedure (using any of the methods describes earlier in this chapter), Excel displays a message box that contains the value of the Ans variable, which is 5.

Here's what's going on: The CubeRoot function is executed using an argument of 125. The function returns a value. That value is assigned to the Ans variable. The MsgBox function then displays the value in the Ans variable. Try changing the argument that's passed to the CubeRoot function and run the CallerSub macro again. It works just like it should.

By the way, the CallerSub procedure could be simplified a bit. The Ans variable is not really required. You could use this single statement to obtain the same result:

```
MsgBox CubeRoot(125)
```

Calling a function from a worksheet formula

Now it's time to call this VBA Function procedure from a worksheet formula. Activate a worksheet in the same workbook that holds the CubeRoot function definition. Then enter the following formula into any cell:

```
=CubeRoot(1728)
```

The cell displays 12, which is indeed the cube root of 1728.

As you might expect, you can use a cell reference as the argument for the CubeRoot function. For example, if cell A1 contains a value, you can enter =CubeRoot(A1). In this case, the function returns the number obtained by calculating the cube root of the value in A1.

You can use this function any number of times in the worksheet. As with Excel's built-in functions, your custom functions also appear in the Insert Function dialog box. Click the Insert Function toolbar button and choose the User Defined category. As shown in Figure 5-6, the Insert Function dialog box lists your very own function.

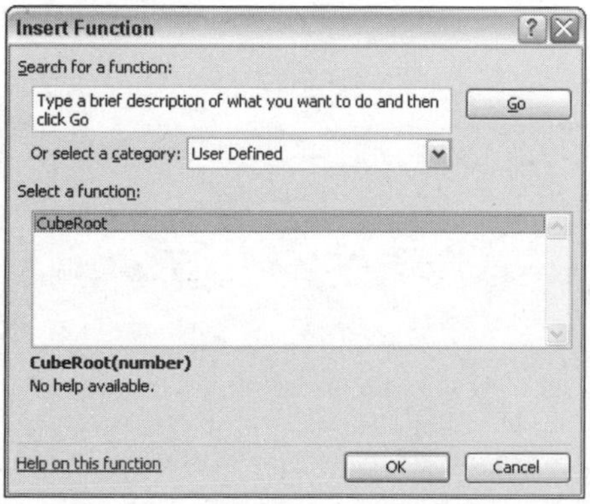

Figure 5-6: The CubeRoot function appears in the User Defined category of the Insert Function dialog box.

If you want the Insert Function dialog box to display a description of the function, follow these steps:

1. **Choose Tools⇨Macro⇨Macros.**

   Excel displays the Macro dialog box, but CubeRoot doesn't appear in the list. (CubeRoot is a Function procedure, and this list shows only Sub procedures.) Don't fret.

2. **Type the word** CubeRoot **in the Macro Name box.**

3. **Click the Options button.**

4. **Enter a description of the function in the Description box.**

5. **Close the Macro Options dialog box.**

6. **Close the Macro dialog box by clicking the Cancel button.**

   This descriptive text now appears in the Insert Function dialog box.

By now, things may be starting to come together for you. (I wish I had had this book when *I* was starting out.) You've found out lots about Sub and Function procedures. You start creating macros in Chapter 6, which discusses the ins and outs of developing macros using the Excel macro recorder.

Chapter 6

Using the Excel Macro Recorder

You can use two methods to create a macro:

✔ Record it using the Excel macro recorder

✔ Write it with VBA

This chapter deals specifically with the ins and outs of using the Excel macro recorder. Recording a macro isn't always the best approach, and some macros simply can't be recorded, no matter how hard you try. You see, however, that the Excel macro recorder is very useful. Even if your recorded macro isn't quite what you want, the recorder is an excellent learning tool.

Is It Live or Is It VBA?

Recording a macro is sort of like using a tape recorder. Turn it on, do your thing, and then turn it off. This analogy, however, goes only so far. Table 6-1 compares tape recording with macro recording.

Table 6-1	Tape Recording versus Macro Recording	
	Tape Recorder	*Excel Macro Recorder*
What equipment is required?	A tape recorder and a microphone.	A computer and a copy of Excel.
What is recorded?	Sounds.	Actions taken in Excel.
Where is the recording stored?	On magnetic tape.	In a VBA module.
How do you play it back?	Rewind the tape and press Play.	Choose Tools⇨Macro⇨Macros (or other methods).
Can you edit the recording?	Yes, if you have the proper equipment.	Yes, if you know what you're doing.
Can you copy the recording?	Yes, if you have a second tape recorder.	Yes (no additional equipment required).
Is the recording accurate?	Depends on the situation and the equipment quality.	Depends on how you set things up.
What if you make a mistake?	Rerecord the tape (or edit it if possible).	Rerecord the macro (or edit it if possible).
Can you view the recording?	No, it's just a bunch of magnetic impulses.	Yes, by activating a VBA module.
Can you make money with the recording?	Yes, if it's good (editing usually required).	Yes, but you need to do a lot of editing first.

Recording Basics

You take the following basic steps when recording a macro. I describe these steps in more detail later in this chapter.

1. **Determine what you want the macro to do.**

2. **Get things set up properly.**

   This step determines how well your macro works.

3. **Determine whether you want cell references in your macro to be relative or absolute.**

4. **Choose Tools⇨Macro⇨Record New Macro.**

   Excel displays its Record Macro dialog box.

5. **Enter a name, shortcut key, macro location, and description.**

   Each of these items — with the exception of the name — is optional.

6. **Click OK in the Record Macro dialog box.**

   Excel automatically inserts a VBA module. From this point, Excel converts your actions into VBA code. It also displays a miniature floating toolbar, which contains two toolbar buttons: Stop Recording and Relative Reference.

7. **Perform the actions you want recorded using the mouse or the keyboard.**

8. **After you're finished, click the Stop Recording button on the miniature toolbar (or choose Tools⇨Macro⇨Stop Recording).**

   Excel stops recording your actions.

9. **Test the macro to make sure it works correctly.**

The macro recorder is best suited for simple, straightforward macros. For example, you might want a macro that applies formatting to a selected range of cells or that sets up row and column headings for a new worksheet.

The macro recorder is for Sub procedures only. You can't use the macro recorder to create Function procedures.

You may also find the macro recorder helpful for developing more-complex macros. Often, I record some actions and then copy the recorded code into another, more complex macro. In most cases, you need to edit the recorded code and add some new VBA statements.

The macro recorder *cannot* generate code for any of the following tasks, which I describe later in the book:

- ✔ Performing any type of repetitive looping
- ✔ Performing any type of conditional actions (using an If-Then statement)
- ✔ Assigning values to variables
- ✔ Specifying data types
- ✔ Displaying pop-up messages
- ✔ Displaying custom dialog boxes

The macro recorder's limited capability certainly doesn't diminish its importance. I make this point throughout the book: *Recording your actions is perhaps the best way to learn VBA.* When in doubt, try recording. Although the result may not be exactly what you want, viewing the recorded code might steer you in the right direction.

Preparing to Record

Before you take the big step and turn on the macro recorder, spend a minute or two thinking about what you're going to do. You record a macro so that Excel can automatically repeat the actions you record.

Ultimately, the success of a recorded macro depends on five factors:

- ✔ How the workbook is set up while you record the macro
- ✔ What is selected when you start recording
- ✔ Whether you use absolute or relative recording mode
- ✔ The accuracy of your recorded actions
- ✔ The context in which you play back the recorded macro

The importance of these factors becomes crystal clear when I walk you through an example.

Relative or Absolute?

When recording your actions, Excel normally records absolute references to cells. (This is the default recording mode.) Very often, this is the *wrong* recording mode. If you use relative recording, Excel records relative references to cells. The distinction is explained in this section.

Recording in absolute mode

Follow these steps to record a simple macro in absolute mode. This macro simply enters three month names into a worksheet:

1. **Choose Tools⇨Macro⇨Record New Macro.**

2. **Type** Absolute **as the name for this macro.**

3. **Click OK to begin recording.**

4. **Activate cell B1 and type** Jan **in that cell.**

5. **Move to cell C1 and type** Feb.

6. **Move to cell D1 and type** Mar.

7. **Click cell B1 to activate it again.**

8. **Stop the macro recorder.**

9. **Press Alt+F11 to activate the VBE.**

10. **Examine the Module1 module.**

Excel generates the following code:

```
Sub Absolute()
'
' Absolute Macro
' Macro recorded by John Walkenbach
'
    Range("B1").Select
    ActiveCell.FormulaR1C1 = "Jan"
    Range("C1").Select
    ActiveCell.FormulaR1C1 = "Feb"
    Range("D1").Select
    ActiveCell.FormulaR1C1 = "Mar"
    Range("B1").Select
End Sub
```

When executed, this macro selects cell B1 and inserts the three month names in the range B1:D1. Then the macro reactivates cell B1

These same actions occur regardless of which cell is active when you execute the macro. A macro recorded using absolute references always produces the same results when it is executed. In this case, the macro always enters the names of the first three months into the range B1:D1.

Recording in relative mode

In some cases you want your recorded macro to work with cell locations in a *relative* manner. You may want the macro to start entering the month names in the active cell. In such a case, you need to use relative recording.

The Stop Recording toolbar, which consists of only two buttons, is displayed when you are recording a macro. You can change the manner in which Excel records your actions by clicking the Relative Reference button on the Stop Recording toolbar. This button is a toggle. When the button appears in a pressed state, the recording mode is relative. When the button appears normally, you are recording in absolute mode.

You can change the recording method at any time, even in the middle of recording.

To see how relative mode recording works, erase the cells in B1:D1 and then perform the following steps:

1. **Activate cell B1.**
2. **Choose Tools⇨Macro⇨Record New Macro.**
3. **Name this macro** Relative.
4. **Click OK to begin recording.**
5. **Click the Relative Reference button to change the recording mode to relative.**

   When you click this button, it looks pressed.
6. **Activate cell B1 and type** Jan **in that cell.**
7. **Move to cell C1 and type** Feb.
8. **Move to cell D1 and type** Mar.
9. **Select cell B1.**
10. **Stop the macro recorder.**

Notice that this procedure differs slightly from the previous example. In this example, you activate the beginning cell *before* you start recording. This is an important step when you record macros that use the active cell as a base.

This macro always starts entering text in the active cell. Try it. Move the cell pointer to any cell and then execute the Relative macro. The month names are always entered beginning at the active cell.

With the recording mode set to relative, the code Excel generates is quite different from absolute mode:

```
Sub Relative()
'
' Relative Macro
' Macro recorded by John Walkenbach
'
    ActiveCell.FormulaR1C1 = "Jan"
    ActiveCell.Offset(0, 1).Range("A1").Select
    ActiveCell.FormulaR1C1 = "Feb"
    ActiveCell.Offset(0, 1).Range("A1").Select
    ActiveCell.FormulaR1C1 = "Mar"
    ActiveCell.Offset(0, -2).Range("A1").Select
End Sub
```

To test this macro, activate any cell except B1. The month names are entered in three cells, beginning with the cell that you activated.

Notice that the code generated by the macro recorder refers to cell A1. This may seem strange because you never used cell A1 during the recording of the macro. This is simply a byproduct of the way the macro recorder works. (I discuss this in more detail in Chapter 8 where I talk about the Offset method.)

What Gets Recorded?

When you turn on the macro recorder, Excel converts your mouse and keyboard actions into valid VBA code. I could probably write several pages describing how Excel does this, but the best way to understand the process is by watching the macro recorder in action. (Figure 6-1 shows how my screen looked while I had the macro recorder turned on.)

Follow these steps:

1. **Start with a blank workbook.**

2. **Make sure that the Excel window is not maximized.**

3. **Press Alt+F11 to activate the VBE (and make sure that *this* program window is not maximized).**

4. **Resize and arrange the Excel window and the VBE window so that both are visible.**

   For best results, position the Excel window on top of the VBE window, and minimize any other applications that are running.

5. **Activate Excel and choose Tools⇨Macro⇨Record New Macro.**

6. **Click OK to start the macro recorder.**

   Excel inserts a new module (named Module1) and starts recording in that module.

7. **Activate the VBE program window.**

8. **In the Project Explorer window, double-click Module1 to display that module in the Code window.**

Now play around for a while: Choose various Excel commands and watch the code being generated in the VBE window. Select cells, enter data, format cells, use the menus and toolbars, create a chart, manipulate graphics objects, and so on — go crazy! I guarantee that you'll be enlightened as you watch Excel spit out the VBA code before your very eyes.

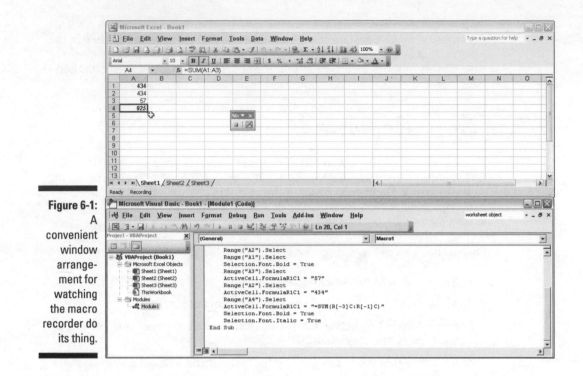

Figure 6-1: A convenient window arrangement for watching the macro recorder do its thing.

Recording Options

When recording your actions to create VBA code, you have several options. Recall that the Tools➪Macro➪Record New Macro command displays the Record Macro dialog box before recording begins, as shown in Figure 6-2.

The Record Macro dialog box, shown in Figure 6-2 gives you quite a bit of control over your macro. In the following sections, I describe these options.

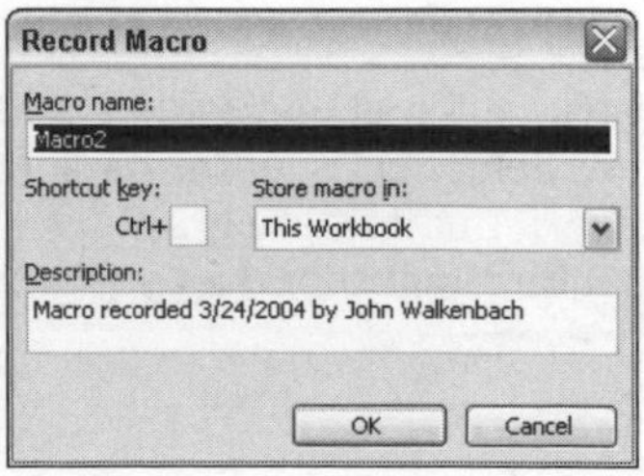

Figure 6-2: The Record Macro dialog box provides several options.

Macro name

You can enter a name for the Sub procedure that you are recording. By default, Excel uses the names Macro1, Macro2, and so on for each macro you record. I usually just accept the default name. If the macro works correctly and I want to save it, I give it a more descriptive name later on. You, however, may prefer to name the macro upfront — the choice is yours.

Shortcut key

The Shortcut key option lets you execute the macro by pressing a shortcut key combination. For example, if you enter w (lowercase), you can execute the macro by pressing Ctrl+w. If you enter W (uppercase), the macro comes alive when you press Ctrl+Shift+W.

You can add or change a shortcut key at any time, so you don't have to set this option when recording a macro. See Chapter 5 for instructions on assigning a shortcut key to an existing macro.

Store Macro In

The Store Macro In option tells Excel where to store the macro that it is recording. By default, Excel puts the recorded macro in a module in the active workbook. If you prefer, you can record it in a new workbook (Excel opens a blank workbook) or in your Personal Macro Workbook.

Your Personal Macro Workbook is a hidden workbook that opens automatically when Excel starts. This is a good place to store macros that you'll use with multiple workbooks. The Personal Macro Workbook is named personal. xls and it is created the first time you specify it as the location for a recorded macro.

Description

When you record a macro, the macro begins with five comment lines (three of them blank) that list the macro name, the user's name, and the date. You can put anything you like here or nothing at all. As far as I'm concerned, the Description option is a waste of time because I always end up deleting these lines in the module.

Is This Thing Efficient?

You might think that recording a macro would generate some award-winning VBA code — better than you could ever write manually. Think again. In many cases, the recorder spits out lots of extraneous garbage, and it often generates code that's less than efficient.

Don't get me wrong. I'm a staunch supporter of the macro recorder. It's a great tool for helping you learn VBA. Except for simple macros, however, I've never used a recorded macro without fixing it up a bit (usually *quite* a bit).

To demonstrate just how inefficient the macro recorder's code can be, try this:

1. **Turn on the macro recorder.**
2. **Choose File⇨Page Setup.**

   The Page Setup dialog box appears.
3. **Make sure the Page tab is selected.**
4. **Change the page orientation to Landscape and click OK.**
5. **Turn off the macro recorder.**

To take a look at the macro, activate the Module1 sheet. This single — and very simple — command generates the following code:

```
Sub Macro1()
'
' Macro1 Macro
' Macro recorded by John Walkenbach
'
    With ActiveSheet.PageSetup
        .PrintTitleRows = ""
        .PrintTitleColumns = ""
    End With
    ActiveSheet.PageSetup.PrintArea = ""
    With ActiveSheet.PageSetup
        .LeftHeader = ""
        .CenterHeader = ""
        .RightHeader = ""
        .LeftFooter = ""
        .CenterFooter = ""
        .RightFooter = ""
        .LeftMargin = Application.InchesToPoints(0.75)
        .RightMargin = Application.InchesToPoints(0.75)
        .TopMargin = Application.InchesToPoints(1)
        .BottomMargin = Application.InchesToPoints(1)
```

```
        .HeaderMargin = Application.InchesToPoints(0.5)
        .FooterMargin = Application.InchesToPoints(0.5)
        .PrintHeadings = False
        .PrintGridlines = False
        .PrintComments = xlPrintNoComments
        .PrintQuality = 600
        .CenterHorizontally = False
        .CenterVertically = False
        .Orientation = xlLandscape
        .Draft = False
        .PaperSize = xlPaperLetter
        .FirstPageNumber = xlAutomatic
        .Order = xlDownThenOver
        .BlackAndWhite = False
        .Zoom = 100
        .PrintErrors = xlPrintErrorsDisplayed
    End With
End Sub
```

You may be surprised by the amount of code generated by this single command. (I was, the first time I tried something like this.) Although you changed only one setting in the Page Setup dialog box, Excel generated code that reproduces *all* the settings in the dialog box.

This is a good example of macro-recording overkill. If you want a macro that simply switches the page setup to landscape mode, simplify this macro considerably by deleting the extraneous code. This makes the macro faster and easier to read. You can simplify this macro as follows:

```
Sub Macro1()
    With ActiveSheet.PageSetup
        .Orientation = xlLandscape
    End With
End Sub
```

I deleted all the code except the line that sets the Orientation property. Actually, you can simplify this macro even more because you don't really need the With.End With construct:

```
Sub Macro1()
    ActiveSheet.PageSetup.Orientation = xlLandscape
End Sub
```

In this case, the macro changes the Orientation property of the PageSetup object on the active sheet. All other properties are unchanged. By the way, xlLandscape is a built-in constant that makes things easier. I discuss built-in constants in Chapter 7.

Rather than record this macro, you could enter it directly into a VBA module. To do so, you have to know which objects, properties, and methods to use. Although the recorded macro isn't all that great, by recording it you realize that the PageSetup object has an Orientation property. This example shows how the macro recorder can help you learn VBA.

This chapter nearly sums it up when it comes to using the macro recorder. The only thing missing is experience. Eventually, you discover which recorded statements you can safely delete. Better yet, you discover how to modify a recorded macro to make it more useful.

Part III

Programming Concepts

The 5th Wave   By Rich Tennant

"We're concerned.—Kyle doesn't seem to be able to hot key between apps like all the other children."

In this part . . .

This is the part of the book that you've been waiting for. In the next eight chapters, you find out about all the essential elements of Excel programming. And in the process, you see some illuminating examples that you can adapt to your own needs.

Chapter 7

Essential VBA Language Elements

● ●

In This Chapter

▶ Knowing when, why, and how to use comments in your code

▶ Using variables and constants

▶ Telling VBA what type of data you're using

▶ Knowing why you may need to use labels in your procedures

● ●

*B*ecause VBA is a real, live programming language, it uses many elements common to all programming languages. In this chapter, I introduce you to several of these elements: comments, variables, constants, data types, arrays, and a few other goodies. If you've programmed using other languages, some of this material will be familiar. If you're a programming newbie, it's time to roll up your sleeves and get busy.

Using Comments in Your VBA Code

A *comment* is the simplest type of VBA statement. Because VBA ignores these statements, they can consist of anything you want. You can insert a comment to remind yourself why you did something or to clarify some particularly elegant code you wrote. Use comments liberally to describe what the code does (which isn't always obvious by reading the code itself). Often, code that makes perfect sense today mystifies you tomorrow. Been there. Done that.

You begin a comment with an apostrophe ('). VBA ignores any text that follows an apostrophe in a line of code. You can use a complete line for your comment or insert your comment at the end of a line of code. The following example shows a VBA procedure with three comments, though they're not necessarily *good* comments:

```
Sub CommentsDemo()
'   This procedure does nothing of value
    x = 0   'x represents nothingness
    'Display the result
    MsgBox x
End Sub
```

The "apostrophe indicates a comment" rule has one exception: VBA doesn't interpret an apostrophe inside a set of quotation marks as a comment indicator. For example, the following statement doesn't contain a comment, even though it has an apostrophe:

```
Msg = "Can't continue"
```

When you're writing code, you may want to test a procedure *without* a particular statement or group of statements. Rather than delete the statements, simply turn them into comments by inserting apostrophes. VBA ignores statements enclosed in apostrophes when executing a routine. Simply remove the apostrophes to convert the comments back to statements.

When testing a procedure you may want to remove some statements temporarily. Rather than delete the statements, you can convert them to comments. Then, when testing is completed, convert the comments back to statements. In the VBE, choose View⇨Toolbars⇨Edit to display the Edit toolbar that you see in Figure 7-1. To convert a block of statements to comments, select the statements and click the Comment Block button. To remove the apostrophes, select the statements and click the Uncomment Block button.

Figure 7-1:
The VBE Edit toolbar contains several useful buttons.

Comment block

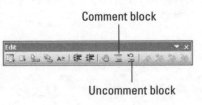

Uncomment block

Although comments can be helpful, not all comments are created equal. For example, the following procedure uses lots of comments, but they add nothing of value. The code is clear enough without the comments.

```
Sub BadComments()
'   Declare variables
    Dim x As Integer
    Dim y As Integer
    Dim z As Integer
'   Start the routine
    x = 100 ' Assign 100 to x
    y = 200 ' Assign 200 to y
'   Add x and y and store in z
    z = x + y
'   Show the result
    MsgBox z
End Sub
```

Everyone develops his or her own style of commenting. To be useful, however, comments should convey information that's not immediately obvious from reading the code. Otherwise, comments just chew up bytes and make files larger than necessary.

The following tips can help you make effective use of comments:

✔ Briefly describe the purpose of each Sub or Function procedure you write.

✔ Use comments to keep track of changes you make to a procedure.

✔ Use a comment to indicate that you're using a function or a construct in an unusual or nonstandard manner.

✔ Use comments to describe the variables you use, especially if you don't use meaningful variable names.

✔ Use a comment to describe any workarounds you develop to overcome bugs in Excel.

✔ Write comments as you develop code, rather than saving the task for a final step.

Using Variables, Constants, and Data Types

VBA's main purpose is to manipulate data. VBA stores the data in your computer's memory; it may or may not end up on disk. Some data, such as worksheet ranges, resides in objects. Other data is stored in variables that you create.

Understanding variables

A *variable* is simply a named storage location in your computer's memory. You have lots of flexibility in naming your variables, so make the variable names as descriptive as possible. You assign a value to a variable using the equal sign operator. (More about this later in the "Using Assignment Statements" section.)

The variable names in these examples are on the left side of the equal signs. Note that the last example uses two variables.

```
x = 1
```

```
InterestRate = 0.075
```

```
LoanPayoffAmount = 243089

DataEntered = False

x = x + 1

UserName = "Bob Johnson"

DateStarted = #3/14/2004#

MyNum = YourNum * 1.25
```

VBA enforces a few rules regarding variable names:

- ✔ You can use letters, numbers, and some punctuation characters, but the first character must be a letter.
- ✔ You cannot use any spaces or periods in a variable name.
- ✔ VBA does not distinguish between uppercase and lowercase letters.
- ✔ You cannot use the following characters in a variable name: #, $, %, &, or ! .
- ✔ Variable names can be no longer than 254 characters. Of course, you're only asking for trouble if you use variable names 254 characters long.

To make variable names more readable, programmers often use mixed case (for example, InterestRate) or the underscore character (interest_rate).

VBA has many reserved words that you can't use for variable names or procedure names:

- ✔ Built-in VBA function names such as Ucase and Sqr
- ✔ VBA language words such as Sub, With, and For

If you attempt to use one of these names as a variable, you may get a compile error (your code won't run). So, if an assignment statement produces an error message, double-check and make sure that the variable name isn't a reserved word.

What are VBA's data types?

When I talk about *data type,* I'm referring to the manner in which a program stores data in memory — for example, as integers, real numbers, or strings. Although VBA can take care of these details automatically, it does so at a cost. (There's no free lunch.) Letting VBA handle your data typing results in slower execution and inefficient memory use. For small applications, this usually doesn't present much of a problem. But for large or complex applications, which may be slow or need to conserve every last byte of memory, you need to be on familiar terms with data types.

VBA's automatically handling all the data details makes life easy for programmers. Not all programming languages provide this luxury. For example, some languages are *strictly typed,* which means the programmer must explicitly define the data type for every variable used.

VBA has a variety of built-in data types. Table 7-1 lists the most common types of data that VBA can handle.

Table 7-1	VBA's Built-in Data Types	
Data Type	*Bytes Used*	*Range of Values*
Boolean	2	True or False
Integer	2	−32,768 to 32,767
Long	4	−2,147,483,648 to 2,147,483,647
Single	4	−3.402823E38 to 1.401298E45
Double (negative)	8	−1.79769313486232E308 to −4.94065645841247E 324
Double (positive)	8	4.94065645841247E−324 to 1.79769313486232E308
Currency	8	−922,337,203,685,477.5808 to 922,337,203,685,477.5807
Date	8	1/1/100 to 12/31/9999
String	1 per char	Varies
Object	4	Any defined object
Variant	Varies	Any data type
User defined	Varies	Varies

In general, choose the data type that uses the smallest number of bytes but can still handle all the data the program assigns to it.

Declaring and scoping variables

If you read the preceding sections, you now know a bit about variables and data types. In this section, you discover how to declare a variable as a certain data type.

If you don't declare the data type for a variable you use in a VBA routine, VBA uses the default data type: variant. Data stored as a variant acts like a chameleon; it changes type depending on what you do with it. For example, if a variable is a variant data type and contains a text string that looks like a number (such as "143"), you can use this variable for string manipulations as well as numeric calculations. VBA automatically handles the conversion, which may seem like an easy way out — but remember that you sacrifice speed and memory.

Before you use variables in a procedure, it's an excellent practice to *declare* your variables — that is, tell VBA each variable's data type. Declaring your variables makes your program run faster and use memory more efficiently. The default data type, variant, causes VBA to repeatedly perform time-consuming checks and reserve more memory than necessary. If VBA knows a variable's data type, it doesn't have to investigate and can reserve just enough memory to store the data.

To force yourself to declare all the variables you use, include the following as the first statement in your VBA module:

```
Option Explicit
```

When this statement is present, you won't be able to run your code if it contains any undeclared variable.

You need to use Option Explicit only once: at the beginning of your module. Keep in mind that the Option Explicit statement applies only to the module in which it resides. If you have more than one VBA module in a project, you need an Option Explicit statement for each module.

Suppose that you use an undeclared variable (that is, a variant) named CurrentRate. At some point in your routine, you insert the following statement:

```
CurentRate = .075
```

This misspelled variable, which is difficult to spot, will probably cause your routine to give incorrect results. If you use Option Explicit at the beginning of your module (and declare the CurrentRate variable), Excel generates an error if it encounters a misspelled variation of that variable.

To ensure that the Option Explicit statement is inserted automatically whenever you insert a new VBA module, turn on the Require Variable Definition option. You'll find it in the Editor tab of the Options dialog box (in the VBE, choose Tools⇨Options). I highly recommend doing so.

You now know the advantages of declaring variables, but *how* do you do this? Before getting into the mechanics, I need to discuss one more topic: a variable's scope.

Recall that a workbook can have any number of VBA modules. And a VBA module can have any number of Sub and Function procedures. A variable's *scope* determines which modules and procedures can use the variable. Table 7-2 describes the scopes in detail.

Table 7-2	Variable's Scope
Scope	*How the Variable Is Declared*
Procedure only	By using a Dim or a Static statement in the procedure that uses the variable
Module only	By using a Dim statement before the first Sub or Function statement in the module
All procedures in all modules	By using a Public statement before the first Sub or Function statement in a module

If you're completely confused at this point, don't despair. I discuss each of these in the following sections.

Procedure-only variables

The lowest level of scope for a variable is at the procedure level. (A *procedure* is either a Sub or a Function procedure.) Variables declared with this scope can be used only in the procedure in which they are declared. When the procedure ends, the variable no longer exists, and Excel frees up its memory. If you execute the procedure again, the variable comes back to life, but its previous value is lost.

The most common way to declare a procedure-only variable is with a Dim statement placed between a Sub statement and an End Sub statement (or between a Function and an End Function statement). The Dim keyword is short for *dimension,* which simply means you are setting aside memory for a particular variable. You usually place Dim statements immediately after the Sub or Function statement and before the procedure's code.

The following example shows some procedure-only variables declared by using Dim statements:

```
Sub MySub()
    Dim x As Integer
    Dim First As Long
    Dim InterestRate As Single
    Dim TodaysDate As Date
    Dim UserName As String
    Dim MyValue
'    ... [The procedure's code goes here] ...
End Sub
```

Notice that the last Dim statement in the preceding example doesn't declare a data type; it declares only the variable itself. The effect is that the variable MyValue is a variant.

By the way, you can also declare several variables with a single Dim statement, as in the following example:

```
Dim x As Integer, y As Integer, z As Integer
Dim First As Long, Last As Double
```

Unlike some languages, VBA doesn't allow you to declare a group of variables to be a particular data type by separating the variables with commas. For example, though valid, the following statement does *not* declare all the variables as integers:

```
Dim i, j, k As Integer
```

In this example, only k is declared to be an integer; the other variables are declared to be variants.

If you declare a variable with procedure-only scope, other procedures in the same module can use the same variable name, but each instance of the variable is unique to its own procedure. In general, variables declared at the procedure level are the most efficient because VBA frees up the memory they use when the procedure ends.

Module-only variables

Sometimes, you want a variable to be available to all procedures in a module. If so, just declare the variable *before* the module's first Sub or Function statement — outside any procedures. This is done in the Declarations section, at the beginning of your module. (This is also where the Option Explicit statement, discussed earlier in this chapter, is located.) Figure 7-2 shows how you know when you are working with the Declarations section.

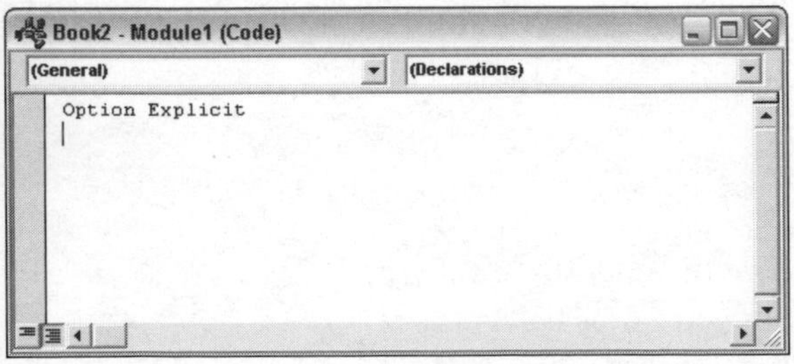

Figure 7-2:
Each VBA module has a Declarations section, which appears before any Sub or Function procedures.

As an example, suppose that you want to declare the CurrentValue variable so that it's available to all the procedures in your module. All you need to do is use the Dim statement in the Declarations section:

```
Dim CurrentValue As Integer
```

With this declaration in place — and in the proper place — the CurrentValue variable can be used from any other procedure within the module, and it retains its value from one procedure to another.

Public variables

If you need to make a variable available to all the procedures in all your VBA modules in a workbook, declare the variable at the module level (in the Declarations section) by using the Public keyword. Here's an example:

```
Public CurrentRate As Long
```

The Public keyword makes the CurrentRate variable available to any procedure in the workbook — even those in other VBA modules. You must insert this statement before the first Sub or Function statement in a module.

If you would like a variable to be available to modules in other workbooks, you must declare the variable as Public and establish a reference to the workbook that contains the variable declaration. Set up a reference by using the Tools⇨References command in VBE.

Static variables

Normally, when a procedure ends all of the variables are reset. *Static variables* are a special case because they retain their value even when the procedure ends. You declare a static variable at the procedure level. A static variable may be useful if you need to track the number of times you execute a procedure. You can declare a static variable and increment it each time you run the procedure.

As shown in the following example, you declare static variables by using the Static keyword:

```
Sub MySub()
    Static Counter As Integer
    Dim Msg As String
    Counter = Counter + 1
    Msg = "Number of executions: " & Counter
    MsgBox Msg
End Sub
```

The code keeps track of the number of times the procedure was executed. The value of the Counter variable is not reset when the procedure ends.

Even though the value of a variable declared as Static is retained after a variable ends, that variable is unavailable to other procedures. In the preceding MySub procedure example, the Counter variable and its value are available only within the MySub procedure. In other words, it's a procedure-level variable.

Working with constants

A variable's value may (and usually does) change while your procedure is executing (that's why they call it a *variable*). Sometimes, you need to refer to a value or string that never changes — a *constant*. A constant is a named element whose value doesn't change.

As shown in the following examples, you declare constants by using the Const statement:

```
Const NumQuarters As Integer = 4
```

```
Const Rate = .0725, Period = 12
```

```
Const ModName As String = "Budget Macros"
```

```
Public Const AppName As String = "Budget Application"
```

Using constants in place of hard-coded values or strings is an excellent programming practice. For example, if your procedure needs to refer to a specific value (such as an interest rate) several times, it's better to declare the value as a constant and refer to its name rather than the value. This makes your code more readable and easier to change; should the need for changes arise, you have to change only one statement rather than several.

Like variables, constants have a scope. Keep these points in mind:

✔ To make a constant available within only a single procedure, declare the constant after the procedure's Sub or Function statement.

✔ To make a constant available to all procedures in a module, declare the constant in the Declarations section for the module.

✔ To make a constant available to all modules in the workbook, use the Public keyword and declare the constant in the Declarations section of any module.

If you attempt to change the value of a constant in a VBA routine, you get an error. This isn't surprising because a constant is constant. Unlike a variable, the value of a constant does not vary. If you need to change the value of a constant, what you really need is a variable.

Excel and VBA contain many predefined constants, which you can use without the need to declare them yourself. In general, you don't need to know the value of these constants to use them. The macro recorder usually uses constants rather than actual values.

The following simple procedure uses a built-in constant (xlCalculationManual) to change the Calculation property of the Application object. (In other words, this changes the Excel recalculation mode to manual.)

```
Sub CalcManual()
    Application.Calculation = xlCalculationManual
End Sub
```

I discovered the xlCalculationManual constant by recording a macro that changed the calculation mode. I also could have looked in the Help system under "Microsoft Excel Constants." As shown in Figure 7-3, the Help system lists all the built-in constants.

The actual value of the built-in xlCalculationManual constant is –4135. Obviously, it's easier to use the constant's name than to look up the value (even if you knew where to look). By the way, the constant for changing to automatic calculation mode is xlCalculationAutomatic; its value is –4105. As you can see, many of the built-in constants are just arbitrary numbers that have special meaning to VBA.

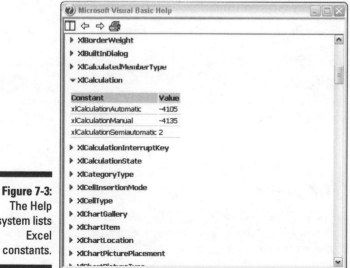

Figure 7-3:
The Help
system lists
Excel
constants.

To find the actual value of a built-in constant, execute a VBA statement such as the following:

```
MsgBox xlCalculationAutomatic
```

Working with strings

Excel can work with both numbers and text, so it should come as no surprise that VBA has this same power. Text is often referred to as a *string*. You can work with two types of strings in VBA:

- ✔ **Fixed-length strings** are declared with a specified number of characters. The maximum length is about 65,526 characters.

- ✔ **Variable-length strings** theoretically can hold as many as two billion characters.

Each character in a string takes one byte of storage. In addition, a variable-length string consumes an additional 16 bytes. Therefore, if you're striving for efficiency, it's better to use fixed-length strings if possible.

When declaring a string variable with a Dim statement, you can specify the maximum length if you know it (it's a fixed-length string) or let VBA handle it dynamically (it's a variable-length string). The following example declares the MyString variable as a string with a maximum length of 50 characters. (Use an asterisk to specify the number of characters, up to the 65,526 character limit.) YourString is also declared as a string but its length is unspecified:

```
Dim MyString As String * 50
Dim YourString As String
```

When declaring a fixed-length string, do not use a comma in the number that specifies the string size. In fact, *never* use commas when entering a value in VBA.

Working with dates

Another data type you may find useful is date. You can use a string variable to store dates, but then you won't be able to perform date calculations. Using the date data type gives your routines greater flexibility. For example, you might need to calculate the number of days between two dates. This would be impossible if you used strings to hold your dates.

A variable defined as a date uses eight bytes of storage and can hold dates ranging from January 1, 0100 to December 31, 9999. That's a span of nearly 10,000 years and more than enough for even the most aggressive financial forecast. You can also use the date data type to work with time data (seeing as VBA lacks a time data type).

These examples declare variables and constants as a date data type:

```
Dim Today As Date
```

```
Dim StartTime As Date
```

```
Const FirstDay As Date = #1/1/2005#
```

```
Const Noon = #12:00:00#
```

In VBA, place dates and times between two hash marks, as shown in the preceding examples.

Date variables display dates according to your system's short date format, and display times according to your system's time format (either 12- or 24-hour). The Windows Registry stores these settings and you can modify them via the Regional and Language Options dialog box in the Windows Control Panel. Therefore, the VBA-displayed date or time format may vary, depending on the settings for the system on which the application is running.

Using Assignment Statements

An *assignment statement* is a VBA statement that assigns the result of an expression to a variable or an object. Excel's Help system defines the term *expression* as

> ". . . a combination of keywords, operators, variables, and constants that yields a string, number, or object. An expression can be used to perform a calculation, manipulate characters, or test data."

I couldn't have said it better myself.

Much of your work in VBA involves developing (and debugging) expressions. If you know how to create formulas in Excel, you'll have no trouble creating expressions. With a worksheet formula, Excel displays the result in a cell. A VBA expression, on the other hand, can be assigned to a variable.

Assignment statement examples

In the assignment statement examples that follow, the expressions are to the right of the equal sign:

```
x = 1
```

```
x = x + 1
```

```
x = (y * 2) / (z * 2)
```

```
HouseCost = 375000
```

```
FileOpen = True
```

```
Range("TheYear").Value = 2005
```

Expressions can be as complex as you need them to be; use the line continuation character (a space followed by an underscore) to make lengthy expressions easier to read.

Often, expressions use functions: VBA's built-in functions, Excel's worksheet functions, or functions that you develop using VBA. I discuss functions in Chapter 9.

About that equal sign

As you can see in the preceding example, VBA uses the equal sign as its assignment operator. You're probably accustomed to using an equal sign as a mathematical symbol for equality. Therefore, an assignment statement like the following may cause you to raise your eyebrows:

```
z = z + 1
```

How can z be equal to itself plus 1? Answer: It can't. In this case, the assignment statement is increasing the value of z by 1. Just remember that an assignment uses the equal sign as an operator, not a symbol of equality.

Other operators

Operators play a major role in VBA. Besides the equal sign operator (discussed in the previous section), VBA provides several other operators. Table 7-3 lists these operators, with which you are familiar from your worksheet formulas experience.

Table 7-3	VBA's Operators
Function	*Operator Symbol*
Addition	+
Multiplication	*
Division	/
Subtraction	-
Exponentiation	^
String concatenation	&
Integer division (the result is always an integer)	\
Modulo arithmetic (returns the remainder of a division operation)	Mod

The term *concatenation* is programmer speak for "put together." Thus, if you concatenate strings, you are combining strings to make a new and improved string.

As shown in Table 7-4, VBA also provides a full set of logical operators. Consult the Help system for complete details.

Table 7-4	VBA's Logical Operators
Operator	*What It Does*
Not	Performs a logical negation on an expression
And	Performs a logical conjunction on two expressions
Or	Performs a logical disjunction on two expressions
XoR	Performs a logical exclusion on two expressions
Eqv	Performs a logical equivalence on two expressions
Imp	Performs a logical implication on two expressions

The precedence order for operators in VBA is exactly the same as in Excel formulas. Exponentiation has the highest precedence. Multiplication and division come next, followed by addition and subtraction. You can use parentheses to change the natural precedence order, making whatever's sandwiched in parentheses come before any operator.

Working with Arrays

Most programming languages support arrays. An *array* is a group of variables that have a common name; you refer to a specific variable in the array by using the array name and an index number. For example, you may define an array of 12 string variables to hold the names of the months of the year. If you name the array *MonthNames,* you can refer to the first element of the array as MonthNames(1), the second element as MonthNames(2), and so on.

Declaring arrays

Before you can use an array, you must declare it. You declare an array with a Dim or a Public statement, just as you declare a regular variable. However, you also need to specify the number of elements in the array. You do this by specifying the first index number, the keyword to, and the last index number — all inside parentheses. The following example shows how to declare an array of 100 integers:

```
Dim MyArray(1 to 100) As Integer
```

When you declare an array, you can choose to specify only the upper index. VBA assumes that 0 is the lower index. Therefore, the following statements both declare the same 101-element array:

```
Dim MyArray(0 to 100) As Integer
```

```
Dim MyArray(100) As Integer
```

If you want VBA to assume that 1 is the lower index for your arrays, simply include the following statement in the Declarations section of your module:

```
Option Base 1
```

This statement forces VBA to use 1 as the first index number for arrays that declare only the upper index. If this statement is present, the following statements are identical, both declaring a 100-element array:

```
Dim MyArray(1 to 100) As Integer
```

```
Dim MyArray(100) As Integer
```

Multidimensional arrays

The arrays created in the previous examples are all one-dimensional arrays. Arrays you create in VBA can have as many as 60 dimensions — although you rarely need more than two or three dimensions in an array. The following example declares a 100-integer array with two dimensions:

```
Dim MyArray(1 to 10, 1 to 10) As Integer
```

You can think of this array as occupying a 10-by-10 matrix. To refer to a specific element in this array, you need to specify two index numbers. The following example shows how you can assign a value to an element in this array:

```
MyArray(3, 4) = 125
```

This statement assigns a value to a single element in the array. If you're thinking of the array in terms of a 10-by-10 matrix, this assigns 125 to the element located in the third row and fourth column of the matrix.

You can think of a three-dimensional array as a cube. Visualizing an array of more than three dimensions is more difficult. Sorry, I haven't yet mastered the fourth dimension and beyond.

Dynamic Arrays

You can also create *dynamic* arrays. A dynamic array doesn't have a preset number of elements. Declare a dynamic array with a blank set of parentheses:

```
Dim MyArray() As Integer
```

Before you can use this array, you must use the ReDim statement to tell VBA how many elements the array has. Usually, the number of elements in the array is determined while your code is running. You can use the ReDim statement any number of times, changing the array's size as often as you need. The following example demonstrates how to change the number of elements in a dynamic array. It assumes that the NumElements variable contains a value, which your code calculated.

```
ReDim MyArray(NumElements)
```

When you redimension an array by using ReDim, you wipe out any values currently stored in the array elements. You can avoid this by using the Preserve keyword. The following example shows how you can preserve an array's values when you redimension the array:

```
ReDim Preserve MyArray(NumElements)
```

If MyArray has ten elements and you execute the preceding statement, the first ten elements remain intact and the array has room for additional elements (up to the number contained in the variable NumElements).

The topic of arrays comes up again in Chapter 10, when I discuss looping.

Using Labels

In early versions of BASIC, every line of code required a line number. For example, if you were writing a BASIC program in the '70s (dressed, of course, in your bell bottoms) it may have looked something like this:

```
010: LET X=5
020: LET Y=3
030: LET Z=X*Y
040: PRINT Z
050: END
```

VBA permits the use of such line numbers and it even permits text labels. You don't typically use a label for each line, but you may occasionally need to use a label. For example, insert a label if you use a GoTo statement (which I discuss in Chapter 10). A label must begin with the first nonblank character in a line and end with a colon.

The information in this chapter becomes clearer as you read subsequent chapters. If you want to find out more about VBA language elements, I refer you to the VBA Help system. You'll find as much detail as you need, or care to know.

Chapter 8

Working with Range Objects

In This Chapter

▶ Finding out more about Range objects

▶ Understanding the various ways of referring to ranges

▶ Discovering some of the more useful Range object properties

▶ Uncovering some of the more useful Range object methods

In Chapter 4, I run the risk of overwhelming you with an introduction to Excel's object model. In that chapter, I also run through the basics of properties and methods. Additionally, I dig a bit deeper and take a closer look at Range objects. Why do you need to know so much about Range objects? Because much of the programming work you do in Excel focuses on Range objects. You can thank me later.

A Quick Review

A *Range object* represents a range contained in a Worksheet object. A Range object can be as small as a single cell or as large as every cell on a worksheet (A1:IV65536 or 16,777,216 cells).

You can refer to a Range object like this:

```
Range("A1:C5")
```

Or if the range has a name (created using Insert⇨Name⇨Define), you can use an expression like this:

```
Range("PriceList")
```

Unless you tell Excel otherwise, it assumes that you're referring to a range on the active worksheet. If anything other than a worksheet is active (such as a chart sheet), the range reference fails, and your macro displays an error message.

As shown in the following example, you can refer to a range outside the active sheet by qualifying the range reference with a worksheet name from the active workbook:

```
Worksheets("Sheet1").Range("A1:C5")
```

If you need to refer to a range in a different workbook (that is, any workbook other than the active workbook), you can use a statement like this:

```
Workbooks("Budget.xls").Worksheets("Sheet1").Range("A1:C5")
```

A Range object can consist of one or more entire rows or columns. You can refer to an entire row (in this case, row 3) by using syntax like this:

```
Range("3:3")
```

You can refer to an entire column (column 4 in this example) like this:

```
Range("D:D")
```

To further confuse matters, you can even work with noncontiguous ranges. (In Excel, you select noncontiguous ranges by holding down the Ctrl key while selecting various ranges.) The following expression refers to a two-area non-contiguous range. Notice that a comma separates the two areas.

```
Range("A1:B8,D9:G16")
```

Finally, recall that Range objects (like all other objects) have properties (which you can examine and change) and methods (which perform actions on the object).

Other Ways to Refer to a Range

The more you work with VBA, the more you realize that it's a fairly well-conceived language and is usually quite logical (despite what you may be thinking right now). Often, VBA provides multiple ways of performing an action. You can choose the most appropriate method for your problem. This section discusses some of the other ways to refer to a range.

This chapter barely scratches the surface for the Range object's properties and methods. As you work with VBA you'll probably need to access other properties and methods. The Help system is the best place to find out about them, but it's also helpful to simply record your actions and examine the code Excel generates.

The Cells property

Rather than use the VBA Range keyword, you can refer to a range via the Cells property.

Notice that I wrote Cells *property,* not Cells *object.* Although Cells may seem like an object, it's really not. Rather, Cells is a property that VBA evaluates; VBA then returns an object (more specifically, a Range object). If this seems strange, don't worry. Even Microsoft appears to be confused about this issue. In some earlier versions of Excel, the Cells property was known as the Cells method. Regardless of what it is, just understand that Cells is a handy way to refer to a range.

The Cells property takes two arguments: row and column. For example, the following expression refers to cell C2 on Sheet2:

```
Worksheets("Sheet2").Cells(2, 3)
```

You can also use the Cells property to refer to a multicell range. The following example demonstrates the syntax you use:

```
Range(Cells(1, 1), Cells(10, 10))
```

This expression refers to a 100-cell range that extends from cell A1 (row 1, column 1) to cell J10 (row 10, column 10).

The following statements both produce the same result; they enter a value of 99 into a 10-by-10 range of cells. More specifically, these statements set the Value property of the Range object:

```
Range("A1:J10").Value = 99
Range(Cells(1, 1), Cells(10, 10)).Value = 99
```

The advantage of using the Cells method to refer to ranges becomes apparent when you use variables rather than actual numbers as the Cells arguments. And things really start to click when you understand looping, which I cover in Chapter 10.

The Offset property

The Offset property provides another handy means for referring to ranges. This property, which operates on a Range object and returns another Range object, lets you refer to a cell that is a particular number of rows and columns away from another cell.

Like the Cells property, the Offset property takes two arguments. The first argument represents the number of rows to offset; the second represents the number of columns to offset.

The following expression refers to a cell one row below cell A1 and two columns to the right of cell A1. In other words, this refers to the cell commonly known as C2:

```
Range("A1").Offset(1, 2)
```

The Offset method can also use negative arguments. A *negative* row offset refers to a row above the range. A negative column offset refers to a column to the left of the range. The following example refers to cell A1:

```
Range("C2").Offset(-1, -2)
```

And, as you may expect, you can use 0 as one or both of the arguments for Offset. The following expression refers to cell A1:

```
Range("A1").Offset(0, 0)
```

The Offset method is most useful when you use variables instead of actual values for the arguments. In Chapter 10, I present some examples that demonstrate this.

Referring to entire columns and rows

If you need to refer to a range that consists of one or more entire columns, you can use an expression like the following:

```
Columns("A:C")
```

And to refer to one or more complete rows, use an expression like this:

```
Rows("1:5")
```

Some Useful Range Object Properties

A Range object has dozens of properties. You can write Excel programs non-stop for the next 40 years and never use them all. In this section, I briefly describe some of the more commonly used Range properties. For complete details, consult the Help system in the VBE.

Some Range properties are *read-only* properties, which means you can't change them. For example, every Range object has an Address property (which holds the range's address). You can access this read-only property, but you can't change it.

The examples that follow are typically statements rather than complete procedures. If you'd like to try any of these (which you should), create a Sub procedure to do so. Also, many of these statements work properly only if a worksheet is the active sheet.

The Value property

The Value property represents the value contained in a cell. It's a read-write property, so your VBA code can either read or change the value.

The following statement displays a message box that shows the value in cell A1 on Sheet1:

```
MsgBox Worksheets("Sheet1").Range("A1").Value
```

It stands to reason that you would read the Value property only for a single-cell Range object. For example, the following statement generates an error:

```
MsgBox Worksheets("Sheet1").Range("A1:C3").Value
```

You can, however, change the Value property for a range of any size. The following statement enters the number 123 into each cell in a range:

```
Worksheets("Sheet1").Range("A1:C3").Value = 123
```

Value is the default property for a Range object. In other words, if you omit a property for a Range, Excel uses its Value property. The following statements both enter a value of 75 into cell A1 on Sheet1:

```
Worksheets("Sheet1").Range("A1").Value = 75
Worksheets("Sheet1").Range("A1") = 75
```

The Text property

The Text property returns a string that represents the text as displayed in a cell — the formatted value. The Text property is read-only. For example, suppose that cell A1 contains the value 12.3 and is formatted to display two decimals and a dollar sign ($12.30). The following statement displays a message box containing $12.30:

```
MsgBox Worksheets("Sheet1").Range("A1").Text
```

But the next statement displays a message box containing 12.3:

```
MsgBox Worksheets("Sheet1").Range("A1").Value
```

The Count property

The Count property returns the number of cells in a Range (all cells, not just the nonblank cells). It's a read-only property. The following statement accesses a range's Count property and displays the result (9) in a message box:

```
MsgBox Range("A1:C3").Count
```

The Column and Row properties

The Column property returns the column number of a single-cell range; the Row property returns the row number of a single-cell range. Both are read-only properties. For example, the following statement displays 6 because the cell is in the sixth column:

```
MsgBox Sheets("Sheet1").Range("F3").Column
```

The next expression displays 3 because cell F3 is in the third row:

```
MsgBox Sheets("Sheet1").Range("F3").Row
```

If the Range object consists of more than one cell, the Column property returns the column number of the first column in the range, and the Row property returns the row number of the first row in the range.

Don't confuse the Column and Row properties with the Columns and Rows properties (discussed earlier in this chapter). The Column and Row properties return a single value. Columns and Rows properties return a Range object.

The Address property

Address, a read-only property, displays the cell address for a Range object in absolute notation (a dollar sign before the column letter and before the row number). The following statement displays the message box shown in Figure 8-1.

```
MsgBox Range(Cells(1, 1), Cells(5, 5)).Address
```

Figure 8-1:
This message box displays the Address property of a 1-by-5 range.

The HasFormula property

The HasFormula property (which is read-only) returns True if the single-cell Range contains a formula. It returns False if the cell does not have a formula. If the range consists of more than one cell, VBA returns True only if all cells in the range contain a formula, or False if all cells in the range don't have a formula. The property returns a Null if there is a mixture of formulas and nonformulas.

Be careful with the type of variables you use to maintain the results returned by the HasFormula property. When working with any property that returns a Null, it is easy to generate errors by using the wrong data types.

For example, assume that cell A1 contains a value and cell A2 contains a formula. The following statements generate an error because the range doesn't consist of all formulas or all nonformulas:

```
Dim FormulaTest As Boolean
FormulaTest = Range("A1:A2").HasFormula
```

To fix this type of situation, the best thing to do is simply make sure the FormulaTest variable is declared as a variant rather than as a Boolean. The following example demonstrates.

```
Dim FormulaTest As Variant
FormulaTest = Range("A1:A2").HasFormula
If TypeName(FormulaTest) = "Null" Then MsgBox "Mixed!"
```

The Font property

As I note earlier in this chapter (see "The Cells property"), a property can return an object. Here's another example: A Range object's Font property returns a Font object.

A Font object, as you may expect, has many accessible properties. To change some aspect of a range's font, you must first access the range's Font object and then manipulate the properties of that object. This might be confusing at first but it eventually makes sense.

The following expression returns a Font object for a range:

```
Range("A1").Font
```

The following statement sets to True the Bold property of the Font object contained in the Range object. In plain English, this makes the cell display in boldface:

```
Range("A1").Font.Bold = True
```

To see other examples of manipulating font objects, record your actions while you modify some of a range's font attributes. See Chapter 6 for more information about recording macros.

The Interior property

Here's another example of a property that returns an object. A Range object's Interior property returns an Interior object (strange name, but that's what it's called). This type of object referencing works the same way as the Font property (which I describe in the preceding section).

For example, the following statement sets to 3 the ColorIndex property of the Interior object contained in the Range object:

```
Range("A1").Interior.ColorIndex = 3
```

In other words, this statement changes the cell's background to red.

The ColorIndex values correspond to the color palette Excel currently uses. The ColorIndex value can be any value from 1 to 56. The easiest way to determine the ColorIndex for a particular color is to record your actions while changing a cell's color. If you need to use standard colors, use the Color property (instead of ColorIndex) along with a built-in constant: vbBlack, vbRed, vbGreen, vbYellow, vbBlue, vbMagenta, vbCyan, or vbWhite. For example, the following statement makes cell A1 yellow:

```
Range("A1").Interior.Color = vbYellow
```

The Formula property

The Formula property represents the formula in a cell. This is a read-write property, so you can access it to insert a formula into a cell. For example, the following statement enters a SUM formula into cell A13:

```
Range("A13").Formula = "=SUM(A1:A12)"
```

Notice that the formula is a text string and is enclosed in quotation marks. If you are using the Formula property to determine the formula already in a cell and the cell doesn't have a formula, the Formula property returns the cell's Value property.

The NumberFormat property

The NumberFormat property represents the number format (expressed as a text string) of the Range object. This is a read-write property, so your VBA code can change the number format. The following statement changes the number format of column A to percent with two decimal places:

```
Columns("A:A").NumberFormat = "0.00%"
```

Follow these steps to see a list of other number formats:

1. **Activate a worksheet.**
2. **Access the Format Cells dialog box by pressing Ctrl+1.**
3. **Click the Number tab.**
4. **Select the Custom category to view some additional number format strings.**

Some Useful Range Object Methods

As you know, a VBA method performs an action. A Range object has dozens of methods but, again, you won't need most of these. In this section, I point out some of the more commonly used Range object methods.

The Select method

Use the Select method to select a range of cells. The following statement selects a range on the active worksheet:

```
Range("A1:C12").Select
```

Before selecting a range, make sure you've activated the range's worksheet; otherwise, you get an error or the wrong range is selected. For example, if Sheet1 contains the range you want to select, use the following statements to select the range:

```
Sheets("Sheet1").Activate
Range("A1:C12").Select
```

Contrary to what you may expect, the following statement generates an error. In other words, you must use two statements instead of just one: one to activate the sheet and another to select the range.

```
Sheets("Sheet1").Range("A1:C12").Select
```

The Copy and Paste methods

You can perform copy and paste operations in VBA by using the Copy and Paste methods. The Copy method is applicable to the Range object, but the Paste method is applicable to the Worksheet object. This short macro copies range A1:A12 and pastes it to the range beginning at cell C1:

```
Sub CopyRange()
    Range("A1:A12").Select
    Selection.Copy
    Range("C1").Select
    ActiveSheet.Paste
End Sub
```

Notice that in the preceding example, which the macro recorder generated, the ActiveSheet object is used with the Paste method. This is a special version of the Worksheet object that refers to the presently selected worksheet. Also notice that the macro selects the range before copying it. However, you don't have to select a range before doing something with it. In fact, the following procedure accomplishes the same task as the preceding example by using a single statement:

```
Sub CopyRange2()
    Range("A1:A12").Copy Range("C1")
End Sub
```

This procedure takes advantage of the fact that the Copy method can use an argument that corresponds to the destination range for the copy operation.

The Clear method

The Clear method deletes the contents of a range and all the cell formatting. For example, if you want to zap everything in column D, the following statement does the trick:

```
Columns("D:D").Clear
```

You should be aware of two related methods. The ClearContents method deletes the contents of the range but leaves the formatting intact. The ClearFormats method deletes the formatting in the range but not the cell contents.

The Delete method

Clearing a range differs from deleting a range. When you *delete* a range, Excel shifts the remaining cells around to fill up the range you deleted.

The following example uses the Delete method to delete row 6:

```
Rows("6:6").Delete
```

When you delete a range that's not a complete row or column, Excel needs to know how to shift the cells. (To see how this works, experiment with the Excel Edit⇨Delete command.)

The following statement deletes a range and then fills the resulting gap by shifting the other cells to the left:

```
Range("C6:C10").Delete xlToLeft
```

The Delete method uses an argument that indicates how Excel should shift the remaining cells. In this case, I use a built-in constant (xlToLeft) for the argument. I could also use xlUp, another named constant.

Chapter 9

Using VBA and Worksheet Functions

- -

In This Chapter

▶ Using functions to make your VBA expressions more powerful

▶ Using the VBA built-in functions

▶ Using Excel worksheet functions in your VBA code

▶ Writing custom functions

- -

*I*n previous chapters, I allude to the fact that you can use functions in your VBA expressions. I provide a full explanation in this chapter. Functions can make your VBA code perform some powerful feats, with little or no programming effort required. If you like that idea, this chapter's for you.

What Is a Function?

All Excel users beyond rank beginners use worksheet functions in their formulas. The most common worksheet function is the SUM function, and you have hundreds of others at your disposal.

A *function* essentially performs a calculation and returns a single value. The SUM function, of course, returns the sum of a range of values. The same holds true for functions used in your VBA expressions: Each function does its thing and returns a single value.

The functions you use in VBA can come from three sources:

- ✔ Built-in functions provided by VBA
- ✔ Worksheet functions provided by Excel
- ✔ Custom functions that you (or someone else) write, using VBA

The rest of this chapter clarifies the differences and (I hope) convinces you of the value of using functions in your VBA code.

Using VBA Functions

VBA provides numerous built-in functions. Some of these functions take arguments and some do not.

VBA function examples

In this section, I present a few examples of using VBA functions in code. In many of these examples, I use the MsgBox function to display a value in a message box. Yes, MsgBox is a VBA function — a rather unusual one, but a function nonetheless. This useful function displays a message in a pop-up dialog box. For more details about the MsgBox function, see Chapter 15.

A workbook that contains all of the examples is available at this book's Web site.

Displaying the system date

The first example uses VBA's Date function to display the current system date in a message box:

```
Sub ShowDate()
    MsgBox Date
End Sub
```

Notice that the Date function doesn't use an argument. Unlike worksheet functions, a VBA function with no argument doesn't require an empty set of parentheses. In fact, if you provide an empty set of parentheses, the VBE will remove them.

To get the system date and time, use the Now function instead of the Date function. Or to get only the time, use the Time function.

Finding a string length

The following procedure uses the VBA Len function, which returns the length of a string. The Len function takes one argument: the string. When you execute this procedure, the message box displays 11 because the argument has 11 characters.

```
Sub GetLength()
    Dim MyString As String
    Dim StringLength As Integer
    MyString = "Hello World"
    StringLength = Len(MyString)
    MsgBox StringLength
End Sub
```

Excel also has a function, which you can use in your worksheet formulas. The Excel version and the VBA function work the same.

Displaying the integer part of a number

The following procedure uses the Fix function, which returns the *integer* portion of a value — the value without any decimal digits:

```
Sub GetIntegerPart()
    Dim MyValue As Double
    Dim IntValue As Integer
    MyValue = 123.456
    IntValue = Fix(MyValue)
    MsgBox IntValue
End Sub
```

In this case, the message box displays 123.

VBA has a similar function called Int. The difference between Int and Fix is how each deals with negative numbers.

- ✔ Int returns the first negative integer that's less than or equal to the argument.

- ✔ Fix returns the first negative integer that's greater than or equal to the argument.

Determining a file size

The following Sub procedure displays the size, in bytes, of the Excel executable file. It finds this value by using the FileLen function.

```
Sub GetFileSize()
    Dim TheFile As String
    TheFile = "c:\MSOFFICE\EXCEL\EXCEL.EXE"
    MsgBox FileLen(TheFile)
End Sub
```

Notice that this routine *hard codes* the filename (that is, it explicitly states the path). Generally, this isn't a good idea. The file might not be on the C drive, or the Excel folder may have a different name. The following statement shows a better approach:

```
TheFile = Application.Path & "\EXCEL.EXE"
```

Path is a property of the Application object. It simply returns the name of the folder in which the application (that is, Excel) is installed (without a trailing backslash).

Identifying the type of a selected object

The following procedure uses the TypeName function, which returns the type of the selected object (as a string):

```
Sub ShowSelectionType()
    Dim SelType As String
    SelType = TypeName(Selection)
    MsgBox SelType
End Sub
```

This could be a Range, a ChartObject, a TextBox, or any other type of object that can be selected.

The TypeName function is very versatile. You can also use this function to determine the data type of a variable.

VBA functions that do more than return a value

A few VBA functions go above and beyond the call of duty. Rather than simply return a value, these functions have some useful side effects. Table 9-1 lists them.

Table 9-1	Functions with Useful Side Benefits
Function	**What It Does**
MsgBox	Displays a handy dialog box containing a message and buttons. The function returns a code that identifies which button the user clicks. See Chapter 15 for details.
InputBox	Displays a simple dialog box that asks the user for some input. The function returns whatever the user enters into the dialog box. I discuss this in Chapter 15.

Function	What It Does
Shell	Executes another program. The function returns the *task ID* (a unique identifier) of the other program (or an error if the function can't start the other program).

Discovering VBA functions

How do you find out which functions VBA provides? Good question. The best source is the Excel Visual Basic Help system. I compiled a partial list of functions, which I share with you in Table 9-2. I omitted some of the more specialized or obscure functions.

For complete details on a particular function, type the function name into a VBA module, move the cursor anywhere in the text, and press F1.

Table 9-2	VBA's Most Useful Built-in Functions
Function	**What It Does**
Abs	Returns a number's absolute value
Array	Returns a variant containing an array
Asc	Converts the first character of a string to its ASCII value
Atn	Returns the arctangent of a number
Choose	Returns a value from a list of items
Chr	Converts an ANSI value to a string
Cos	Returns a number's cosine
CurDir	Returns the current path
Date	Returns the current system date
DateAdd	Returns a date to which a specified time interval has been added — for example, one month from a particular date
DateDiff	Returns an integer showing the number of specified time intervals between two dates, for example the number of months between now and your birthday
DatePart	Returns an integer containing the specified part of a given date — for example, a date's day of the year

(continued)

Table 9-2 *(continued)*

Function	What It Does
DateSerial	Converts a date to a serial number
DateValue	Converts a string to a date
Day	Returns the day of the month from a date value
Dir	Returns the name of a file or directory that matches a pattern
Erl	Returns the line number that caused an error
Err	Returns the error number of an error condition
Error	Returns the error message that corresponds to an error number
Exp	Returns the base of the natural logarithm (e) raised to a power
FileLen	Returns the number of bytes in a file
Fix	Returns a number's integer portion
Format	Displays an expression in a particular format
GetSetting	Returns a value from the Windows registry
Hex	Converts from decimal to hexadecimal
Hour	Returns the hours portion of a time
InputBox	Displays a box to prompt a user for input
InStr	Returns the position of a string within another string
Int	Returns the integer portion of a number
IPmt	Returns the interest payment for an annuity or loan
IsArray	Returns True if a variable is an array
IsDate	Returns True if an expression is a date
IsEmpty	Returns True if a variable has not been initialized
IsError	Returns True if an expression is an error value
IsMissing	Returns True if an optional argument was not passed to a procedure
IsNull	Returns True if an expression contains no valid data
IsNumeric	Returns True if an expression can be evaluated as a number

Function	*What It Does*
IsObject	Returns True if an expression references an OLE Automation object
LBound	Returns the smallest subscript for a dimension of an array
LCase	Returns a string converted to lowercase
Left	Returns a specified number of characters from the left of a string
Len	Returns the number of characters in a string
Log	Returns the natural logarithm of a number to base e
LTrim	Returns a copy of a string, with any leading spaces removed
Mid	Returns a specified number of characters from a string
Minute	Returns the minutes portion of a time value
Month	Returns the month from a date value
MsgBox	Displays a message box and (optionally) returns a value
Now	Returns the current system date and time
RGB	Returns a numeric RGB value representing a color
Right	Returns a specified number of characters from the right of a string
Rnd	Returns a random number between 0 and 1
RTrim	Returns a copy of a string, with any trailing spaces removed
Second	Returns the seconds portion of a time value
Sgn	Returns an integer that indicates a number's sign
Shell	Runs an executable program
Sin	Returns a number's sine
Space	Returns a string with a specified number of spaces
Sqr	Returns a number's square root
Str	Returns a string representation of a number
StrComp	Returns a value indicating the result of a string comparison
String	Returns a repeating character or string
Tan	Returns a number's tangent

(continued)

Table 9-2 *(continued)*

Function	What It Does
Time	Returns the current system time
Timer	Returns the number of seconds since midnight
TimeSerial	Returns the time for a specified hour, minute, and second
TimeValue	Converts a string to a time serial number
Trim	Returns a string without leading or trailing spaces
TypeName	Returns a string that describes a variable's data type
UBound	Returns the largest available subscript for an array's dimension
UCase	Converts a string to uppercase
Val	Returns the numbers contained in a string
VarType	Returns a value indicating a variable's subtype
Weekday	Returns a number representing a day of the week
Year	Returns the year from a date value

Using Worksheet Functions in VBA

Although VBA offers a decent assortment of built-in functions, you might not always find exactly what you need. Fortunately, you can also use most of Excel's worksheet functions in your VBA procedures. The only worksheet functions that you cannot use are those that have an equivalent VBA function.

VBA makes Excel's worksheet functions available through the WorksheetFunction object, which is contained in the Application object. (Remember, the Application object is Excel.) Therefore, any statement that uses a worksheet function must use the Application. WorksheetFunction qualifier. In other words, you must precede the function name with Application.WorksheetFunction (with a dot separating the two). The following is an example:

```
Total = Application.WorksheetFunction.Sum(Range("A1:A12"))
```

You can omit the Application part of the expression because it's assumed. You can also omit the WorksheetFunction part of the expression; VBA will determine that you want to use an Excel worksheet function. But if you do so, then you must include the Application part. In other words, these three expressions all work exactly the same:

```
Total = Application.WorksheetFunction.Sum(Range("A1:A12"))
Total = WorksheetFunction.Sum(Range("A1:A12"))
Total = Application.Sum(Range("A1:A12"))
```

My personal preference is to use the WorksheetFunction part just to make it perfectly clear that the code is using an Excel function.

Worksheet function examples

In this section, I demonstrate how to use worksheet functions in your VBA expressions.

Finding the maximum value in a range

Here's an example showing how to use the MAX worksheet function in a VBA procedure. This procedure displays the maximum value in the range named NumberList on the active worksheet:

```
Sub ShowMax()
    Dim TheMax As Double
    TheMax = WorksheetFunction.Max(Range("NumberList"))
    MsgBox TheMax
End Sub
```

You can use the MIN function to get the smallest value in a range. And, as you might expect, you can use other worksheet functions in a similar manner. For example, you can use the LARGE function to determine the *k*th-largest value in a range. The following expression demonstrates this:

```
SecondHighest = WorksheetFunction. _
    Large(Range("NumberList"),2)
```

Notice that the LARGE function uses two arguments; the second argument represents the *k*th part — 2 in this case (the second-largest value).

Calculating a mortgage payment

The next example uses the PMT worksheet function to calculate a mortgage payment. I use three variables to store the data that's passed to the Pmt function as arguments. A message box displays the calculated payment.

```
Sub PmtCalc()
    Dim IntRate As Double
    Dim LoanAmt As Double
    Dim Periods As Integer
    IntRate = 0.0825 / 12
    Periods = 30 * 12
    LoanAmt = 150000
    MsgBox WorksheetFunction.Pmt(IntRate, Periods, -LoanAmt)
End Sub
```

As the following statement shows, you can also insert the values directly as the function arguments:

```
MsgBox WorksheetFunction.Pmt(0.0825 /12, 360, -150000)
```

However, using variables to store the parameters makes the code easier to read and modify, if necessary.

Using a lookup function

The following example uses the simple lookup table shown in Figure 9-1. Range A1:B13 is named PriceList.

```
Sub GetPrice()
    Dim PartNum As Variant
    Dim Price As Double
    PartNum = InputBox("Enter the Part Number")
    Sheets("Prices").Activate
    Price = WorksheetFunction. _
        VLookup(PartNum, Range("PriceList"), 2, False)
    MsgBox PartNum & " costs " & Price
End Sub
```

You can download this workbook from the book's Web site.

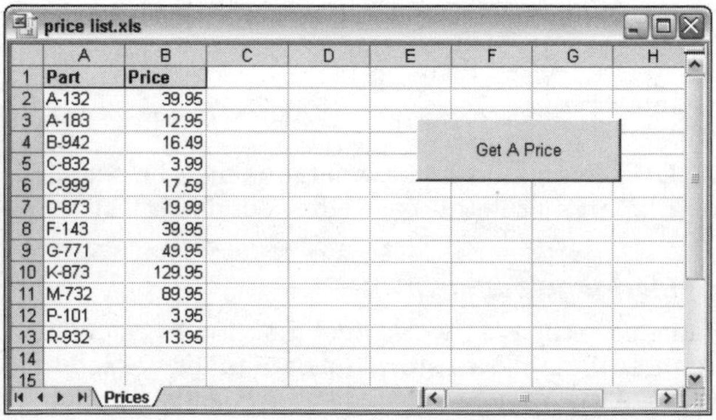

Figure 9-1:
The range,
named
PriceList,
contains
prices for
parts.

	A	B
1	Part	Price
2	A-132	39.95
3	A-183	12.95
4	B-942	16.49
5	C-832	3.99
6	C-999	17.59
7	D-873	19.99
8	F-143	39.95
9	G-771	49.95
10	K-873	129.95
11	M-732	89.95
12	P-101	3.95
13	R-932	13.95
14		
15		

price list.xls

Get A Price

Prices

The procedure starts this way:

1. VBA's InputBox function asks the user for a part number.

   Figure 9-2 shows the Microsoft Excel dialog box that displays when this statement is executed.

2. This statement assigns the part number the user enters for the PartNum variable.

3. The next statement activates the Prices worksheet, just in case it's not already the active sheet.

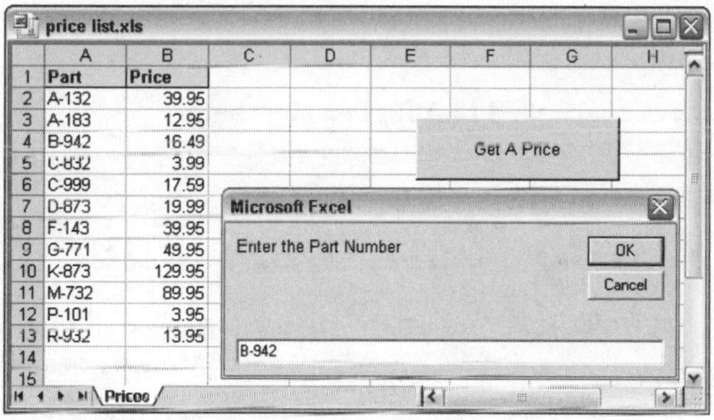

Figure 9-2:
Use the InputBox function to get the user's input.

4. The code uses the VLOOKUP function to find the part number in the table.

   Notice that the arguments you use in this statement are the same as those you would use with the function in a worksheet formula. This statement assigns the result of the function to the Price variable.

5. The code displays the price for the part via the MsgBox function.

This procedure doesn't have any error handling, and it fails miserably if you enter a nonexistent part number. (Try it.) Add some error-handling statements for a more robust procedure. I discuss error handling in Chapter 12.

Entering worksheet functions

You can't use the Excel Paste Function dialog box to insert a worksheet function into a VBA module. Instead, enter such functions the old-fashioned way: by hand. However, you *can* use the Paste Function dialog box to identify the function you want to use and find out about its arguments.

1. **Activate a worksheet.**

2. **Choose Insert⇨Function as you normally would.**

3. **Figure out how the function works.**

4. **Type the function and its arguments into your module.**

Follow these steps to display the VBE's Auto List Members option, which displays a drop-down list of all worksheet functions:

1. **Type** Application.WorksheetFunction, **followed by a period.**

2. **If this feature isn't working, choose the VBE's Tools⇨ Options command.**

3. **Click the Editor tab.**

4. **Place a check mark next to Auto List Members.**

More about Using Worksheet Functions

Newcomers to VBA often confuse VBA's built-in functions and Excel's workbook functions. A good rule to remember is that VBA doesn't try to reinvent the wheel. For the most part, VBA doesn't duplicate Excel worksheet functions.

Bottom line? If you need to use a function, first determine whether VBA has something that meets your needs. If not, check out the worksheet functions. If all else fails, you may be able to write a custom function by using VBA.

The WorksheetFunction object contains the worksheet functions available to VBA procedures. To see a list of these functions, you can use the Object Browser as shown in Figure 9-3. Follow these steps to display a complete list of worksheet functions available in VBA:

1. **In the VBE, press F2.**

   The Object Browser appears.

2. **In the Project/Library drop-down list (the one in the upper-left corner of the Object Browser), select Excel.**

3. **In the list labeled Classes, select WorksheetFunction.**

   The Members of list shows all the worksheet functions you can use in your code.

For most worksheet functions that are unavailable as methods of the Application object, you can use an equivalent VBA built-in operator or function. For example, the MOD worksheet function is unavailable in the WorksheetFunction object because VBA has an equivalent, built-in Mod operator. This is by design — a VBA operator works faster than an Excel function in a VBA module.

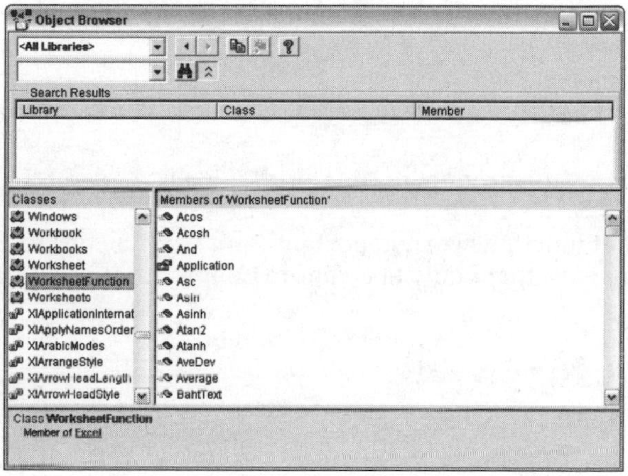

Figure 9-3:
Use the
Object
Browser to
show the
worksheet
function
available
in VBA.

Using Custom Functions

I've covered VBA functions and Excel worksheet functions. The third category of functions you can use in your VBA procedures is custom functions. A *custom function* is one you develop yourself using (what else?) VBA. To use a custom function, you must define it in the workbook in which you use it.

Here's an example of defining a simple Function procedure and then using it in a VBA Sub procedure:

```
Function MultiplyTwo(num1, num2)
    MultiplyTwo = num1 * num2
End Function

Sub ShowResult()
    Dim n1 As Double, n2 As Double
    Dim Result As Double
    n1 = 123
    n2 = 544
    Result = MultiplyTwo(n1, n2)
    MsgBox Result
End Sub
```

The custom function MultiplyTwo has two arguments. The ShowResult Sub procedure uses this Function procedure by passing two arguments to it (in parentheses). The ShowResult procedure then displays a message box showing the value returned by the MultiplyTwo function.

The MultiplyTwo function is fairly useless. It's much more efficient to perform the multiplication in the ShowResult Sub procedure. I include it simply to give you an idea of how a Sub procedure can make use of a custom function.

You can use custom functions also in your worksheet formulas. For example, if MultiplyTwo is defined in your workbook, you can write a formula such as this one:

```
=MultiplyTwo(A1,A2)
```

This formula returns the product of the values in cells A1 and A2.

Custom worksheet functions is an important (and very useful) topic. So important (and useful) that I devote an entire chapter to it. See Chapter 21.

Chapter 10

Controlling Program Flow and Making Decisions

In This Chapter

▶ Discovering methods for controlling the flow of your VBA routines

▶ Finding out about the dreaded GoTo statement

▶ Using If-Then and Select Case structures

▶ Performing looping in your procedures

S ome VBA procedures start at the code's beginning and progress line by line to the end, never deviating from this top-to-bottom program flow. Macros that you record always work like this. In many cases, however, you need to control the flow of your code by skipping over some statements, executing some statements multiple times, and testing conditions to determine what the procedure does next. Ready or not, you find out how to do all that stuff in this chapter.

Going with the Flow, Dude

Some programming newbies can't understand how a dumb computer can make intelligent decisions. The secret is in several programming constructs that most programming languages support. Table 10-1 provides a quick summary of these constructs. (I explain all of these later in this chapter.)

Table 10-1	Programming Constructs for Making Decisions
Construct	*How It Works*
GoTo statement	Jumps to a particular statement
If-Then structure	Does something if something else is true
Select Case	Does any of several things, depending on something's value
For-Next loop	Executes a series of statements a specified number of times
Do-While loop	Does something as long as something else remains true
Do-Until loop	Does something until something else becomes true

The GoTo Statement

A GoTo statement offers the most straightforward means for changing a program's flow. The GoTo statement simply transfers program control to a new statement, which is preceded by a label.

Your VBA routines can contain as many labels as you like. A *label* is just a text string followed by a colon. (See Chapter 7 for more label information.)

The following procedure shows how a GoTo statement works:

```
Sub GoToDemo()
    UserName = InputBox("Enter Your Name: ")
    If UserName <> "Bill Gates" Then GoTo WrongName
    MsgBox ("Welcome Bill...")
'   ...[More code here] ...
    Exit Sub
WrongName:
    MsgBox "Sorry. Only Bill Gates can run this."
End Sub
```

The procedure uses the InputBox function to get the user's name. If the user enters a name other than Bill Gates, the program flow jumps to the WrongName label, displays an apologetic message, and the procedure ends. On the other hand, if Mr. Gates signs on, the procedure displays a welcome message and then executes some additional code (not shown in the example). The Exit Sub statement ends the procedure before the second MsgBox function has a chance to work.

This simple routine works, but VBA provides several better (and more structured) alternatives than GoTo. In general, you should use GoTo only when you have no other way to perform an action. In practice, the only time you really need to use a GoTo statement is for trapping errors. (I cover this in Chapter 12.)

Many hard-core programming types have a deep-seated hatred for GoTo statements because using them tends to result in difficult-to-read "spaghetti code." Therefore, you should avoid this subject when talking with other programmers.

Decisions, decisions

In this section, I discuss two programming structures that can empower your VBA procedures with some impressive decision-making capabilities: If-Then and Select Case.

The If-Then structure

Okay, I'll say it: If-Then is VBA's most important control structure. You'll probably use this command on a daily basis (at least *I* do). As in many other aspects of life, effective decision making is the key to success in writing programs. If this book has the effect I intend, you'll soon share my philosophy that a successful Excel application boils down to making decisions and acting upon them.

What is structured programming? Does it matter?

If you hang around with programmers, sooner or later you hear the term *structured programming*. This term has been around for decades, and programmers generally agree that structured programs are superior to unstructured programs. So, what is structured programming? And can you write such things using VBA?

The basic premise of structured programming is that a routine or code segment should have only one entry point and one exit point. In other words, a block of code should be a stand-alone unit. A program cannot jump into the middle of this unit, nor can it exit at any point except the single exit point. When you write structured code, your program progresses in an orderly manner and is easy to follow — unlike a program that jumps around in a haphazard fashion. This pretty much rules out using the GoTo statement.

In general, a structured program is easier to read and understand. More importantly, it's also easier to modify when the need arises.

VBA is indeed a structured language. It offers standard structured constructs such as If-Then-Else, For-Next loops, Do-Until loops, Do-While loops, and Select Case structures. Furthermore, it fully supports module code constructions. If you're new to programming, you should try to develop good structure programming habits early on. End of lecture.

The If-Then structure has this basic syntax:

```
If condition Then statements [Else elsestatements]
```

Use the If-Then structure when you want to execute one or more statements conditionally. The optional Else clause, if included, lets you execute one or more statements if the condition you're testing is not true. Sound confusing? Don't worry; a few examples make this crystal clear.

If-Then examples

The following routine demonstrates the If-Then structure without the optional Else clause:

```
Sub GreetMe()
    If Time < 0.5 Then MsgBox "Good Morning"
End Sub
```

The GreetMe procedure uses VBA's Time function to get the system time. If the current system time is less than .5 (in other words, before noon), the routine displays a message. If Time is greater than or equal to .5, the routine ends and nothing happens.

To display a different greeting if Time is greater than or equal to .5, add another If-Then statement after the first one:

```
Sub GreetMe()
    If Time < 0.5 Then MsgBox "Good Morning"
    If Time >= 0.5 Then MsgBox "Good Afternoon"
End Sub
```

Notice that I used >= (greater than or equal to) for the second If-Then statement. This covers the extremely remote chance that the time is precisely 12:00 p.m.

An If-Then-Else example

Another approach to the preceding problem uses the Else clause. Here's the same routine recoded to use the If-Then-Else structure:

```
Sub GreetMe()
    If Time < 0.5 Then MsgBox "Good Morning" Else _
    MsgBox "Good Afternoon"
End Sub
```

Notice that I use the line continuation character (underscore) in the preceding example. The If-Then-Else statement is actually a single statement. But VBA provides a slightly different way of coding If-Then-Else constructs that use an End If statement. Therefore, the GreetMe procedure can be rewritten as:

```
Sub GreetMe()
    If Time < 0.5 Then
        MsgBox "Good Morning"
    Else
        MsgBox "Good Afternoon"
    End If
End Sub
```

In fact, you can insert any number of statements under the If part, and any number of statements under the Else part.

What if you need to expand the GreetMe routine to handle three conditions: morning, afternoon, and evening? You have two options: Use three If-Then statements or use a *nested* If-Then-Else structure. *Nesting* means placing an If-Then-Else structure within another If-Then-Else structure. The first approach, the three statements, is simplest:

```
Sub GreetMe2()
  Dim Msg As String
  If Time < 0.5 Then Msg = "Morning"
  If Time >= 0.5 And Time < 0.75 Then Msg = "Afternoon"
  If Time >= 0.75 Then Msg = " Evening"
  MsgBox "Good " & Msg
End Sub
```

The Msg variable gets a different text value, depending on the time of day. The final MsgBox statement displays the greeting: Good Morning, Good Afternoon, or Good Evening.

The following routine performs the same action but uses a nested If-Then-Else structure:

```
Sub GreetMe3()
  Dim Msg As String
  If Time < 0.5 Then Msg = "Morning" Else
    If Time >= 0.5 And Time < 0.75 Then Msg = "Afternoon"
            Else
        If Time >= 0.75 Then Msg = "Evening"
  MsgBox "Good " & Msg
End Sub
```

The example works fine but could be simplified a bit by omitting the last If-Then part. Because the routine has already tested for two conditions (morning and afternoon), the only remaining condition is evening. Here's the modified procedure:

```
Sub GreetMe4()
  Dim Msg As String
  If Time < 0.5 Then Msg = "Morning" Else
    If Time >= 0.5 And Time < 0.75 Then _
      Msg = "Afternoon" Else Msg = "Evening"
  MsgBox "Good " & Msg
End Sub
```

Using ElseIf

In both of the previous examples, every statement in the routine is executed — even in the morning. A more efficient structure would exit the routine as soon as a condition is found to be true. In the morning, for example, the procedure should display the Good Morning message and then exit — without evaluating the other superfluous conditions.

With a tiny routine like this, you don't have to worry about execution speed. But for larger applications in which speed is important, you should know about another syntax for the If-Then structure. The ElseIf syntax follows:

```
If condition Then
    [statements]
[ElseIf condition-n Then
    [elseifstatements]] . . .
[Else
    [elsestatements]]
End If
```

Here's how you can rewrite the GreetMe routine using this syntax:

```
Sub GreetMe5()
  Dim Msg As String
  If Time < 0.5 Then
    Msg = "Morning"
      ElseIf Time >= 0.5 And Time < 0.75 Then
        Msg = "Afternoon"
          Else
            Msg = "Evening"
  End If
  MsgBox "Good " & Msg
End Sub
```

When a condition is true, VBA executes the conditional statements and the If structure ends. In other words, VBA doesn't waste time evaluating the extraneous conditions, which makes this procedure a bit more efficient than the previous examples. The trade-off (there are always trade-offs) is that the code is more difficult to understand. (Of course, you already knew that.)

Another If-Then example

Here's another example that uses the simple form of the If-Then structure. This procedure prompts the user for a quantity and then displays the appropriate discount, based on the quantity the user enters:

```
Sub ShowDiscount()
    Dim Quantity As Integer
    Dim Discount As Double
    Quantity = InputBox("Enter Quantity:")
    If Quantity > 0 Then Discount = 0.1
    If Quantity >= 25 Then Discount = 0.15
    If Quantity >= 50 Then Discount = 0.2
    If Quantity >= 75 Then Discount = 0.25
    MsgBox "Discount: " & Discount
End Sub
```

A workbook that contains this section's examples can be downloaded from this book's Web site.

Notice that each If-Then statement in this routine is executed and the value for Discount can change as the statements are executed. However, the routine ultimately displays the correct value for Discount.

The following procedure performs the same tasks by using the alternative ElseIf syntax. In this case, the routine ends immediately after executing the statements for a true condition.

```
Sub ShowDiscount2()
  Dim Quantity As Integer
  Dim Discount As Double
  Quantity = InputBox("Enter Quantity: ")
  If Quantity > 0 And Quantity < 25 Then
    Discount = 0.1
      ElseIf Quantity >= 25 And Quantity < 50 Then
        Discount = 0.15
          ElseIf Quantity >= 50 And Quantity < 75 Then
            Discount = 0.2
              ElseIf Quantity >= 75 Then
                Discount = 0.25
  End If
  MsgBox "Discount: " & Discount
End Sub
```

Personally, I find these multiple If-Then structures rather cumbersome. I generally use the If-Then structure for only simple binary decisions. When a decision involves three or more choices, the Select Case structure offers a simpler, more efficient approach.

The Select Case structure

The Select Case structure is useful for decisions involving three or more options (although it also works with two options, providing an alternative to the If-Then-Else structure).

The syntax for the Select Case structure follows:

```
Select Case testexpression
[Case expressionlist-n
    [statements-n]] . . .
[Case Else
    [elsestatements]]
End Select
```

Don't be scared off by this official syntax. Using the Select Case structure is quite easy.

A Select Case example

The following example shows how to use the Select Case structure. This also shows another way to code the examples presented in the previous section:

```
Sub ShowDiscount3()
    Dim Quantity As Integer
    Dim Discount As Double
    Quantity = InputBox("Enter Quantity: ")
    Select Case Quantity
        Case 0 To 24
            Discount = 0.1
        Case 25 To 49
            Discount = 0.15
        Case 50 To 74
            Discount = 0.2
        Case Is >= 75
            Discount = 0.25
    End Select
    MsgBox "Discount: " & Discount
End Sub
```

In this example, the Quantity variable is being evaluated. The routine is checking for four different cases (0 to 24, 25 to 49, 50 to 74, and 75 or greater).

Any number of statements can follow each Case statement, and they all are executed if the case is true. If you use only one statement, as in this example, you can put the statement on the same line as the Case keyword, preceded by a colon — the VBA statement separator character. In my opinion, this makes the code more compact and a bit clearer. Here's how the routine looks using this format:

```
Sub ShowDiscount4 ()
    Dim Quantity As Integer
    Dim Discount As Double
    Quantity = InputBox("Enter Quantity: ")
    Select Case Quantity
        Case  0 To 24: Discount = 0.1
        Case 25 To 49: Discount = 0.15
        Case 50 To 74: Discount = 0.2
        Case Is >= 75: Discount = 0.25
    End Select
    MsgBox "Discount: " & Discount
End Sub
```

When VBA executes a Select Case structure, the structure is exited as soon as VBA finds a true case.

A nested Select Case example

As demonstrated in the following example, you can nest Select Case structures. This routine examines the active cell and displays a message describing the cell's contents. Notice that the procedure has three Select Case structures and each has its own End Select statement.

```
Sub CheckCell()
   Dim Msg As String
   Select Case IsEmpty(ActiveCell)
      Case True
         Msg = "is blank."
      Case Else
         Select Case ActiveCell.HasFormula
            Case True
               Msg = "has a formula"
            Case False
               Select Case IsNumeric(ActiveCell)
                  Case True
                     Msg = "has a number"
                  Case Else
                     Msg = "has text"
               End Select
         End Select
   End Select
   MsgBox "Cell " & ActiveCell.Address & " " & Msg
End Sub
```

This example is available at this book's Web site.

The logic goes something like this:

1. Find out whether the cell is empty.

2. If it's not empty, see whether it contains a formula.

3. If there's no formula, find out whether it contains a numeric value or text.

When the routine ends, the Msg variable contains a string that describes the cell's contents. As shown in Figure 10-1, the MsgBox function displays that message.

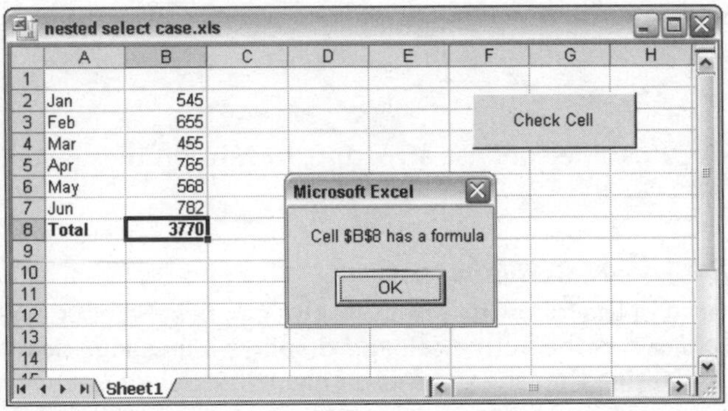

Figure 10-1:
A message
displayed
by the
CheckCell
procedure.

You can nest Select Case structures as deeply as you need, but make sure that each Select Case statement has a corresponding End Select statement.

As you can see, indenting makes this potentially confusing code much more understandable. If you don't believe me, take a look at the same procedure without any indentation:

```
Sub CheckCell()
Dim Msg As String
Select Case IsEmpty(ActiveCell)
Case True
Msg = "is blank."
Case Else
Select Case ActiveCell.HasFormula
Case True
Msg = "has a formula"
Case False
Select Case IsNumeric(ActiveCell)
Case True
Msg = "has a number"
Case Else
Msg = "has text"
```

```
    End Select
    End Select
    End Select
    MsgBox "Cell " & ActiveCell.Address & " " & Msg
    End Sub
```

Fairly incomprehensible, eh?

Knocking Your Code for a Loop

The term *looping* refers to repeating a block of VBA statements numerous times. You may know how many times your program needs to loop, or variables used in your program's may determine this.

There are two types of loops: good loops and bad loops. (Good loops get rewarded, and bad loops get sent to their room.)

The following code demonstrates a bad loop. The procedure simply enters consecutive numbers into a range. It starts by prompting the user for two values: a starting value and the total number of cells to fill. (Because InputBox returns a string, I convert the strings to integers by using the CInt function.) This loop uses the GoTo statement to control the flow. The CellCount variable keeps track of how many cells are filled. If this value is less than the number requested by the user, program control loops back to DoAnother.

```
Sub BadLoop()
    Dim StartVal As Integer
    Dim NumToFill As Long
    Dim CellCount As Long
    StartVal = CInt(InputBox("Enter the starting value: "))
    NumToFill = CInt(InputBox("How many cells? "))
    ActiveCell = StartVal
    CellCount = 1
DoAnother:
    ActiveCell.Offset(CellCount, 0) = StartVal + CellCount
    CellCount = CellCount + 1
    If CellCount < NumToFill Then GoTo DoAnother _
        Else Exit Sub
End Sub
```

This routine works as intended, so why is it an example of bad looping? As I mention earlier in this chapter, avoid using a GoTo statement unless it's absolutely necessary. Using GoTo statements to perform looping

    ✔ Is contrary to the concept of structured programming. (See the sidebar earlier in this chapter, "What is structured programming? Does it matter?")

    ✔ Makes the code more difficult to read.

    ✔ Is more prone to errors than using structured looping procedures.

VBA has enough structured looping commands that you almost never have to rely on GoTo statements for your decision making. Again, the exception is for error handling.

Now you can move on to a discussion of good looping structures.

For-Next loops

The simplest type of loop is a For-Next loop. Here's the syntax for this structure:

```
For counter = start To end [Step stepval]
    [statements]
    [Exit For]
    [statements]
Next [counter]
```

The looping is controlled by a counter variable, which starts at one value and stops at another value. The statements between the For statement and the Next statement are the statements that get repeated in the loop. To see how this works, keep reading.

A For-Next example

The following example shows a For-Next loop that doesn't use the optional Step value or the optional Exit For statement. This routine loops 100 times and uses the VBA Rnd function to enter a random number into 100 cells:

```
Sub FillRange()
    Dim Count As Integer
    For Count = 1 To 100
        ActiveCell.Offset(Count - 1, 0) = Rnd
    Next Count
End Sub
```

In this example, Count (the loop counter variable) starts with a value of 1 and increases by 1 each time through the loop. Because I didn't specify a Step value, VBA uses the default value (1). The Offset method uses the value of

Count as an argument. The first time through the loop, the procedure enters a number into the active cell offset by zero rows. The second time through (Count = 2), the procedure enters a number into the active cell offset by one row (Count –1), and so on.

Because the loop counter is a normal variable, you can change its value within the block of code between the For and the Next statements. This, however, is a *very bad* practice. Changing the counter within the loop can have unpredictable results. Take special precautions to ensure that your code does not directly change the value of the loop counter.

A For-Next example with a Step

You can use a Step value to skip some values in a For-Next loop. Here's the same procedure as in the preceding section, rewritten to insert random numbers into every other cell:

```
Sub FillRange()
    Dim Count As Integer
    For Count = 1 To 100 Step 2
        ActiveCell.Offset(Count - 1, 0) = Rnd
    Next Count
End Sub
```

This time, Count starts out as 1 and then takes on a value of 3, 5, 7, and so on. The final Count value is 99. The Step value determines how the counter is incremented.

This chapter introduces looping via the BadLoop example, which uses a GoTo statement. Here's the same example, which is available on this book's Web site, converted into a good loop by using the For-Next structure:

```
Sub FillRange()
    Dim StartVal As Integer
    Dim NumToFill As Long
    Dim CellCount As Long
    StartVal = CInt(InputBox("Enter the starting value: "))
    NumToFill = CInt(InputBox("How many cells? "))
    For CellCount = 1 To NumToFill
        ActiveCell.Offset(CellCount - 1, 0) = _
            StartVal + CellCount - 1
    Next CellCount
End Sub
```

A For-Next example with an Exit For statement

A For-Next loop can also include one or more Exit For statements within the loop. When VBA encounters this statement, the loop terminates immediately.

The following example, available on the book's Web site, demonstrates the Exit For statement. This routine identifies which of the active worksheet's cells in column A has the largest value:

```
Sub ExitForDemo()
    Dim MaxVal As Double
    Dim Row As Long
    MaxVal = Application.WorksheetFunction. _
        Max(Range("A:A"))
    For Row = 1 To 65536
        If Range("A1").Offset(Row - 1, 0).Value = MaxVal Then
            Range("A1").Offset(Row - 1, 0).Activate
            MsgBox "Max value is in Row " & Row
            Exit For
        End If
    Next Row
End Sub
```

The routine calculates the maximum value in the column by using Excel's MAX function and assigns the result to the MaxVal variable. The For-Next loop then checks each cell in the column. If the cell being checked is equal to MaxVal, the routine doesn't need to continue looping (its job is finished), so the Exit For statement terminates the loop. Before terminating the loop, the procedure activates the cell with the maximum value and informs the user of its location.

A nested For-Next example

So far, all this chapter's examples use relatively simple loops. However, you can have any number of statements in the loop and nest For-Next loops inside other For-Next loops.

The following example uses a nested For-Next loop to insert random numbers into a 12-row-by-5-column range of cells, as shown in Figure 10-2. Notice that the routine executes the *inner loop* (the loop with the Row counter) once for each iteration of the *outer loop* (the loop with the Col counter). In other words, the routine executes the Cells(Row, Col) = Rnd statement 60 times.

```
Sub FillRange2()
    Dim Col As Integer
    Dim Row As Long
    For Col = 1 To 5
        For Row = 1 To 12
            Cells(Row, Col) = Rnd
        Next Row
    Next Col
End Sub
```

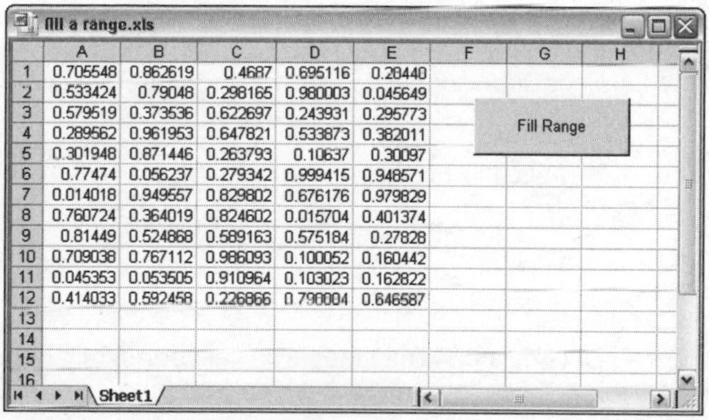

Figure 10-2:
These cells
were filled
using a
nested For-
Next loop.

The next example uses nested For-Next loops to initialize a three-dimensional array with zeros. This routine executes the statement in the middle of all the loops (the assignment statement) 1,000 times, each time with a different combination of values for i, j, and k:

```
Sub NestedLoops()
    Dim MyArray(10, 10, 10)
    Dim i As Integer
    Dim j As Integer
    Dim k As Integer
    For i = 1 To 10
        For j = 1 To 10
            For k = 1 To 10
                MyArray(i, j, k) = 0
            Next k
        Next j
    Next i
End Sub
```

Refer to Chapter 7 for information about arrays.

Do-While loop

VBA supports another type of looping structure known as a Do-While loop. Unlike a For-Next loop, a Do-While loop continues until a specified condition is met. Here's the Do-While loop syntax:

```
Do [While condition]
    [statements]
    [Exit Do]
    [statements]
Loop
```

The following example uses a Do-While loop. This routine uses the active cell as a starting point and then travels down the column, multiplying each cell's value by 2. The loop continues until the routine encounters an empty cell.

```
Sub DoWhileDemo()
    Do While ActiveCell.Value <> Empty
        ActiveCell.Value = ActiveCell.Value * 2
        ActiveCell.Offset(1, 0).Select
    Loop
End Sub
```

Some people prefer to code a Do-While loop as a Do-Loop While loop. This example performs exactly as the previous procedure but uses a different loop syntax:

```
Sub DoLoopWhileDemo()
    Do
        ActiveCell.Value = ActiveCell.Value * 2
        ActiveCell.Offset(1, 0).Select
    Loop While ActiveCell.Value <> Empty
End Sub
```

Remember this key difference between the Do-While and Do-Loop While loops: The Do-While loop always performs its conditional test first. If the test is not true, the instructions inside the loop are never executed. The Do-Loop While loop, on the other hand, always performs its conditional test after the instructions inside the loop are executed. Thus, the loop instructions are always executed at least once, regardless of the test. This difference can make a profound difference in how your program functions.

Do-Until loop

The Do-Until loop structure is similar to the Do-While structure. The two structures differ in their handling of the tested condition. A program continues to execute a Do-While loop *while* the condition remains true. In a Do-Until loop, the program executes the loop *until* the condition is true.

Here's the Do-Until syntax:

```
Do [Until condition]
      statements]
    [Exit Do]
    [statements]
Loop
```

The following example is the same one presented for the Do-While loop but recoded to use a Do-Until loop:

```
Sub DoUntilDemo()
    Do Until IsEmpty (ActiveCell.Value)
        ActiveCell.Value = ActiveCell.Value * 2
        ActiveCell.Offset(1, 0).Select
    Loop
End Sub
```

You may encounter a different form of the Do-Until loop — a Do-Loop Until loop. The following example, which has the same effect as the preceding procedure, demonstrates an alternate syntax for this type of loop:

```
Sub DoLoopUntilDemo()
    Do
        ActiveCell.Value = ActiveCell.Value * 2
        ActiveCell.Offset(1, 0).Select
    Loop Until IsEmpty (ActiveCell.Value)
End Sub
```

There is a subtle difference in how the Do-Until loop and the Do-Loop Until loop operate. In the former, the test is performed at the beginning of the loop, before anything in the body of the loop is executed. This means that it is possible that the code in the loop body will not be executed if the test condition is met. In the latter version, the condition is tested at the end of the loop. This means, at a minimum, the Do-Loop Until loop always results in the body of the loop being executed once.

Looping through a Collection

VBA supports yet another type of looping — looping through each object in a collection. Recall that a collection consists of a number of the same type of object. For example, each workbook has a collection of worksheets (the Worksheets collection), and Excel has a collection of all open workbooks (the Workbooks collection).

When you need to loop through each object in a collection, use the For Each-Next structure. The syntax is

```
For Each element In collection
    [statements]
    [Exit For]
    [statements]
Next [element]
```

The following example loops through each worksheet in the active workbook and deletes the first row of each worksheet:

```
Sub DeleteRow1()
    Dim WkSht As Worksheet
    For Each WkSht In ActiveWorkbook.Worksheets
        WkSht.Rows(1).Delete
    Next WkSht
End Sub
```

In this example, the variable WkSht is an object variable that represents each worksheet in the workbook. Nothing is special about the variable name WkSht — you can use any variable name that you like.

The example that follows loops through the cells in a range, checking each one. The code switches the sign of the values (negative values are made positive; positive values are made negative). It does this by multiplying each value times –1. Note that I used an If-Then construct, along with the VBA IsNumeric function, to ensure that the cell contains a numeric value:

```
Sub ChangeSign()
    Dim Cell As Range
    For Each Cell In Range("A1:E50")
        If IsNumeric(Cell.Value) Then
            Cell.Value = Cell.Value * -1
        End If
    Next Cell
End Sub
```

Here's another example that loops through each chart on Sheet1 (that is, each member of the ChartObjects collection) and changes each chart to a line chart. In this example, Cht is a variable that represents each ChartObject. If Sheet1 has no ChartObjects, nothing happens.

```
Sub ChangeCharts()
    Dim Cht As ChartObject
    For Each Cht In Sheets("Sheet1").ChartObjects
        Cht.Chart.ChartType = xlLine
    Next Cht
End Sub
```

Chapter 11

Automatic Procedures and Events

● ●

● ●

*Y*ou have a number of ways to execute a VBA Sub procedure. One way is to arrange for the Sub to be executed automatically. In this chapter, I cover the ins and outs of this potentially useful feature, explaining how to set things up so that a macro is executed automatically when a particular event occurs. (No, this chapter is not about capital punishment.)

Preparing for the Big Event

What types of events am I talking about here? Good question. An *event* is basically something that happens in Excel. Following are a few examples of the types of events that Excel can deal with:

✔ A workbook is opened or closed.

✔ A window is activated.

✔ A worksheet is activated or deactivated.

✔ Data is entered into a cell or the cell is edited.

✔ A workbook is saved.

✔ A worksheet is calculated.

✔ An object, such as button, is clicked.

✔ A particular key or key combination is pressed.

✔ A cell is double-clicked.

✔ A particular time of day occurs.

✔ An error occurs.

Most Excel programmers never need to worry about most of the events in this list. You should, however, at least know that these events exist because they may come in handy someday. In this chapter, I discuss the most commonly used events. To simplify things, I talk about two types of events: workbook and worksheet.

Table 11-1 lists most of the workbook-related events. You can access the complete list if you follow these directions:

1. **Choose the ThisWorkbook object in the Project window.**

2. **Display the Code window.**

   Choose View➪Code or press F7 to do this.

3. **Choose the Workbook object in the Object drop-down list (at the top-left of the Code window).**

4. **Expand the Procedure drop-down list (at the top-right of the Code window).**

Table 11-1	Workbook Events
Event	*When It's Triggered*
Activate	The workbook is activated.
AddinInstall	An add-in is installed (relevant only for add-ins).
AddinUninstall	The add-in is uninstalled (relevant only for add-ins).
BeforeClose	The workbook is closed.
BeforePrint	The workbook is printed.
BeforeSave	The workbook is saved.
Deactivate	The workbook is deactivated.
NewSheet	A new sheet is added to the workbook.
Open	The workbook is opened.
SheetActivate	A sheet in the workbook is activated.
SheetBefore DoubleClick	A cell in the workbook is double-clicked.
SheetBefore RightClick	A cell in the workbook is right-clicked.

Event	When It's Triggered
SheetCalculate	A sheet in the workbook is recalculated.
SheetChange	A change is made to a cell in the workbook.
SheetDeactivate	A sheet in the workbook is deactivated.
SheetFollowHyperlink	A hyperlink in a worksheet is clicked.
SheetSelectionChange	The selection is changed.
WindowActivate	The workbook window is activated.
WindowDeactivate	The workbook window is deactivated.
WindowResize	The workbook window is resized.

Table 11-2 lists most of the worksheet events. These events are accessible if you follow these directions:

1. **Choose a Worksheet object in the Project window.**

2. **Display the Code window.**

3. **Choose the Worksheet object in the Object list (at the top of the Code window).**

4. **Expand the Procedure drop-down list.**

Table 11-2	Worksheet Events
Event	**When It's Triggered**
Activate	The worksheet is activated.
BeforeDoubleClick	A cell in the worksheet is double-clicked.
BeforeRightClick	A cell in the worksheet is right-clicked.
Calculate	The worksheet is recalculated.
Change	A change is made to a cell in the worksheet.
Deactivate	The worksheet is deactivated.
FollowHyperlink	A hyperlink is activated.
SelectionChange	The selection is changed.

Are events useful?

At this point, you may be wondering how these events can be useful. Here's a quick example.

Suppose you have a workbook that other people use for data entry. Any values entered must be greater than 1,000. You can write a simple macro that Excel executes whenever someone enters data into a cell. (Entering data is an event.) If the user enters a value less than 1,000, the macro displays a dialog box reprimanding the user.

The Data⇨Validation command in Excel provides another way to perform this type of data-entry checking — without even using VBA. However, as you see later in this chapter (see "A data validation example"), using VBA for data validation offers some distinct advantages.

This is just one example of how you can take advantage of an event. Keep reading for some more examples.

Programming event-handler procedures

A VBA procedure that executes in response to an event is called an *event-handler procedure*. These are always Sub procedures (as opposed to Function procedures). Writing these event-handlers is relatively straightforward after you understand how the process works. It all boils down to a few steps, all of which I explain later:

1. **Identify the event you want to trigger the procedure.**

2. **Press Alt+F11 to Activate the Visual Basic Editor.**

3. **In the VBE Project Window, double-click the appropriate object listed under Microsoft Excel Objects.**

   For workbook-related events, the object is ThisWorkbook. For a workbook-related event, the object is a Worksheet object (such as Sheet1).

4. **In the Code window for the object, write the event-handler procedure that is executed when the event occurs.**

   This procedure will have a special name that identifies it as an event-handler procedure.

These steps become clearer as you progress through the chapter. Trust me.

Where Does the VBA Code Go?

It's very important to understand where your event-handler procedures go. They must reside in the Code window of an Object module. They simply won't work if you put them in a standard VBA module.

Figure 11-1 shows the VBE window with one project displayed in the Project window. (Refer to Chapter 3 for some background on the VBE.) Notice that the project consists of several objects:

- ✔ One object for each worksheet in the workbook (in this case, three Sheet objects)

- ✔ An object labeled ThisWorkbook

- ✔ A VBA module that I inserted manually using the Insert⇨Module command

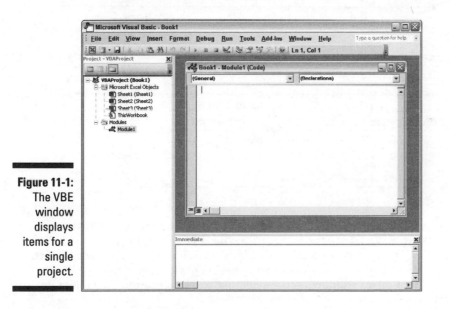

Figure 11-1:
The VBE window displays items for a single project.

Double-clicking any of these objects displays the code associated with the item, if any.

The event-handler procedures that you write go into the Code window for the ThisWorkbook item (for workbook-related events) or one of the Sheet objects (for worksheet-related events).

Writing an Event-Handler Procedure

The VBE helps you out when you're ready to write an event-handler procedure; it displays a list of all events that Excel can recognize.

Figure 11-2 shows a Code window for the ThisWorkbook object (the code window is maximized to fill the entire code window area). To display this empty Code window, double-click the ThisWorkbook object in the Project window. This Code window has two drop-down lists at the top.

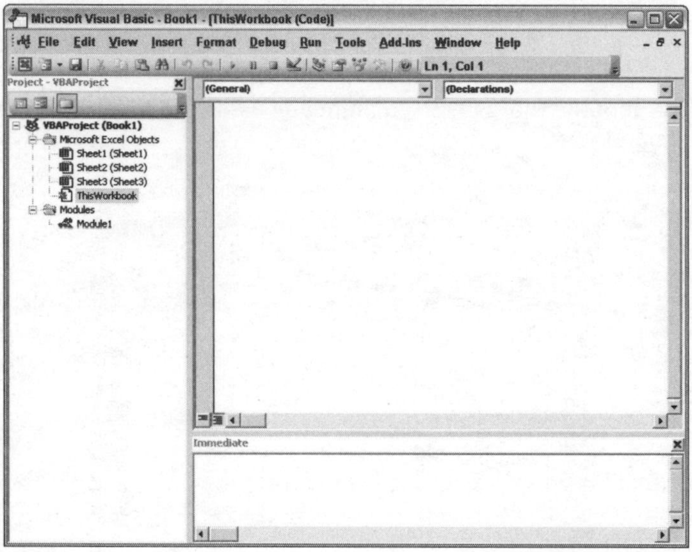

Figure 11-2:
An empty
Code
window
for the This
Workbook
object.

By default, the Object (left) drop-down list in the Code window displays General. To write an event-handler procedure, you need to select Workbook from the Object drop-down list. (Workbook is the only other item in the list.) If the event-handler is for a worksheet, double-click the appropriate Sheet item in the Project window before selecting Worksheet from the Object drop-down list.

Figure 11-3 shows the right drop-down list, which consists of all the workbook-related events that Excel recognizes. When you select an event from the list, VBE automatically starts creating an event-handler procedure for you. (When you first selected Workbook from the Object list, VBE assumed that you wanted to create an event-handler procedure for the Open event and created it. You can see this in Figure 11-3.)

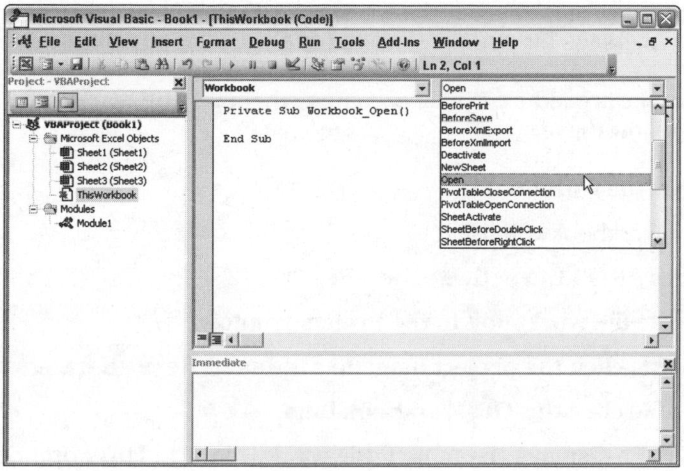

Figure 11-3:
The drop-down list displays all the workbook-related events.

VBE's help goes only so far, however. It writes the Sub statement and the End Sub statement. Writing the VBA code that goes between these two statements is your job.

Some event-handler procedures use one or more arguments in the Sub statement. For example, if you select SheetActivate from the event list for a Workbook object, VBE writes the following Sub statement:

```
Private Sub Workbook_SheetActivate(ByVal Sh As Object)
```

In this case, Sh is the argument passed to the procedure and is a variable that represents the sheet in the activated workbook. Examples in this chapter clarify this point.

Introductory Examples

In this section, I provide a few examples so that you can get the hang of this event-handling business.

The Open event for a workbook

One of the most commonly used events is the Workbook Open event. Assume that you have a workbook that you use every day. The Workbook_Open procedure in this example is executed every time the workbook is opened. The procedure checks the day of the week; if it's Friday, the code displays a reminder message for you.

To create the procedure that is executed whenever the Workbook Open event occurs, follow these steps:

1. **Open the workbook.**

   Any workbook will do.

2. **Press Alt+F11 to activate the VBE.**

3. **Locate the workbook in the Project window.**

4. **Double-click the project name to display its items, if necessary.**

5. **Double-click the ThisWorkbook item.**

   The VBE displays an empty Code window for the ThisWorkbook object.

6. **In the Code window, select Workbook from the Object (left) drop-down list.**

   The VBE enters the beginning and ending statements for a Workbook_Open procedure.

7. **Enter the following statements:**

```
Private Sub Workbook_Open()
    Dim Msg As String
    If WeekDay(Now) = 6 Then
        Msg = "Today is Friday. Make sure that you "
        Msg = Msg & "do your weekly backup!"
        MsgBox Msg
    End If
End Sub
```

The Code window should look like Figure 11-4.

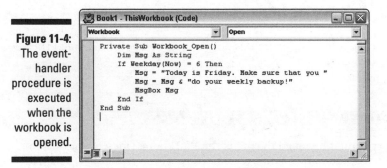

Figure 11-4:
The event-handler procedure is executed when the workbook is opened.

Workbook_Open is executed automatically whenever the workbook is opened. It uses VBA's WeekDay function to determine the day of the week. If it's Friday (day 6), a message box reminds the user to perform a weekly file backup. If it's not Friday, nothing happens.

If today isn't Friday, you might have a hard time testing this procedure. Here's a chance to test your own skill at VBA. You can modify this procedure any way you like. For example, the following version displays a message every time the workbook is opened. This gets annoying after a while, trust me.

```
Private Sub Workbook_Open()
    Msg = "This is Frank's cool workbook!"
    MsgBox Msg
End Sub
```

A Workbook_Open procedure can do almost anything. These event-handlers are often used for the following:

- Displaying welcome messages (such as the one to Frank)
- Opening other workbooks
- Activating a particular worksheet in the workbook
- Setting up custom menus
- Displaying or hiding toolbars

Keep in mind that event-handler procedures are not executed if the user disables macros when the workbook is opened. In other words, you can't count on the fact that your event-handler procedures will always work.

The BeforeClose event for a workbook

Here's an example of the Workbook_BeforeClose event-handler procedure, which is automatically executed immediately before the workbook is closed. This procedure is located in the Code window for a ThisWorkbook object:

```
Private Sub Workbook_BeforeClose(Cancel As Boolean)
    Dim Msg As String
    Dim Ans As Integer
    Dim FName As String
    Msg = "Would you like to make a backup of this file?"
    Ans = MsgBox(Msg, vbYesNo)
    If Ans = vbYes Then
        FName = "F:\BACKUP\" & ThisWorkbook.Name
        ThisWorkbook.SaveCopyAs FName
    End If
End Sub
```

This routine uses a message box to ask the user whether he would like to make a backup copy of the workbook. If the answer is yes, the code uses the SaveCopyAs method to save a backup copy of the file on drive F. If you adapt this procedure for your own use, you probably need to change the drive and path.

Excel programmers often use a Workbook_BeforeClose procedure to clean up after themselves. For example, if you use a Workbook_Open procedure to change some settings when you open a workbook (hiding the status bar, for example), it's only appropriate that you return the settings to their original state when you close the workbook. You can perform this electronic house-keeping with a Workbook_BeforeClose procedure.

The BeforeSave event for a workbook

The BeforeSave event, as its name implies, is triggered before a workbook is saved. This event occurs when you use either the File⇨Save or File⇨Save As command.

The following procedure, which is placed in the Code window for a ThisWorkbook object, demonstrates the BeforeSave event. The routine updates the value in a cell (cell A1 on Sheet1) every time the workbook is saved. In other words, cell A1 serves as a counter to keep track of the number of times the file was saved.

```
Private Sub Workbook_BeforeSave(ByVal SaveAsUI _
    As Boolean, Cancel As Boolean)
      Sheets("Sheet1").Range("A1").Value = _
        Sheets("Sheet1").Range("A1").Value +1
End Sub
```

Notice that the Workbook_BeforeSave procedure has two arguments, SaveAsUI and Cancel. To demonstrate how these arguments work, examine the following macro, which is executed before the workbook is saved. This procedure prevents the user from saving the workbook with a different name. If the user chooses the File⇨Save As command, then the SaveAsUI argument is True.

When the code executes, it checks the SaveAsUI value. If this variable is True, the procedure displays a message and sets Cancel to True, which cancels the Save operation.

```
Private Sub Workbook_BeforeSave(ByVal SaveAsUI _
    As Boolean, Cancel As Boolean)
      If SaveAsUI Then
          MsgBox "You cannot save a copy of this workbook!"
          Cancel = True
      End If
End Sub
```

Examples of Activation Events

Another category of events consists of activating and deactivating objects — specifically, sheets and windows.

Activate and Deactivate events in a sheet

Excel can detect when a particular sheet is activated or deactivated and execute a macro when either of these events occurs. These event-handler procedures go in the Code window for a Sheet object.

The following example shows a simple procedure that is executed whenever a particular sheet is activated. This code simply pops up a message box that displays the name of the active sheet:

```
Private Sub Worksheet_Activate()
    MsgBox "You just activated " & ActiveSheet.Name
End Sub
```

Here's another example that activates cell A1 whenever the sheet is activated:

```
Private Sub Worksheet_Activate()
    Range("A1").Activate
End Sub
```

Although the code in these two procedures is about as simple as it gets, event-handler procedures can be as complex as you like.

The following procedure (which is stored in the Code window for the Sheet1 object) uses the Deactivate event to prevent a user from activating any other sheet in the workbook. If Sheet1 is deactivated (that is, another sheet is activated), the user gets a message and Sheet1 is activated.

```
Private Sub Worksheet_Deactivate()
    MsgBox "You must stay on Sheet1"
    Sheets("Sheet1").Activate
End Sub
```

Activate and Deactivate events in a workbook

The previous examples use events associated with a worksheet. The ThisWorkbook object also handles events that deal with sheet activation and deactivation. The following procedure, which is stored in the Code window for the ThisWorkbook object, is executed when *any* sheet in the workbook is activated. The code displays a message with the name of the activated sheet.

```
Private Sub Workbook_SheetActivate(ByVal Sh As Object)
    MsgBox Sh.Name
End Sub
```

The Workbook_SheetActivate procedure uses the Sh argument. Sh is a variable that represents the active Sheet object. The message box displays the Sheet object's Name property.

The next example is contained in a ThisWorkbook Code window. It consists of two event-handler procedures. Workbook_SheetDeactivate is executed when a sheet is deactivated. It stores the sheet that is deactivated in an object variable. (The Set keyword creates an object variable.) The Workbook_SheetActivate code checks the type of sheet that is activated (using the TypeName function). If the sheet is a chart sheet, the user gets a message and the *previous* sheet (which is stored in the OldSheet variable) is reactivated. The effect is that users cannot activate a chart sheet (and are always returned to the previous sheet if they try).

A workbook that contains this code is available at this book's Web site.

```
Dim OldSheet As Object

Private Sub Workbook_SheetDeactivate(ByVal Sh As Object)
    Set OldSheet = Sh
End Sub
Private Sub Workbook_SheetActivate(ByVal Sh As Object)
    If TypeName(Sh) = "Chart" Then
        MsgBox "Sorry, you can't activate any charts."
        OldSheet.Activate
    End If
End Sub
```

Workbook activation events

Excel also recognizes the event that occurs when you activate or deactivate a particular workbook. The following code, which is contained in the Code window for the ThisWorkbook object, is executed whenever the workbook is activated. The procedure simply maximizes the workbook's window.

```
Private Sub Workbook_Activate()
    ActiveWindow.WindowState = xlMaximized
End Sub
```

The Workbook_Deactivate code, shown next, is executed when a workbook is deactivated. This procedure minimizes the workbook's window:

```
Private Sub Workbook_Deactivate()
    ThisWorkbook.Windows(1).WindowState = xlMinimized
End Sub
```

Notice that I didn't use ActiveWindow in this code. That's because the workbook is no longer the active window when it's deactivated. Therefore, I used ThisWorkbook, which refers to the workbook that contains the code.

Other Worksheet-Related Events

In the preceding section I present examples for worksheet activation and deactivation events. In this section I discuss three additional events that occur in worksheets: double-clicking a cell, right-clicking a cell, and changing a cell.

The BeforeDoubleClick event

You can set up a VBA procedure to be executed when the user double-clicks a cell. In the following example (which is stored in the Code window for a Sheet object), double-clicking a cell makes the cell bold (if it's not bold) or not bold (if it is bold):

```
Private Sub Worksheet_BeforeDoubleClick _
    (ByVal Target As Excel.Range, Cancel As Boolean)
    Target.Font.Bold = Not Target.Font.Bold
    Cancel = True
End Sub
```

The Worksheet_BeforeDoubleClick procedure has two arguments: Target and Cancel. Target represents the cell (a Range object) that was double-clicked. If Cancel is set to True, the default double-click action doesn't occur.

Notice that I set the Cancel argument to True. This prevents the default action from occurring. In other words, double-clicking the cell won't put Excel into cell edit mode.

The BeforeRightClick event

The BeforeRightClick event is similar to the BeforeDoubleClick event, except that it consists of right-clicking a cell. The following procedure checks to see whether the cell that was right-clicked contains a numeric value. If so, the code displays the Format Number dialog box and sets the Cancel argument to True (avoiding the normal shortcut menu display). If the cell does not contain a numeric value, nothing special happens — the shortcut menu is displayed as usual.

```
Private Sub Worksheet_BeforeRightClick _
    (ByVal Target As Excel.Range, Cancel As Boolean)
    If IsNumeric(Target) And Not IsEmpty(Target) Then
        Application.Dialogs(xlDialogFormatNumber).Show
        Cancel = True
    End If
End Sub
```

Notice that the code, which is available on this book's Web site, makes an additional check to see if the cell is empty. This is because VBA considers empty cells to be numeric.

The Change event

The Change event occurs whenever any cell on the worksheet is changed. In the following example, the Worksheet_Change procedure effectively prevents a user from entering a non-numeric value into cell A1. This code is stored in the Code window for a Sheet object.

```
Private Sub Worksheet_Change(ByVal Target As Range)
    If Target.Address = "$A$1" Then
        If Not IsNumeric(Target) Then
            MsgBox "Enter a number in cell A1."
            Range("A1").ClearContents
            Range("A1").Activate
        End If
    End If
End Sub
```

The single argument for the Worksheet_Change procedure represents the range that was changed. The first statement sees whether the cell's address is A1. If so, the code uses the IsNumeric function to determine whether the cell contains a numeric value. If not, a message appears and the cell's value is erased. Cell A1 is then activated — useful if the cell pointer moved to a different cell after the entry was made. If the change occurs in any cell except A1, nothing happens.

Why not use the Excel Data⇨Validation command?

You may be familiar with the Data⇨Validation command. This is a handy feature that makes it easy to ensure that only data of the proper type is entered into a particular cell or range. Although the Data⇨Validation command is useful, it's definitely not foolproof. To demonstrate, start with a blank worksheet and perform the following steps:

1. **Select the range A1:C12.**

2. **Choose Data⇨Validation.**

3. **Set up your validation criteria to accept only whole numbers between 1 and 12, as shown in Figure 11-5.**

Now, enter some values in the range A1:C12. The data validation works as it should. But to see it fall apart at the seams, try this:

1. **Enter –1 into any cell outside the validation range (any cell not in A1:C12).**

2. **Choose Edit⇨Copy to copy the negative number to the Clipboard.**

3. **Select any cell in the validation range.**

4. **Choose Edit⇨Paste.**

You find that the paste operation is allowable. Look a little closer, however, and you find that the cell into which you pasted the negative value no longer has any validation criteria. Pasting wipes out the data validation criteria! The severity of this flaw depends on your application. In the next section I describe how to use the Change event to provide for better validating.

Pasting wipes out data validation because Excel considers validation a format for a cell. This means it is in the same classification as font size, color, or other similar attributes. When you paste a cell, you are replacing the formats in the target cell with those of the source cell. Unfortunately, those formats also include your validation rules.

A data validation example

The next procedure demonstrates a better alternative to the Excel Data⮡ Validation command. It ensures that only positive values are entered into the range A1:C12.

A workbook that contains this code is available at this book's Web site:

```
Private Sub Worksheet_Change(ByVal Target As Range)
    Dim ValRange As Range
    Dim cell As Range
    Dim DataOK As Boolean
    Dim Msg As String
    Set ValRange = Range("A1:C12")
    DataOK = True
    For Each cell In Target
        If Union(cell, ValRange).Address = _
            ValRange.Address Then
            If cell.Value < 0 Then
                cell.ClearContents
                DataOK = False
            End If
        End If
    Next cell
    If Not DataOK Then
        Msg = "Only positive values are acceptable in "
        Msg = Msg & ValRange.Address
        MsgBox Msg, vbCritical
    End If
End Sub
```

The procedure starts by creating an object variable (ValRange) that represents the range to be validated. DataOK is a Boolean variable initially set to True. The For-Next loop examines each cell in Target (which is the cell or range that was changed). I use the Union function to determine whether the cell is contained in ValRange. If so, an If statement determines whether the cell's value is less than 0. If so, the contents are erased and DataOK is set to False.

When all the cells have been checked, another If statement checks the DataOK value. If it was set to False, one or more cells in the changed range were negative. Therefore, the user gets a message. This routine works even when data is copied and pasted to the validation range.

Events Not Associated with Objects

The events that I discuss previously in this chapter are associated with either a workbook object or a worksheet object. In this section, I discuss two types of events that are not associated with objects: time and keypresses.

Because time and keypresses aren't associated with a particular object such as a workbook or a worksheet, you program these events in a normal VBA module (unlike the other events discussed in this chapter).

The OnTime event

The OnTime event occurs when a particular time of day occurs. The following example demonstrates how to program Excel so that it beeps and then displays a message at 3:00 p.m.:

```
Sub SetAlarm()
    Application.OnTime 0.625, "DisplayAlarm"
End Sub

Sub DisplayAlarm()
    Beep
    MsgBox "Wake up. It's time for your afternoon break!"
End Sub
```

In this example, I use the OnTime method of the Application object. This method takes two arguments: the time (0.625 or 3:00 p.m.) and the code to execute when the time occurs (DisplayAlarm).

This procedure is quite useful if you tend to get so wrapped up in your work that you forget about meetings and appointments. Just set an OnTime event to remind yourself.

Most people (this author included) find it difficult to think of time in terms of the Excel numbering system. Therefore, you may want to use the VBA TimeValue function to represent the time. TimeValue converts a string that looks like a time into a value that Excel can handle. The following statement shows an easier way to program an event for 3:00 p.m.:

```
Application.OnTime TimeValue("3:00:00 pm"), "DisplayAlarm"
```

If you want to schedule an event relative to the current time — for example, 20 minutes from now — you can use a statement like this:

```
Application.OnTime Now + TimeValue("00:20:00"),
          "DisplayAlarm"
```

You can also use the OnTime method to run a VBA procedure on a particular day. You must make sure that your computer keeps running and that the workbook with the procedure is open. The following statement runs the DisplayAlarm procedure at 5:00 p,m, on December 31, 2005:

```
Application.OnTime DateValue("12/31/2005 5:00 pm"),
          "DisplayAlarm"
```

This particular code line could come in handy to warn you that you need to go home and get ready for the New Year's Eve festivities.

The OnTime method has two additional arguments. If you plan to use this method, you should refer to the online help for complete details.

Keypress events

While you work, Excel constantly monitors what you type. Because of this, you can set up a keystroke or a key combination to execute a procedure.

Here's an example that reassigns the PgDn and PgUp keys:

```
Sub Setup_OnKey()
    Application.OnKey "{PgDn}", "PgDn_Sub"
    Application.OnKey "{PgUp}", "PgUp_Sub"
End Sub

Sub PgDn_Sub()
    On Error Resume Next
    If TypeName(ActiveSheet) = "Worksheet" _
      Then ActiveCell.Offset(1, 0).Activate
End Sub

Sub PgUp_Sub()
    On Error Resume Next
    If TypeName(ActiveSheet) = "Worksheet" _
      Then ActiveCell.Offset(-1, 0).Activate
End Sub
```

After setting up the OnKey events by executing the Setup_OnKey procedure, pressing PgDn moves you down one row. Pressing PgUp moves you up one row.

Notice that the key codes are enclosed in braces, not parentheses. For a complete list of keyboard codes, consult the Help system. Search for *OnKey*.

In this example, I use On Error Resume Next to ignore any errors that are generated. For example, if the active cell is in the first row, trying to move up one row causes an error that can safely be ignored. Also, notice that the procedures check to see which type of sheet is active. The routine reassigns the PgUp and PgDn keys only when a worksheet is the active sheet.

By executing the following routine, you cancel the OnKey events:

```
Sub Cancel_OnKey()
    Application.OnKey "{PgDn}"
    Application.OnKey "{PgUp}"
End Sub
```

Using an empty string as the second argument for the OnKey method does *not* cancel the OnKey event. Rather, it causes Excel to simply ignore the keystroke. For example, the following statement tells Excel to ignore Alt+F4. The percent sign represents the Alt key:

```
    Application.OnKey "%{F4}", ""
```

Although you can use the OnKey method to assign a shortcut key for executing a macro, you should use the Macro Options dialog box for this task. For more details, see Chapter 5.

Chapter 12

Error-Handling Techniques

. . . .

In This Chapter

▶ Understanding the difference between programming errors and run-time errors

▶ Trapping and handling run-time errors

▶ Using the VBA On Error and Resume statements

▶ Finding how you can use an error to your advantage

. . . .

*W*hen working with VBA, you should be aware of two broad classes of errors: programming errors and *run-time errors*. (I cover programming errors, also known as *bugs,* in the next chapter.) A well-written program handles errors the way Fred Astaire danced: gracefully. Fortunately, VBA includes several tools to help you identify errors — and then handle them gracefully.

Types of Errors

If you've tried any of the examples in this book, you have probably encountered one or more error messages. Some of these errors result from bad VBA code. For example, you may spell a keyword incorrectly or type a statement with the wrong syntax. If you make such an error, you won't even be able to execute the procedure until you correct it.

This chapter does not deal with those types of errors. Instead, I discuss run-time errors — the errors that occur while Excel executes your VBA code. More specifically, this chapter covers the following:

✔ Identifying errors

✔ Doing something about the errors that occur

✔ Recovering from errors

✔ Creating intentional errors (Yes, sometimes an error can be a good thing.)

The ultimate goal of error handling is to write code that avoids displaying Excel's error messages as much as possible. In other words, you want to anticipate potential errors and deal with them before Excel has a chance to rear its ugly head with a (usually) less-than-informative error message.

An Erroneous Example

To get things started, I developed a short VBA macro. Activate the VBE, insert a module, and enter the following code:

```
Sub EnterSquareRoot()
    Dim Num As Double
'    Prompt for a value
    Num = InputBox("Enter a value")

'    Insert the square root
    ActiveCell.Value = Sqr(Num)
End Sub
```

As shown in Figure 12-1, this procedure asks the user for a value. It then enters the square root of that value into the active cell.

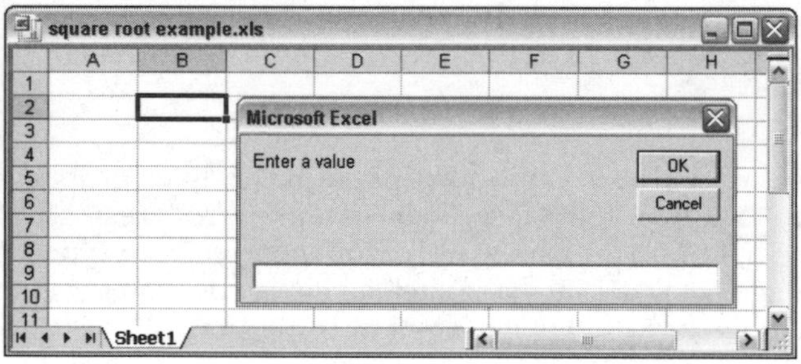

Figure 12-1: The InputBox function displays a dialog box that asks the user for a value.

You can execute this procedure directly from the VBE by pressing F5. Alternatively, you may want to add a button to a worksheet (use the Forms toolbar to do this) and then assign the macro to the button. (Excel prompts you for the macro to assign.) Then you can run the procedure by simply clicking the button.

The macro's not quite perfect

Enter this code and try it out. It works pretty well, doesn't it? Now try entering a negative number when you are prompted for a value. Oops. Trying to calculate the square root of a negative number is illegal on this planet. Excel responds with the message shown in Figure 12-2, indicating that your code generated a run-time error. For now, just click the End button. Or click the Debug button; Excel suspends the macro so you can use the debugging tools. (I describe the debugging tools in Chapter 13.)

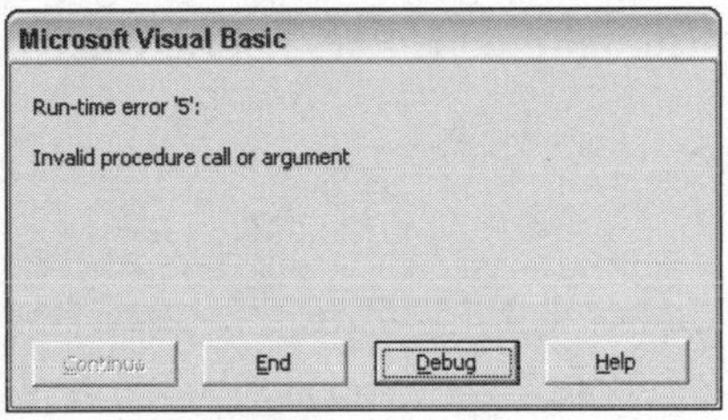

Figure 12-2:
Excel
displays this
error
message
when the
procedure
attempts to
calculate
the square
root of a
negative
number.

Most folks don't find the Excel error messages (for example, *Invalid procedure call or argument*) very helpful. To improve the procedure, you need to anticipate this error and handle it more gracefully.

Here's a modified version of EnterSquareRoot:

```
Sub EnterSquareRoot2()
    Dim Num As Double
'   Prompt for a value
    Num = InputBox("Enter a value")

'   Make sure the number is nonnegative
    If Num < 0 Then
        MsgBox "You must enter a positive number."
        Exit Sub
    End If

'   Insert the square root
    ActiveCell.Value = Sqr(Num)
End Sub
```

An If-Then structure checks the value contained in the Num variable. If Num is less than 0, the procedure displays a message box containing information that humans can actually understand. The procedure ends with the Exit Sub statement, so the error never has a chance to occur.

The macro is still not perfect

So the modified EnterSquareRoot procedure is perfect, right? Not really. Try entering text instead of a value. Or click the Cancel button in the input box. Both of these actions generate an error *(Type mismatch)*.

The following modified code uses the IsNumeric function to make sure that Num contains a numeric value. If the user doesn't enter a number, the procedure displays a message and then stops. Also, notice that the Num variable is now defined as a Variant. If it were defined as a Double, the code would generate an unhandled error if the user entered a nonnumeric value into the input box.

```
Sub EnterSquareRoot3()
    Dim Num As Variant
'   Prompt for a value
    Num = InputBox("Enter a value")

'   Make sure Num is a number
    If Not IsNumeric(Num) Then
        MsgBox "You must enter a number."
        Exit Sub
    End If

'   Make sure the number is nonnegative
    If Num < 0 Then
        MsgBox "You must enter a positive number."
        Exit Sub
    End If

'   Insert the square root
    ActiveCell.Value = Sqr(Num)
End Sub
```

Is the macro perfect yet?

Now this code is absolutely perfect, right? Not quite. Try running the procedure while the active sheet is a Chart sheet. As shown in Figure 12-3, Excel displays another message that's as illuminating as the other error messages you've seen. This error occurs because there is no active cell on a Chart sheet.

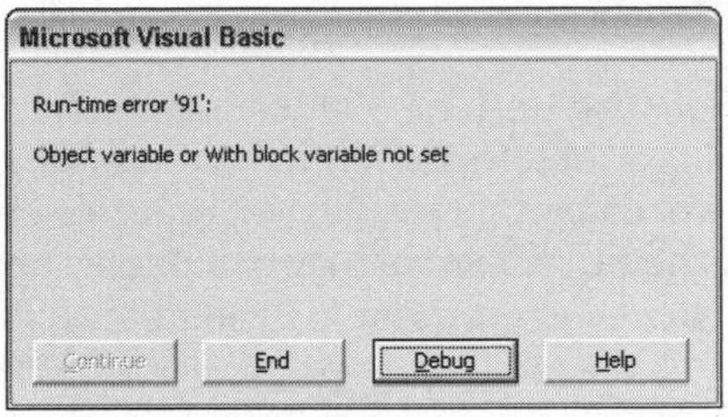

Figure 12-3:
Running the
procedure
when a
chart is
selected
generates
this error.

Microsoft Visual Basic

Run-time error '91':

Object variable or With block variable not set

| Continue | End | Debug | Help |

The following listing uses the TypeName function to make sure the selection
is a range. If anything other than a range is selected, this procedure displays
a message and then exits:

```
Sub EnterSquareRoot4()
    Dim Num As Variant
'   Make sure a worksheet is active
    If TypeName(Selection) <> "Range" Then
        MsgBox "Select a range first."
        Exit Sub
    End If

'   Prompt for a value
    Num = InputBox("Enter a value")

'   Make sure Num is a number

    If Not IsNumeric(Num) Then
        MsgBox "You must enter a number."
        Exit Sub
    End If

'   Make sure the number is nonnegative
    If Num < 0 Then
        MsgBox "You must enter a positive number."
        Exit Sub
    End If

'   Insert the square root
    ActiveCell.Value = Sqr(Num)
End Sub
```

Giving up on perfection

By now, this procedure simply *must* be perfect. Think again, pal. Protect the worksheet (using the Tools⇔Protection⇔Protect Sheet command) and then run the code. Yep, a protected worksheet generates yet another error. And I probably haven't thought of all the other errors that can occur. Keep reading for another way to deal with errors — even those you can't anticipate.

Handling Errors Another Way

How can you identify and handle every possible error? The answer is that often you can't. Fortunately, VBA provides another way to deal with errors.

Revisiting the EnterSquareRoot procedure

Examine the following code. I modified the routine from the previous section by adding an On Error statement to trap all errors and then checking to see whether the InputBox was cancelled.

```
Sub EnterSquareRoot5()
    Dim Num As Variant
    Dim Msg As String

'   Set up error handling
    On Error GoTo BadEntry

'   Prompt for a value
    Num = InputBox("Enter a value")

'   Exit if cancelled
    If Num = "" Then Exit Sub

'   Insert the square root
    ActiveCell.Value = Sqr(Num)
    Exit Sub

BadEntry:
    Msg = "An error occurred." & vbNewLine
    Msg = Msg & "Make sure a range is selected "
    Msg = Msg & "and you enter a nonnegative value."
    MsgBox Msg
End Sub
```

On Error not working?

If an On Error statement isn't working as advertised, you need to change one of your settings.

1. Activate the VBE.

2. Choose the Tools⇨Options command.

3. Click the General tab of the Options dialog box.

4. Make sure that the Break On All Errors setting is deselected.

If this setting is selected, Excel essentially ignores any On Error statements. You normally want to keep the Error Trapping options set to Break on Unhandled Errors.

This routine traps *any* type of run-time error. After trapping a run-time error, the revised EnterSquareRoot procedure displays the message box shown in Figure 12-4.

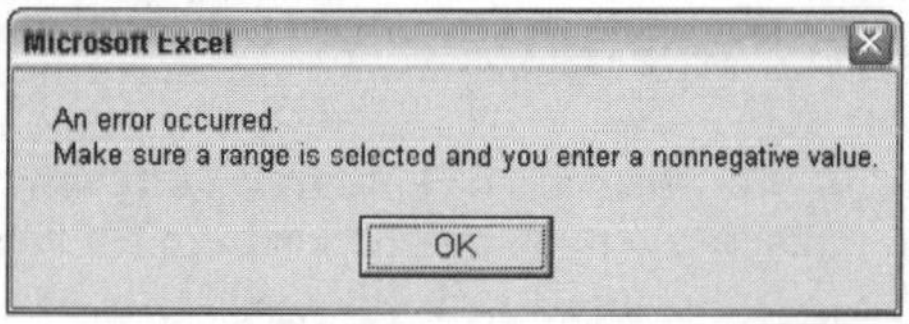

Figure 12-4:
A run-time error in the procedure generates this helpful error message.

> **Microsoft Excel**
>
> An error occurred.
> Make sure a range is selected and you enter a nonnegative value.
>
> [OK]

About the On Error statement

Using an On Error statement in your VBA code causes Excel to bypass its built-in error handling and use your own error-handling code. In the previous example, a run-time error causes macro execution to jump to the statement labeled BadEntry. As a result, you avoid Excel's unfriendly error messages and you can display your own (friendlier, I hope) message to the user.

Notice that the example uses an Exit Sub statement right before the BadEntry label. This statement is necessary because you don't want to execute the error-handling code if an error does *not* occur.

Handling Errors: The Details

You can use the On Error statement in three ways, as shown in Table 12-1.

Table 12-1	Using the On Error Statement
Syntax	*What It Does*
On Error	After executing this statement, VBA resumes GoTo label execution at the specified line. You must include a colon after the label so that VBA recognizes it as a label.
On Error Resume Next	After executing this statement, VBA simply ignores all errors and resumes execution with the next statement.
On Error GoTo 0	After executing this statement, VBA resumes its normal error-checking behavior. Use this statement after using one of the other On Error statements or when you want to remove error handling in your procedure.

Resuming after an error

In some cases, you simply want your routine to end gracefully when an error occurs. For example, you may display a message describing the error and then exit the procedure. (The EnterSquareRoot5 example uses this technique.) In other cases, you want to recover from the error, if possible.

To recover from an error, you must use a Resume statement. This clears the error condition and lets you continue execution at some location. You can use the Resume statement in three ways, as shown in Table 12-2.

Table 12-2	Using the Resume Statement
Syntax	*What It Does*
Resume	Execution resumes with the statement that caused the error. Use this if your error-handling code corrects the problem and it's okay to continue.
Resume Next	Execution resumes with the statement immediately following the statement that caused the error. This essentially ignores the error.
Resume *label*	Execution resumes at the *label* you specify.

The following example uses a Resume statement after an error occurs:

```
Sub EnterSquareRoot6()
    Dim Num As Variant
    Dim Msg As String
    Dim Ans As Integer
TryAgain:
'    Set up error handling
    On Error GoTo BadEntry

'    Prompt for a value
    Num = InputBox("Enter a value")
    If Num = "" Then Exit Sub

'    Insert the square root
    ActiveCell.Value = Sqr(Num)

    Exit Sub

BadEntry:
    Msg = "An error occurred. Try again?"
    Ans = MsgBox(Msg, vbYesNo)
    If Ans = vbYes Then Resume TryAgain
End Sub
```

This procedure has another label: TryAgain. If an error occurs, execution continues at the BadEntry label and the code displays the message shown in Figure 12-5. If the user responds by clicking Yes, the Resume statement kicks in and execution jumps back to the TryAgain label. If the user clicks No, the procedure ends.

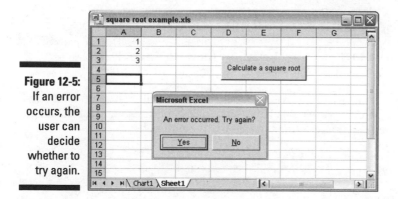

Figure 12-5: If an error occurs, the user can decide whether to try again.

Remember that the Resume statement clears the error condition before continuing. To see what I mean, try substituting the following statement for the second-to-last statement in the preceding example:

```
If Ans = vbYes Then GoTo TryAgain
```

The code, which is available on this book's Web site, doesn't work correctly if you use GoTo instead of Resume. To demonstrate, enter a negative number: You get the error prompt. Click Yes to try again and then enter *another* negative number. This second error is not trapped because the original error condition was not cleared.

Error handling in a nutshell

To help you keep all this error-handling business straight, I've prepared a quick-and-dirty summary. An error-handling routine has the following characteristics:

- It begins immediately after the label specified in the On Error statement.

- It should be reached by your macro only if an error occurs. This means that you must use a statement such as Exit Sub or Exit Function immediately before the label.

- It may require a Resume statement. If you choose not to abort the procedure when an error occurs, you must execute a Resume statement before returning to the main code.

Knowing when to ignore errors

In some cases, it's perfectly okay to ignore errors. That's when the On Error Resume Next statement comes into play.

The following example loops through each cell in the selected range and converts the value to its square root. This procedure generates an error message if any cell in the selection contains a nonpositive number:

```
Sub SelectionSqrt()
    Dim cell As Range
    If TypeName(Selection) <> "Range" Then Exit Sub
    For Each cell In Selection
        cell.Value = Sqr(cell.Value)
    Next cell
End Sub
```

In this case, you may want to simply skip any cell that contains a value you can't convert to a square root. You could create all sorts of error-checking capabilities by using If-Then structures, but you can devise a better (and simpler) solution by simply ignoring the errors that occur.

The following routine accomplishes this by using the On Error Resume Next statement:

```
Sub SelectionSqrt()
    Dim cell As Range
    If TypeName(Selection) <> "Range" Then Exit Sub
    On Error Resume Next
    For Each cell In Selection
        cell.Value = Sqr(cell.Value)
    Next cell
End Sub
```

In general, you can use an On Error Resume Next statement if you consider the errors inconsequential to your task.

Identifying specific errors

All errors are not created equal. Some are serious and some are less serious. Although you may ignore errors you consider inconsequential, you must deal with other, more serious errors. In some cases, you need to identify the specific error that occurred.

When an error occurs, Excel stores the error number in an Error object named Err. This object's Number property contains the error number. You can get a description of the error by using the VBA Error function. For example, the following statement displays the error number and a description:

```
MsgBox Err.Number & ": " & Error(Err.Number)
```

Figure 12-6 shows an example of this. Keep in mind, however, that the Excel error messages are not always very useful — but you already know that.

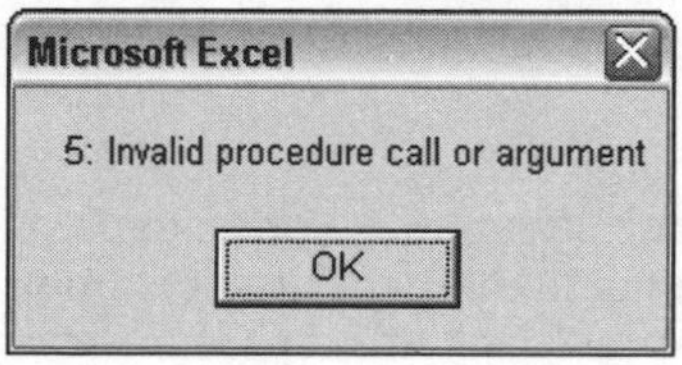

Figure 12-6:
Displaying
an error
number
and a
description.

Microsoft Excel

5: Invalid procedure call or argument

OK

The following procedure demonstrates how to determine which error occurred. In this case, you can safely ignore errors caused by trying to get the square root of a nonpositive number (that is, error 5) or errors caused by trying to get the square root of a nonnumeric value (error 13). On the other hand, you need to inform the user if the worksheet is protected and the selection contains one or more locked cells. (Otherwise, the user may think the macro worked when it really didn't.) This event causes error 1004.

```
Sub SelectionSqrt()
    Dim cell As Range
    Dim ErrMsg As String
    If TypeName(Selection) <> "Range" Then Exit Sub
    On Error GoTo ErrorHandler
    For Each cell In Selection
        cell.Value = Sqr(cell.Value)
    Next cell
    Exit Sub

ErrorHandler:
    Select Case Err
        Case 5 'Negative number
            Resume Next
        Case 13 'Type mismatch
            Resume Next
        Case 1004 'Locked cell, protected sheet
            MsgBox "The cell is locked. Try again."
            Exit Sub
        Case Else
            ErrMsg= Error(Err.Number)
            MsgBox "ERROR: " & ErrMsg
            Exit Sub
    End Select
End Sub
```

When a run-time error occurs, execution jumps to the ErrorHandler label. The Select Case structure tests for three common error numbers. If the error number is 5 or 13, execution resumes at the next statement. (In other words, the error is ignored.) But if the error number is 1004, the routine advises the user and then ends. The last case, a catch-all for unanticipated errors, traps all other errors and displays the actual error message.

An Intentional Error

Sometimes you can use an error to your advantage. For example, suppose you have a macro that works only if a particular workbook is open. How can you determine whether that workbook is open? Perhaps the best solution is to write a general-purpose function that accepts one argument (a workbook name) and returns True if the workbook is open, False if it's not.

Here's the function:

```
Function WorkbookOpen(book As String) As Boolean
    Dim WBName As String
    On Error GoTo NotOpen
    WBName = Workbooks(book).Name
    WorkbookOpen = True
    Exit Function

NotOpen:
    WorkbookOpen = False
End Function
```

This function takes advantage of the fact that Excel generates an error if you refer to a workbook that is not open. For example, the following statement generates an error if a workbook named MyBook.xls is not open:

```
WBName = Workbooks("MyBook.xls").Name
```

In the WorkbookOpen function, the On Error statement tells VBA to resume the macro at the NotOpen statement if an error occurs. Therefore, an error means the workbook is not open, and the function returns False. If the workbook is open, no error occurs and the function returns True.

Here's another variation on the WorkbookOpen function. This version uses On Error Resume Next to ignore the error. But the code checks Err's Number property. If Err.Number is 0, no error occurred and the workbook is open. If Err.Number is anything else, it means that an error occurred (and the workbook is not open).

```
Function WorkbookOpen(book) As Boolean
    Dim WBName As String
    On Error Resume Next
    WBName = Workbooks(book).Name
    If Err.Number = 0 Then WorkbookOpen = True _
      Else WorkbookOpen = False
End Function
```

The following example demonstrates how to use this function in a Sub procedure:

```
Sub Macro1()
    If Not WorkbookOpen("Prices.xls") Then
        MsgBox "Please open the Prices workbook first!"
        Exit Sub
    End If

'   [Other code goes here]
End Sub
```

The Macro1 procedure (which must be in the same project as WorkbookOpen) calls the WorkbookOpen function and passes the workbook name (Prices.xls) as an argument. The WorkbookOpen function returns either True or False. Therefore, if the workbook is not open, the procedure informs the user of that fact. If the workbook is open, the macro continues.

Error handling can be a tricky proposition — after all, many different errors can occur and you can't anticipate them all. In general, you should trap errors and correct the situation before Excel intervenes, if possible. Writing effective error-trapping code requires a thorough knowledge of Excel and a clear understanding of how the VBA error handling works. Subsequent chapters contain more examples of error handling.

Chapter 13

Bug Extermination Techniques

● ●

In This Chapter

▶ Defining a bug and why you should squash it

▶ Recognizing types of program bugs you may encounter

▶ Using techniques for debugging your code

▶ Using the VBA built-in debugging tools

● ●

*I*f the word *bugs* conjures up an image of a cartoon rabbit, this chapter can set you straight. Simply put, a bug is an error in your programming. Here I cover the topic of programming bugs — how to identify them and how to wipe them off the face of your module.

Species of Bugs

Welcome to Entomology 101. The term *program bug,* as you probably know, refers to a problem with software. In other words, if software doesn't perform as expected, it has a bug. Fact is, all major software has bugs — lots of bugs. It has been said that software that doesn't contain bugs is probably so trivial that it's not worth using. Excel itself has hundreds (if not thousands) of bugs. Fortunately, the vast majority of these bugs are relatively obscure and appear in only very unusual circumstances.

When you write VBA programs, your code probably will have bugs. This is a fact of life and not necessarily a reflection of your programming ability. The bugs may fall into any of the following categories:

✔ **Logic flaws in your code.** You can often avoid these bugs by carefully thinking through the problem your program addresses.

✔ **Incorrect context bugs.** This type of bug surfaces when you attempt to do something at the wrong time. For example, you may try to write data to cells in the active sheet when the active sheet is not a worksheet.

✔ **Extreme-case bugs.** These bugs rear their ugly heads when you encounter data you didn't anticipate, such as very large or very small numbers.

✔ **Wrong data type bugs.** This type of bug occurs when you try to process data of the wrong type, such as attempting to take the square root of a text string.

✔ **Wrong version bugs.** This type of bug involves incompatibilities between different Excel versions. For example, you may develop a workbook using Excel 2003 and then find out that the workbook doesn't work with Excel 95 or 97. You can usually avoid such problems by avoiding version-specific features. Often, the easiest approach is to develop your application using the lowest version number of Excel that users might have.

✔ **Beyond-your-control bugs.** These are the most frustrating. An example occurs when Microsoft upgrades Excel and makes a minor, undocumented change that causes your macro to bomb.

Debugging is the process of identifying and correcting bugs in your program. Developing debugging skills takes time, so don't be discouraged if this process is difficult at first.

It's important to understand the distinction between *bugs* and *syntax errors*. A syntax error is a language error. For example, you might misspell a keyword, omit the Next statement in a For-Next loop, or have a mismatched parenthesis. Before you can even execute the procedure, you must correct these syntax errors. A program bug is much subtler. You can execute the routine, but it doesn't perform as expected.

Identifying Bugs

Before you can do any debugging, you must determine whether a bug actually exists. You can tell that your macro contains a bug if it doesn't work the way it should. (Gee, this book is just filled with insight, isn't it?) Usually, but not always, you can easily discern this.

A bug often (but not always) becomes apparent when Excel displays a runtime error message. Figure 13-1 shows an example. Notice that this error message includes a button labeled Debug. More about this later in the "About the Debugger" section.

It's important to remember that bugs often appear when you least expect them. For example, just because your macro works fine with one data set doesn't mean you can assume it will work equally as well with all data sets. The best debugging approach is thorough testing, under a variety of real-life conditions.

Microsoft Visual Basic

Run-time error '5':

Invalid procedure call or argument

| Continue | End | Debug | Help |

Debugging Techniques

In this section, I discuss the four most common methods for debugging Excel VBA code:

✔ Examining the code

✔ Inserting MsgBox functions at various locations in your code

✔ Inserting Debug.Print statements

✔ Using the Excel built-in debugging tools

Examining your code

Perhaps the most straightforward debugging technique is simply taking a close look at your code to see whether you can find the problem. If you're lucky, the error jumps right out and you can quickly correct it.

Notice I said "If you're lucky." That's because often you discover errors when you have been working on your program for eight hours straight, it is 2:00 a.m., and you are running on caffeine and willpower. At times like that, you are lucky if you can even see your code, let alone find the bugs. Thus, don't be surprised if examining your code alone doesn't expunge all the bugs it contains.

Using the MsgBox function

A common problem in many programs involves one or more variables not taking on the values you expect. In such cases, monitoring the variable(s) while your code runs is a helpful debugging technique. Do this by inserting temporary MsgBox functions in your routine. For example, if you have a variable named CellCount, you can insert the following statement:

```
MsgBox CellCount
```

When you execute the routine, the MsgBox function displays CellCount's value.

It's often helpful to display the values of two or more variables in the message box. The following statement displays the current value of LoopIndex and CellCount, as shown in Figure 13-2:

```
MsgBox LoopIndex & " " & CellCount
```

Figure 13-2:
Using a
message
box to
display the
value of two
variables.

Microsoft Excel

24 96

OK

Notice that I combine the two variables with the concatenation operator (&) and insert a space character between them. Otherwise, the message box strings the two values together, making them look like a single value. You can also use the built-in constant, vbNewLine, in place of the space character. vbNewLine inserts a line-feed break, which displays the text on a new line. The following statement displays three variables, each on a separate line:

```
MsgBox LoopIndex & vbNewLine & CellCount & vbNewLine & MyVal
```

This technique isn't limited to monitoring variables. You can use a message box to display all sorts of useful information while your code is running. For example, if your code loops through a series of sheets, the following statement displays the name and type of the active sheet:

```
MsgBox ActiveSheet.Name & " " & TypeName(ActiveSheet)
```

I use MsgBox functions frequently when I debug my code. Just make sure that you remove them after you identify and correct the problem.

Inserting Debug.Print statements

As an alternative to using MsgBox functions in your code, you can insert one or more temporary Debug.Print statements. Use these statements to print the value of one or more variables in the Immediate window. Here's an example that displays the value of three variables:

```
Debug.Print LoopIndex, CellCount, MyVal
```

Notice that the variables are separated with a comma. You can display as many variables as you like using a single Debug.Print statement. If VBE's Immediate window is not visible, press Ctrl+G.

After you've debugged your code, make sure to remove all of the Debug.Print statements.

Using the VBA debugger

The Excel designers are intimately familiar with the concept of bugs. Consequently, Excel includes a set of debugging tools that can help you correct problems in your VBA code. The VBA debugger is the topic of the next section.

About the Debugger

In this section, I discuss the gory details of using the Excel debugging tools. These tools are much more powerful than the techniques I discuss in the previous section. But along with power comes responsibility. Using the debugging tools takes a bit of setup work.

Setting breakpoints in your code

Earlier in this chapter, I discuss using MsgBox functions in your code to monitor the values of certain variables. Displaying a message box essentially halts your code in midexecution, and clicking the OK button resumes execution.

Wouldn't it be nice if you could halt a routine's execution, take a look at *any* of your variables, and then continue execution? Well, that's exactly what you can do by setting a breakpoint.

You can set a breakpoint in your VBA code in several ways:

✔ Move the cursor to the statement at which you want execution to stop; then press F9.

✔ Click in the gray margin to the left of the statement at which you want execution to stop.

✔ Position the insertion point in the statement at which you want execution to stop. Then use the Debug⇨Toggle Breakpoint command.

✔ Right-click a statement and choose Toggle⇨Breakpoint from the shortcut menu

The results of setting a breakpoint are shown in Figure 13-3. Excel highlights the line to remind you that you set a breakpoint there and also inserts a large dot in the gray margin.

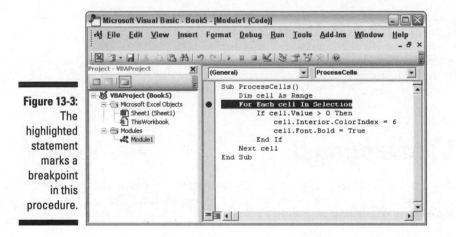

Figure 13-3: The highlighted statement marks a breakpoint in this procedure.

When you execute the procedure, Excel goes into *Break mode* when the line with the breakpoint is executed. In Break mode, the word [break] is displayed in the VBE title bar. To get out of Break mode and continue execution, press F5 or click the Run Sub/UserForm button in the VBE toolbar. Refer to "Stepping through your code" later in this chapter to find out more.

To quickly remove a breakpoint, click the large dot in the gray margin or move the cursor to the highlighted line and press F9. To remove all breakpoints in the module, press Ctrl+Shift+F9.

What is Break mode? You can think of it as a state of suspended animation. Your VBA code stops running and the current statement is highlighted in bright yellow. In Break mode, you can

✔ Type VBA statements in the Immediate window. (See the next section for details.)

✔ Step through your code one line at a time to check various things while the program is paused.

In Break mode, you can move the mouse pointer over a variable to displays its value in a small pop-up window. Figure 13-4 shows an example.

Figure 13-4:
In Break
mode, move
the mouse
pointer over
a variable to
display its
current
value. In this
example,
the cell has
a value
of 43.

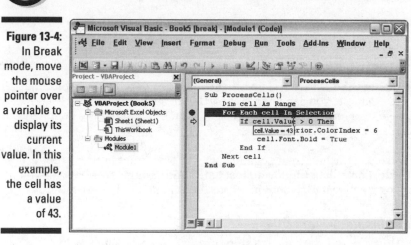

Using the Immediate window

The Immediate window may not be visible in the VBE. You can display the VBE's Immediate window at any time by pressing Ctrl+G.

In Break mode, the Immediate window (see Figure 13-5) is particularly useful for finding the current value of any variable in your program. For example, if you want to know the current value of a variable named CellCount, enter the following in the Immediate window and press Enter:

```
Print CellCount
```

You can save a few milliseconds by using a question mark in place of the word *Print,* like this:

```
? CellCount
```

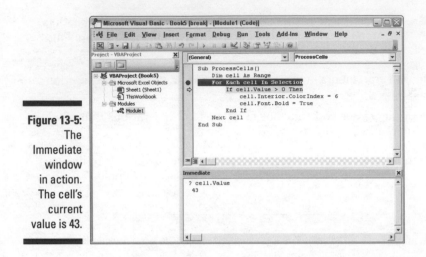

Figure 13-5:
The
Immediate
window
in action.
The cell's
current
value is 43.

The Immediate window lets you do other things besides checking variable values. For example, you can change the value of a variable, activate a different sheet, or even open a new workbook. Just make sure that the command you enter is a valid VBA statement.

You can also use the Immediate window when Excel is not in Break mode. I often use the Immediate window to test small code snippets (whatever you can cram on a single line) before incorporating them into my procedures.

Stepping through your code

While in Break mode, you can also step through your code line by line. One statement is executed for each time you press F8. Throughout this line-by-line execution of your code, you can activate the Immediate window at any time to check the status of your variables.

Using the Watch window

In some cases, you may want to know whether a certain variable or expression takes on a particular value. For example, suppose that a procedure loops through 1,000 cells. You notice that a problem occurs during the 900th iteration of the loop. Well, you could insert a breakpoint in the loop, but that would mean responding to 899 prompts before the code finally gets to the iteration you want to see (and that gets boring real fast). A more efficient solution involves setting a *watch expression*.

For example, you can create a watch expression that puts the procedure into Break mode whenever a certain variable takes on a specific value — for example, Counter=900. To create a watch expression, choose Debug➪Add Watch to display the Add Watch dialog box. See Figure 13-6.

Add Watch

Expression:

cell.value<0

OK

Cancel

Help

Context

Procedure: ProcessCells

Module: Module1

Project: VBAProject

Watch Type

○ Watch Expression

● Break When Value Is True

○ Break When Value Changes

The Add Watch dialog has three parts:

- ✔ **Expression:** Enter a valid VBA expression or a variable here. For example, *Counter=900* or just *Counter*.

- ✔ **Context:** Select the procedure and the module you want to watch. Note that you can select All Procedures and All Modules.

- ✔ **Watch Type:** Select the type of watch by clicking an option button. Your choice here depends on the expression you enter. The first choice, Watch Expression, does not cause a break; it simply displays the expression's value when a break occurs.

Execute your procedure after setting up your watch expression(s). Things run normally until your watch expression is satisfied (based on the Watch Type you specified). When that happens, Excel enters Break mode (unless the Watch Type is set to Watch Expression). From there, you can step through the code or use the Immediate pane to debug your code.

When you create a watch, VBE displays the Watches window shown in Figure 13-7. This window displays the value of all watches that you've defined.

Watches

Expression	Value	Type	Context
cell.Value < 0	False	Variant/Boolean	Module1.ProcessCells

The best way to understand how this Watch business works is to use it and try various options. Before long, you realize what a useful tool it is.

Bug Reduction Tips

I can't tell you how to completely eliminate bugs in your programs, but I can provide a few tips to help you keep those bugs to a minimum:

- **Use an Option Explicit statement at the beginning of your modules.** This statement requires you to define the data type for every variable you use. This creates a bit more work for you, but you avoid the common error of misspelling a variable name. And it has a nice side benefit: Your routines run a bit faster.

- **Format your code with indentation.** Using indentations helps delineate different code segments. If your program has several nested For-Next loops, for example, consistent indentation helps you keep track of them all.

- **Be careful with the On Error Resume Next statement.** As I discuss in Chapter 12, this statement causes Excel to ignore any errors and continue executing the routine. In some cases, using this statement causes Excel to ignore errors that it shouldn't ignore. Your code may have bugs and you may not even realize it.

- **Use lots of comments.** Nothing is more frustrating than revisiting code you wrote six months ago and not having a clue as to how it works. By adding a few comments to describe your logic, you can save lots of time down the road.

- **Keep your Sub and Function procedures simple.** By writing your code in small modules, each of which has a single, well-defined purpose, you simplify the debugging process.

- **Use the macro recorder to help identify properties and methods.** When I can't remember the name or the syntax of a property or method, I often simply record a macro and look at the recorded code.

- **Understand Excel's debugger.** Although it can be a bit daunting at first, the Excel debugger is a useful tool. Invest some time and get to know it.

Debugging code is not one of my favorite activities (it ranks right up there with getting audited by the IRS), but it's a necessary evil that goes along with programming. As you gain more experience with VBA, you spend less time debugging and become more efficient at doing so.

Chapter 14

VBA Programming Examples

In This Chapter
- Exploring VBA examples
- Making your VBA code run as fast as possible

My philosophy for learning how to write Excel macros places heavy emphasis on examples. I find that a well-thought-out example often communicates a concept much better than a lengthy description of the underlying theory. Because you're reading this book, you probably agree with me. This chapter presents several examples that demonstrate common VBA techniques.

I organize these examples into the following categories:

- Working with ranges
- Changing Excel settings
- Working with charts
- Speeding up your VBA code

Although you might be able to use some of the examples directly, in most cases you must adapt them to your own needs.

Working with Ranges

Most of your VBA programming probably involves worksheet ranges. (For a refresher course on Range objects, refer to Chapter 8. When you work with Range objects, keep the following points in mind:

- Your VBA doesn't need to select a range to work with it.
- If your code does select a range, its worksheet must be active.

✔ The macro recorder doesn't always generate the most efficient code. Often, you can create your macro by using the recorder and then edit the code to make it more efficient.

✔ It's a good idea to use named ranges in your VBA code. For example, using Range(Total) is better using than Range(D45). In the latter case, if you add a row above row 45, you need to modify the macro so it uses the correct range address (D46).

✔ When running a macro that works on the current range selection, the user might select entire columns or rows. In most cases, you don't want to loop through every cell in the selection (that could take a long time). Your macro should create a subset of the selection consisting of only the nonblank cells.

✔ Excel allows multiple selections. For example, you can select a range, press Ctrl, and select another range. (Do your range selection with the mouse, of course.) You can test for this in your macro and take appropriate actions.

The examples in this section, which are available at this book's Web site, demonstrate these points.

If you prefer to enter these examples yourself, press Alt+F11 to activate the VBE. Then insert a VBA module and type the code. Make sure that the workbook is set up properly. For example, if the example uses two sheets named Sheet1 and Sheet2, make sure that the workbook has sheets with those names.

Copying a range

Copying a range ranks right up there as one of the most favorite Excel activities of all time. When you turn on the macro recorder and copy a range from A1:A5 to B1:B5, you get this VBA macro:

```
Sub CopyRange()
    Range("A1:A5").Select
    Selection.Copy
    Range("B1").Select
    ActiveSheet.Paste
    Application.CutCopyMode = False
End Sub
```

Notice the last statement. This statement was generated by pressing Esc, which cancels the marching ants display that appears in the worksheet when you copy a range.

This macro works fine, but you can copy a range more efficiently than this. You can produce the same result with the following one-line macro, which doesn't select any cells:

```
Sub CopyRange2()
    Range("A1:A5").Copy Range("B1")
End Sub
```

This procedure takes advantage of the fact that the Copy method can use an argument that specifies the destination. This example also demonstrates that the macro recorder doesn't always generate the most efficient code.

Copying a variable-sized range

In many cases, you need to copy a range of cells but don't know the exact row and column dimensions. For example, you might have a workbook that tracks weekly sales. The number of rows changes as you add new data.

Figure 14-1 shows a range on a worksheet. This range consists of several rows, and the number of rows can change from day to day. Because you don't know the exact range address at any given time, writing a macro to copy the range can be challenging. Are you up for the challenge?

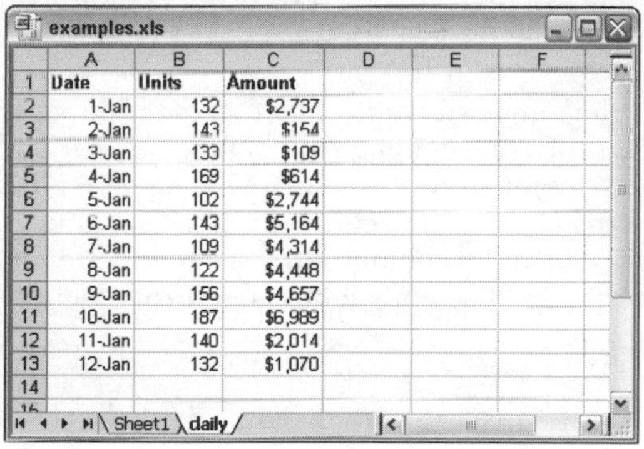

Figure 14-1:
This range can consist of any number of rows.

	A	B	C
1	Date	Units	Amount
2	1-Jan	132	$2,737
3	2-Jan	143	$154
4	3-Jan	133	$109
5	4-Jan	169	$614
6	5-Jan	102	$2,744
7	6-Jan	143	$5,164
8	7-Jan	109	$4,314
9	8-Jan	122	$4,448
10	9-Jan	156	$4,657
11	10-Jan	187	$6,989
12	11-Jan	140	$2,014
13	12-Jan	132	$1,070
14			

The following macro demonstrates how to copy this range from Sheet1 to Sheet2 (beginning at cell A1). It uses the CurrentRegion property, which returns a Range object that corresponds to the block of cells around a particular cell. In this case, that's A1.

```
Sub CopyCurrentRegion()
    Range("A1").CurrentRegion.Copy
    Sheets("Sheet2").Select
    Range("A1").Select
    ActiveSheet.Paste
    Sheets("Sheet1").Select
    Application.CutCopyMode = False
End Sub
```

Using the CurrentRegion property is equivalent to choosing the Edit➪Go To command, clicking the Special button, and selecting the Current region option. To see how this works, record your actions while issuing that command. Generally, the CurrentRegion consists of a rectangular block of cells surrounded by one or more blank rows or columns.

You can make this macro even more efficient by not selecting the destination. The following macro takes advantage of the fact that the Copy method can use an argument for the destination range:

```
Sub CopyCurrentRegion2()
    Range("A1").CurrentRegion.Copy _
        Sheets("Sheet2").Range("A1")
    Application.CutCopyMode = False
End Sub
```

Selecting to the end of a row or column

You're probably in the habit of using key combinations such as Ctrl+Shift+Right Arrow and Ctrl+Shift+Down Arrow to select a range that consists of everything from the active cell to the end of a row or a column. Not surprisingly, you can write macros that perform these types of selections.

You can use the CurrentRegion property to select an entire block of cells. But what if you want to select, say, one column from a block of cells? Fortunately, VBA can accommodate this type of action. The following VBA procedure selects the range beginning at the active cell and extending down to the cell just above the first blank cell in the column. After selecting the range, you can do whatever you want with it — copy it, move it, format it, and so on.

```
Sub SelectDown()
    Range(ActiveCell, ActiveCell.End(xlDown)).Select
End Sub
```

This example uses the End method of the ActiveCell object, which returns a Range object. The End method takes one argument, which can be any of the following constants:

✔ xlUp

✔ xlDown

✔ xlToLeft

✔ xlToRight

Keep in mind that it's unnecessary to select a range before doing something with it. The following macro applies bold formatting to a variable-sized range without selecting the range:

```
Sub MakeBold()
    Range(ActiveCell, ActiveCell.End(xlDown)) _
        .Font.Bold = True
End Sub
```

Selecting a row or column

The following procedure demonstrates how to select the column containing the active cell. It uses the EntireColumn property, which returns a Range object that consists of a full column:

```
Sub SelectColumn()
    ActiveCell.EntireColumn.Select
End Sub
```

As you may expect, VBA also offers an EntireRow property, which returns a Range object that consists of an entire row.

Moving a range

You move a range by cutting it to the Clipboard and then pasting it in another area. If you record your actions while performing a move operation, the macro recorder generates code like the following:

```
Sub MoveRange()
    Range("A1:C6").Select
    Selection.Cut
    Range("A10").Select
    ActiveSheet.Paste
End Sub
```

As with the copying example earlier in this chapter, this is not the most efficient way to move a range of cells. In fact, you can move a range with a single VBA statement, as follows:

```
Sub MoveRange2()
    Range("A1:C6").Cut Range("A10")
End Sub
```

This macro takes advantage of the fact that the Cut method can use an argument that specifies the destination. Notice also that the range was not selected. The cell pointer remains in its original position.

Looping through a range efficiently

Many macros perform an operation on each cell in a range, or they might perform selected actions based on each cell's content. These macros usually include a For-Next loop that processes each cell in the range.

The following example demonstrates how to loop through a range of cells. In this case, the range is the current selection. A variable named Cell refers to the cell being processed. Within the For-Next loop, the single statement evaluates the cell and changes its interior color if the cell contains a positive value.

```
Sub ProcessCells()
    Dim Cell As Range
    For Each Cell In Selection
        If Cell.Value > 0 Then Cell.Interior.ColorIndex = 6
    Next Cell
End Sub
```

This example works, but what if the selection consists of an entire column or row? This is not uncommon because Excel lets you perform operations on entire columns or rows. In such a case, the macro seems to take forever because it loops through each cell in the selection — even the blank cells. To make the macro more efficient, you need a means for processing only the nonblank cells.

The following routine does just that by using the SpecialCells method. (Refer to the VBA Help system for specific details about its arguments.) This routine uses the Set keyword to create two new objects: the selection's subset that consists of cells with constants and the selection's subset that consists of cells with formulas. The routine processes each of these subsets, with the net effect of skipping all blank cells. Pretty slick, eh?

```
Sub SkipBlanks()
    Dim ConstantCells As Range
    Dim FormulaCells As Range
    Dim cell As Range
'   Ignore errors
    On Error Resume Next
'   Process the constants
    Set ConstantCells = Selection _
        .SpecialCells(xlConstants)
    For Each cell In ConstantCells
```

```
            If cell.Value > 0 Then
                cell.Interior.ColorIndex = 6
            End If
        Next cell
'       Process the formulas
        Set FormulaCells = Selection _
            .SpecialCells(xlFormulas)
        For Each cell In FormulaCells
            If cell.Value > 0 Then
                cell.Interior.ColorIndex = 6
            End If
        Next cell
End Sub
```

The SkipBlanks procedure works equally fast, regardless of what you select. For example, you can select the range, all columns in the range, all rows in the range, or even the entire worksheet. It's a vast improvement over the ProcessCells procedure presented earlier in this section.

Notice that I use the following statement in this code:

```
On Error Resume Next
```

This statement tells Excel to ignore any errors that occur and simply process the next statement (see Chapter 12 for a discussion of error handling). This statement is necessary because the SpecialCells method produces an error if no cells qualify.

Using the SpecialCells method is equivalent to choosing the Edit⇨Go To command, clicking the Special button, and selecting the Constants option or the Formulas option. To get a feel for how this works, record your actions while you issue that command and select various options.

Prompting for a cell value

As shown in Figure 14-2, you can use VBA's InputBox function to get a value from the user. Then you can insert that value into a cell. The following procedure demonstrates how to ask the user for a value and place the value in cell A1 of the active worksheet, using only one statement:

```
Sub GetValue()
    Range("A1").Value = InputBox( _
        "Enter the value for cell A1")
End Sub
```

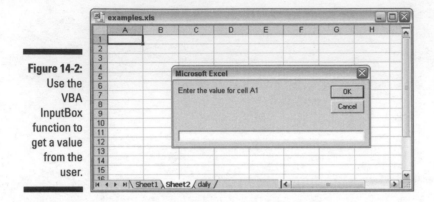

Figure 14-2:
Use the
VBA
InputBox
function to
get a value
from the
user.

If you try out this example, you find that clicking the Cancel button in the Input Box erases the current value in cell A1. The following macro demonstrates a better approach: using a variable (x) to store the value entered by the user. If the value is not empty (that is, the user didn't click Cancel), the value of x is placed into cell A1. Otherwise, nothing happens.

```
Sub GetValue2()
    Dim x as Variant
    x = InputBox("Enter the value for cell A1")
    If x <> "" Then Range("A1").Value = x
End Sub
```

The variable x is defined as a variant because it could be a number or an empty string (if the user clicks Cancel).

Determining the selection type

If you design your macro to work with a range selection, the macro must be able to determine whether a range is actually selected. If something other than a range is selected (such as a chart or a shape), the macro will probably bomb. The following procedure uses the VBA TypeName function to identify the type of object that is currently selected:

```
Sub SelectionType()
    MsgBox TypeName(Selection)
End Sub
```

If a Range object is selected, the MsgBox displays Range. If your macro works only with ranges, you can use an If statement to ensure that a range is selected. This example displays a message and exits the procedure if the current selection is not a Range object:

```
Sub CheckSelection()
    If TypeName(Selection) <> "Range" Then
        MsgBox "Select a range."
        Exit Sub
    End If
'   ... [Other statements go here]
End Sub
```

Identifying a multiple selection

As you know, Excel allows multiple selections by pressing Ctrl while choosing objects or ranges. This can cause problems with some macros. For example, you can't copy a multiple selection that consists of nonadjacent ranges. (Try it if you don't believe me.)

The following macro demonstrates how to determine whether the user made a multiple selection, so your macro can take appropriate action:

```
Sub MultipleSelection()
    If Selection.Areas.Count > 1 Then
        MsgBox "Multiple selections not allowed."
        Exit Sub
    End If
'   ... [Other statements go here]
End Sub
```

This example uses the Areas method, which returns a collection of all objects in the selection. The Count property returns the number of objects in the collection.

Changing Excel Settings

Some of the most useful macros are simple procedures that change one or more of Excel's settings. For example, simply changing the recalculation mode from automatic to manual requires numerous steps. You can save yourself some keystrokes and menu choices (not to mention time) by creating a macro that automates this task.

This section presents two examples that show you how to change settings in Excel. You can apply the general principles demonstrated by these examples to other operations that change settings.

Changing Boolean settings

Like a light switch, a *Boolean* setting is either on or off. For example, you might want to create a macro that turns the worksheet row and column headings on and off. With the headings turned on, Excel generates the following code if you record your actions while accessing the Options dialog box:

```
ActiveWindow.DisplayHeadings = False
```

On the other hand, if the headings are turned off when you record the macro, Excel generates the following code:

```
ActiveWindow.DisplayHeadings = True
```

This may lead you to suspect that you need two macros: one to turn on the headings and one to turn them off. Not true. The following procedure uses the Not operator to effectively toggle the heading display from True to False and from False to True:

```
Sub ToggleHeadings()
    If TypeName(ActiveSheet) <> "Worksheet" Then Exit Sub
    ActiveWindow.DisplayHeadings = Not _
        ActiveWindow.DisplayHeadings
End Sub
```

The first statement ensures that the active sheet is a worksheet. (Chart sheets don't have headings.) If a worksheet is not active, the procedure ends. You can use this technique with any settings that have Boolean (True or False) values.

Changing non-Boolean settings

Use a Select Case structure for non-Boolean settings. This example toggles the calculation mode between manual and automatic and displays a message indicating the current mode:

```
Sub ToggleCalcMode()
    Select Case Application.Calculation
        Case xlManual
            Application.Calculation = xlCalculationAutomatic
            MsgBox "Automatic Calculation Mode"
        Case xlAutomatic
            Application.Calculation = xlCalculationManual
            MsgBox "Manual Calculation Mode"
    End Select
End Sub
```

You can adapt this technique for changing other non-Boolean settings.

Working with Charts

Charts are packed with different objects, so manipulating charts with VBA can be quite confusing. To get a feel for this, turn on the macro recorder, create a chart, and perform some routine chart-editing tasks. You may be surprised by the amount of code Excel generates. After you understand the objects in a chart, however, you can create some useful macros.

To write macros that manipulate charts, you must understand some terminology. An *embedded chart* on a worksheet is a ChartObject object. You can activate a ChartObject much like you activate a sheet. The following statement activates the ChartObject named Chart 1:

```
ActiveSheet.ChartObjects("Chart 1").Activate
```

After you activate the chart, you can refer to it in your VBA code as the ActiveChart. If the chart is on a separate chart sheet, it becomes the active chart as soon as you activate that chart sheet.

When you click an embedded chart, Excel actually selects an object *inside* the ChartObject object. You can select the ChartObject itself by pressing Ctrl while clicking the embedded chart. Select the ChartObject if you want to change an embedded chart's name. After selecting the ChartObject object, use the Name box (the control to the left of the formula bar) to change the name.

Modifying the chart type

Here's a confusing statement for you: A ChartObject object acts as a container for a Chart object.

To modify a chart with VBA, you don't have to activate the chart. Rather, the Chart method can return the chart contained in the ChartObject. Are you thoroughly confused yet? The following two procedures have the same effect — they change the chart named Chart 1 to an area chart. The first procedure activates the chart first; the second one doesn't. The built-in constant xlArea represents an area chart.

```
Sub ModifyChart1()
    ActiveSheet.ChartObjects("Chart 1").Activate
    ActiveChart.Type = xlArea
    ActiveWindow.Visible = False
End Sub
```

```
Sub ModifyChart2()
    ActiveSheet.ChartObjects("Chart 1").Chart.Type = xlArea
End Sub
```

Looping through the ChartObjects collection

This example changes the chart type of every embedded chart on the active sheet. The procedure uses a For-Next loop to cycle through each object in the ChartObjects collection, access the Chart object in each, and change its Type property.

```
Sub ChartType()
    Dim cht As ChartObject
    For Each cht In ActiveSheet.ChartObjects
        cht.Chart.Type = xlArea
    Next cht
End Sub
```

The following macro performs the same function but works on all the chart sheets in the active workbook:

```
Sub ChartType2()
    Dim cht As Chart
    For Each cht In ActiveWorkbook.Charts
        cht.Type = xlArea
    Next cht
End Sub
```

Modifying properties

The following example changes the Legend font for all charts on the active sheet. It uses a For-Next loop to process all ChartObject objects:

```
Sub LegendMod()
    Dim cht As ChartObject
    For Each cht In ActiveSheet.ChartObjects
        With cht.Chart.Legend.Font
            .Name = "Arial"
            .FontStyle = "Bold"
            .Size = 12
        End With
    Next cht
End Sub
```

Note that the Font object is contained in the Legend object, which is contained in the Chart object, which is contained in the ChartObjects collection. Now do you understand why it's called an *object hierarchy?*

Applying chart formatting

This example applies several different types of formatting to the active chart:

```
Sub ChartMods()
    ActiveChart.Type = xlArea
    ActiveChart.ChartArea.Font.Name = "Arial"
    ActiveChart.ChartArea.Font.FontStyle = "Regular"
    ActiveChart.ChartArea.Font.Size = 9
    ActiveChart.PlotArea.Interior.ColorIndex = xlNone
    ActiveChart.Axes(xlValue).TickLabels.Font.Bold = True
    ActiveChart.Axes(xlCategory).TickLabels.Font.Bold = _
        True
    ActiveChart.Legend.Position = xlBottom
End Sub
```

You must activate a chart before executing this macro. Activate an embedded chart by clicking it. To activate a chart on a chart sheet, activate the chart sheet.

To ensure that a chart is selected, you can add some error-handling code. (See Chapter 12 for details about error handling.) Here's the modified macro, which displays a message if a chart is not selected:

```
Sub ChartMods2()
    On Error GoTo ErrorHandler
    ActiveChart.Type = xlArea
    ActiveChart.ChartArea.Font.Name = "Arial"
    ActiveChart.ChartArea.Font.FontStyle = "Regular"
    ActiveChart.ChartArea.Font.Size = 9
    ActiveChart.PlotArea.Interior.ColorIndex = xlNone
    ActiveChart.Axes(xlValue).TickLabels.Font.Bold = True
    ActiveChart.Axes(xlCategory).TickLabels.Font.Bold = _
        True
    ActiveChart.Legend.Position = xlBottom
    Exit Sub
ErrorHandler:
    MsgBox "Select a chart first."
End Sub
```

I created this macro by recording my actions as I formatted a chart. Then I cleaned up the recorded code by removing irrelevant lines.

VBA Speed Tips

VBA is fast, but it's not always fast enough. (Computer programs are never fast enough.) This section presents some programming examples you can use to speed up your macros.

Turning off screen updating

When executing a macro, you can watch everything that occurs in the macro. Although this can be instructive, after getting the macro working properly, it's often annoying and can slow things down considerably. Fortunately, you can disable the screen updating that normally occurs when you execute a macro. To turn off screen updating, use the following statement:

```
Application.ScreenUpdating = False
```

If you want the user to see what's happening at any point during the macro, use the following statement to turn screen updating back on:

```
Application.ScreenUpdating = True
```

To demonstrate the difference in speed, execute this simple macro, which fills a range with numbers:

```
Sub FillRange()
    Dim r as Long, c As Integer
    Dim Number as Long
    Number = 0
    For r = 1 To 50
        For c = 1 To 50
            Number = Number + 1
            Cells(r, c).Value = Number
        Next c
    Next r
End Sub
```

You see each value being entered into the cells. Now insert the following statement at the beginning of the procedure and execute it again:

```
Application.ScreenUpdating = False
```

The range is filled up much faster, and you don't see the end result until the macro is finished running.

Turning off automatic calculation

If you have a worksheet with many complex formulas, you may find that you can speed things up considerably by setting the calculation mode to manual while your macro is executing. When the macro finishes, set the calculation mode back to automatic.

The following statement sets the Excel calculation mode to manual:

```
Application.Calculation = xlCalculationManual
```

Execute the next statement to set the calculation mode to automatic:

```
Application.Calculation = xlCalculationAutomatic
```

Eliminating those pesky alert messages

As you know, a macro can automatically perform a series of actions. In many cases, you can start a macro and then go hang out at the water cooler while Excel does its thing. Some operations performed in Excel, however, display messages that require a human response. For example, if your macro deletes a sheet, Excel displays the message shown in Figure 14-3. These types of messages mean you can't leave Excel unattended while it executes your macro.

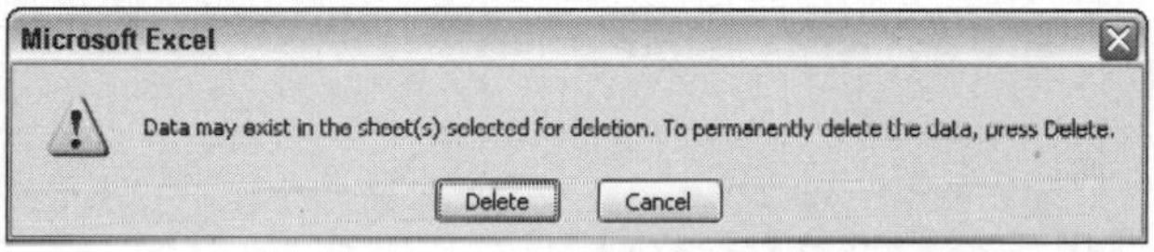

Figure 14-3:
You can instruct Excel to not display these types of alerts while running a macro.

To avoid these alert messages, insert the following VBA statement in your macro:

```
Application.DisplayAlerts = False
```

When the procedure ends, Excel automatically resets the DisplayAlerts property to True (its normal state).

Simplifying object references

As you probably already know, references to objects can become very lengthy. For example, a fully qualified reference to a Range object may look like this:

```
Workbooks("MyBook.xls").Worksheets("Sheet1") _
    .Range("InterestRate")
```

If your macro frequently uses this range, you may want to create an object variable by using the Set command. For example, the following statement assigns this Range object to an object variable named Rate:

```
Set Rate = Workbooks("MyBook.xls") _
    .Worksheets("Sheet1").Range("InterestRate")
```

After defining this object variable, you can use the variable Rate rather than the lengthy reference. For example, you can change the value of the cell named InterestRate:

```
Rate.Value = .085
```

This is much easier to type (and understand) than the following statement:

```
Workbooks("MyBook.xls").Worksheets("Sheet1"). _
    Range("InterestRate") = .085
```

In addition to simplifying your coding, using object variables also speeds up your macros considerably. After creating object variables, I've seen some macros execute twice as fast as before.

Declaring variable types

You don't usually have to worry about the type of data you assign to a variable. Excel handles all the details for you behind the scenes. For example, if you have a variable named MyVar, you can assign a number of any type to that variable. You can even assign a text string to it later in the procedure.

But if you want your procedures to execute as fast as possible (and avoid some potentially nasty problems), tell Excel what type of data will be assigned to each of your variables. This is known as *declaring* a variable's type. (Refer to Chapter 7 for complete details.) Get into the habit of declaring all variables that you use.

In general, you should use the data type that requires the smallest number of bytes yet can still handle all the data assigned to it. When VBA works with data, execution speed depends on the number of bytes VBA has at its disposal. In other words, the fewer bytes data uses, the faster VBA can access and manipulate the data.

If you use an object variable (as described in the preceding section), you can declare the variable as a particular object type. Here's an example:

```
Dim Rate as Range
Set Rate = Workbooks("MyBook.xls") _
    .Worksheets("Sheet1").Range("InterestRate")
```

Using the With-End With structure

Do you need to set a number of properties for an object? Your code runs faster if you use the With-End With structure. An additional benefit is that your code may be easier to read.

The following code does not use With-End With:

```
Selection.HorizontalAlignment = xlCenter
Selection.VerticalAlignment = xlCenter
Selection.WrapText = True
Selection.Orientation = 0
Selection.ShrinkToFit = False
Selection.MergeCells = False
```

Here's the same code, rewritten to use With-End With.

```
With Selection
    .HorizontalAlignment = xlCenter
    .VerticalAlignment = xlCenter
    .WrapText = True
    .Orientation = 0
    .ShrinkToFit = False
    .MergeCells = False
End With
```

If this structure seems familiar to you, it's probably because the macro recorder uses With-End With whenever it can.

Part IV
Developing Custom Dialog Boxes

The 5th Wave   By Rich Tennant

FIRED

YOU

"NIFTY CHART, FRANK, BUT NOT ENTIRELY NECESSARY."

In this part . . .

The four chapters in this part show you how to develop custom dialog boxes (also known as UserForms). This VBA feature is fairly easy to use, after you get a few basic concepts under your belt. And, if you're like me, you may actually *enjoy* creating dialog boxes.

Chapter 15

Custom Dialog Box Alternatives

. . . .

. . . .

ou can't use Excel very long without being exposed to dialog boxes. They seem to pop up almost every time you select a command. Excel — like most Windows programs — uses dialog boxes to obtain information, clarify commands, and display messages. If you develop VBA macros, you can create your own dialog boxes that work just like those built into Excel.

This chapter doesn't tell you anything about creating custom dialog boxes. Rather, it describes some techniques you can use in place of custom dialog boxes. (The next three chapters tell you everything you need to know to jazz up your applications with some award-winning dialog boxes.)

Why Create Dialog Boxes?

Some of the VBA macros you create behave the same every time you execute them. For example, you may develop a macro that enters a list of your employees into a worksheet range. This macro always produces the same result and requires no additional user input.

You might develop other macros, however, that behave differently under various circumstances or that offer the user options. In such cases, the macro may benefit from a custom dialog box. A custom dialog box provides a simple means for getting information from the user. Your macro then uses that information to determine what it should do.

Custom dialog boxes can be quite useful, but creating them takes time. Before I cover the topic of creating custom dialog boxes in the next chapter, you need to know about some time-saving alternatives.

VBA lets you display four different types of dialog boxes that you can sometimes use in place of a custom dialog box. You can customize these built-in dialog boxes in some ways, but they certainly don't offer the options available in a custom dialog box. In some cases, however, they're just what the doctor ordered.

In this chapter you read about

- ✔ The MsgBox function
- ✔ The InputBox function
- ✔ The GetOpenFileName method
- ✔ The GetSaveAsFileName method

I also describe how to use VBA to display the Excel built-in dialog boxes — the dialog boxes that Excel itself uses to get information from you.

The MsgBox Function

You're probably already familiar with the VBA MsgBox function — I use it quite a bit in the examples throughout this book. The MsgBox function, which accepts the arguments shown in Table 15-1, is handy for displaying information and getting simple user input.

Here's a simplified version of the syntax for the MsgBox function:

```
MsgBox(prompt[, buttons][, title])
```

Table 15-1	MsgBox Function Arguments
Argument	*What It Does*
prompt	Supplies the text Excel displays in the message box
buttons	Specifies which buttons appear in the message box (optional)
title	Defines the text that appears in the message box's title bar (optional)

Displaying a simple message box

You can use the MsgBox function by itself or assign its result (that is, the button clicked by the user) to a variable. If you use this function by itself, don't include parentheses around the arguments. The following example simply displays a message and does not return a result:

```
Sub MsgBoxDemo()
    MsgBox "Click OK to continue."
End Sub
```

Figure 15-1 shows how this message box looks.

Getting a response from a message box

Your VBA code can also determine which button was clicked in a message box. You can assign the result of the MsgBox function to a variable. In the following code, I use some built-in constants (which I describe later in Table 15-2) that make it easy to work with the values returned by MsgBox:

```
Sub GetAnswer()
    Dim Ans As Integer
    Ans = MsgBox("Continue?", vbYesNo)
    Select Case Ans
        Case vbYes
'           ...[code if Ans is Yes]...
        Case vbNo
'           ...[code if Ans is No]...
    End Select
End Sub
```

When you execute this procedure, the Ans variable is assigned a value of either vbYes or vbNo, depending on which button the user clicks. The Select Case statement uses the Ans value to determine which action the routine should perform.

You can also use the MsgBox function result without using a variable, as the following example demonstrates:

```
Sub GetAnswer2()
    If MsgBox("Continue?", vbYesNo) = vbYes Then
'           ...[code if Yes is clicked]...
    Else
'           ...[code if Yes is not clicked]...
    End If
End Sub
```

Customizing message boxes

The flexibility of the buttons argument makes it easy to customize your message boxes. You can specify which buttons to display, determine whether an icon appears, and decide which button is the default. Table 15-2 lists some of the built-in constants you can use for the buttons argument. If you prefer, you can use the value rather than a constant (but I think using the built-in constants is a lot easier).

Table 15-2	Constants Used in the MsgBox Function	
Constant	*Value*	*What It Does*
vbOKOnly	0	Displays OK button only
vbOKCancel	1	Displays OK and Cancel buttons
vbAbortRetryIgnore	2	Displays Abort, Retry, and Ignore buttons
vbYesNoCancel	3	Displays Yes, No, and Cancel buttons
vbYesNo	4	Displays Yes and No buttons
vbRetryCancel	5	Displays Retry and Cancel buttons
vbCritical	16	Displays Critical Message icon
vbQuestion	32	Displays Warning Query icon
vbExclamation	48	Displays Warning Message icon
vbInformation	64	Displays Information Message icon
vbDefaultButton1	0	First button is default
vbDefaultButton2	256	Second button is default
vbDefaultButton3	512	Third button is default
vbDefaultButton4	768	Fourth button is default
vbSystemModal	4096	System modal; all applications are suspended until the user responds to the message box

To use more than one of these constants as an argument, just connect them with a + operator. For example, to display a message box with Yes and No buttons and an exclamation icon, use the following expression as the second MsgBox argument:

```
vbYesNo + vbExclamation
```

Or, if you like to make things more difficult for yourself, use a value of 52 (4 + 48).

The following example uses a combination of constants to display a message box with a Yes button and a No button (vbYesNo) as well as a question mark icon (vbQuestion). The constant vbDefaultButton2 designates the second button (No) as the default button — that is, the button that is clicked if the user presses Enter. For simplicity, I assign these constants to the Config variable and then use Config as the second argument in the MsgBox function:

```
Sub GetAnswer3()
    Dim Config As Integer
    Dim Ans As Integer
    Config = vbYesNo + vbQuestion + vbDefaultButton2
    Ans = MsgBox("Process the monthly report?", Config)
    If Ans = vbYes Then RunReport
End Sub
```

Figure 15-2 shows the message box Excel displays when you execute the GetAnswer3 procedure. If the user clicks the Yes button, the routine executes the procedure named RunReport (which is not shown). If the user clicks the No button (or presses Enter), the routine ends with no action. Because I omitted the title argument in the MsgBox function, Excel uses the default title, Microsoft Excel.

Figure 15-2:
The MsgBox function's buttons argument determines what appears in the message box.

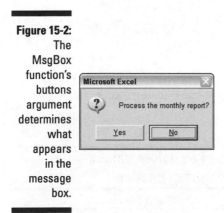

The following routine provides another example of using the MsgBox function:

```
Sub GetAnswer4()
    Dim Msg As String, Title As String
    Dim Config As Integer, Ans As Integer
    Msg = "Do you want to process the monthly report?"
    Msg = Msg & vbNewLine & vbNewLine
    Msg = Msg & "Processing the monthly report will "
    Msg = Msg & "take approximately 15 minutes. It "
    Msg = Msg & "will generate a 30-page report for "
    Msg = Msg & "all sales offices for the current "
    Msg = Msg & "month."
    Title = "XYZ Marketing Company"
    Config = vbYesNo + vbQuestion
    Ans = MsgBox(Msg, Config, Title)
    If Ans = vbYes Then RunReport
End Sub
```

This example demonstrates an efficient way to specify a longer message in a message box. I use a variable (Msg) and the concatenation operator (&) to build the message in a series of statements. The vbNewLine constant inserts a line break character that starts a new line. I also use the title argument to display a different title in the message box. Figure 15-3 shows the message box Excel displays when you execute this procedure.

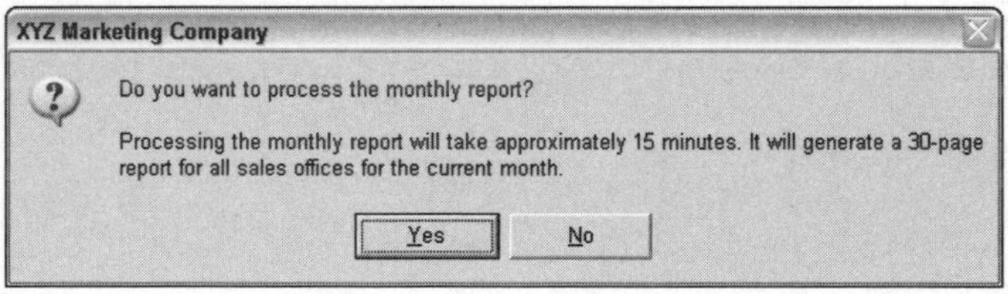

Figure 15-3:
The dialog box displayed by the MsgBox function.

Previous examples have used constants (such as vbYes and vbNo) for the return value of a MsgBox function. Besides these two constants, Table 15-3 lists a few others.

Table 15-3   Constants Used as Return Values for the MsgBox Function

Constant	Value	What It Means
vbOK	1	User clicked OK.
vbCancel	2	User clicked Cancel.
vbAbort	3	User clicked Abort.

Constant	Value	What It Means
vbRetry	4	User clicked Retry.
vbIgnore	5	User clicked Ignore.
vbYes	6	User clicked Yes.
vbNo	7	User clicked No.

The InputBox Function

The VBA InputBox function is useful for obtaining a single value from the user. This is a good alternative to developing a custom dialog box when you need to get only one value.

InputBox syntax

Here's a simplified version of the syntax for the InputBox function:

```
InputBox(prompt[, title][, default])
```

The InputBox function accepts the arguments listed in Table 15-4.

Table 15-4	InputBox Function Arguments
Argument	**What It Does**
prompt	Supplies the text displayed in the input box
title	Specifies the text displayed in the input box's title bar (optional)
default	Defines the default value (optional)

An InputBox example

Here's an example showing how you can use the InputBox function:

```
TheName = InputBox("What is your name?", "Greetings")
```

When you execute this VBA statement, Excel displays the dialog box shown in Figure 15-4. Notice that this example uses only the first two arguments and does not supply a default value. When the user enters a value and clicks OK, the routine assigns the value to the variable TheName.

Figure 15-4:
The
InputBox
function
displays this
dialog box.

Figure 15-4: The InputBox function displays this dialog box.

Greetings	☒
What is your name?	OK
	Cancel
John Walkenbach	

The following example uses the third argument and provides a default value. The default value is the username stored by Excel (the Application object's UserName property).

```
Sub GetName()
    Dim DefName As String
    Dim TheName As String
    DefName = Application.UserName
    TheName = InputBox("What is your name?", _
        "Greetings", DefName)
End Sub
```

REMEMBER

VBA's InputBox function always returns a string, so you might need to convert the result to a value. You can convert a string to a value by using the Val function.

The following example uses the Val function to convert the user's entry to a value:

```
Sub GetName2AddSheet()
    Dim Prompt As String
    Dim Caption As String
    Dim DefValue as Integer
    Dim NumSheets As Integer
    Prompt = "How many sheets do you want to add?"
    Caption = "Tell me..."
    DefValue = 1
    NumSheets = Val(InputBox(Prompt, Caption, DefValue))
    If NumSheets > 0 Then Sheets.Add Count:=NumSheets
End Sub
```

Figure 15-5 shows the dialog box that this routine produces.

Figure 15-5:
Another
example of
using the
InputBox
function.

Tell me...   ☒

How many sheets do you want to add?   OK
                                         Cancel

1

The information presented in this section applies to VBA's InputBox function.
In addition, you have access to the InputBox method, which is a method of
the Application object. One advantage of using the InputBox method is that
your code can prompt for a range selection. Here's a quick example that
prompts the user to select a range. (The Help system has complete details.)

```
Sub GetRange()
    Dim Rng As Range
    On Error Resume Next
    Set Rng = Application.InputBox _
      (prompt:="Specify a range:", Type:=8)
    If Rng Is Nothing Then Exit Sub
    MsgBox "You selected range " & Rng.Address
End Sub
```

The GetOpenFilename Method

If your VBA procedure needs to prompt the user for a filename, you could use
the InputBox function. An InputBox usually isn't the best tool for this job,
however, because most users find it difficult to remember paths and directory names, and typographic errors often result.

For a better solution to this problem, use the GetOpenFilename method of
the Application object, which ensures that your application gets a valid filename, including its complete path. The GetOpenFilename method displays
the familiar Open dialog box (the same dialog box Excel displays when you
choose File➪Open). The GetOpenFilename method doesn't actually open the
specified file. This method simply returns the user-selected filename. Then
you can write code to do whatever you want with the filename.

The syntax

The official syntax for this method is as follows:

```
object.GetOpenFilename([fileFilter], [filterIndex], [title],
        [buttonText], [multiSelect])
```

The GetOpenFileName method takes the optional arguments shown in Table 15-5.

Table 15-5	GetOpenFileName Method Arguments
Argument	*What It Does*
fileFilter	Determines the types of files that appear in the dialog box (for example, *.TXT). You can specify several different filters from which the user can choose.
filterIndex	Determines which of the file filters the dialog box displays by default.
title	Specifies the caption for the dialog box's title bar.
buttonText	Ignored (used only for the Macintosh version of Excel).
multiSelect	If True, the user can select multiple files.

A GetOpenFilename example

The fileFilter argument determines what appears in the dialog box's files of Type drop-down list. This argument consists of pairs of file filter strings followed by the wildcard file filter specification, with commas separating each part and pair. If omitted, this argument defaults to the following:

```
All Files (*.*), *.*
```

Notice that this string consists of two parts:

```
All Files (*.*)
```

and

```
*.*
```

The first part of this string is the text displayed in the Files of Type drop-down list. The second part determines which files the dialog box displays. For example, *.* means *all files.*

The code in the following example brings up a dialog box that asks the user for a filename. The procedure defines five file filters. Notice that I use the VBA line continuation sequence to set up the Filter variable; doing so helps simplify this rather complicated argument.

```
Sub GetImportFileName()
    Dim Finfo As String
    Dim FilterIndex As Integer
    Dim Title As String
    Dim FileName As Variant

'   Set up list of file filters
    FInfo = "Text Files (*.txt),*.txt," & _
            "Lotus Files (*.prn),*.prn," & _
            "Comma Separated Files (*.csv),*.csv," & _
            "ASCII Files (*.asc),*.asc," & _
            "All Files (*.*),*.*"

'   Display *.* by default
    FilterIndex = 5

'   Set the dialog box caption
    Title = "Select a File to Import"

'   Get the filename
    FileName = Application.GetOpenFilename(FInfo, _
        FilterIndex, Title)

'   Handle return info from dialog box
    If FileName = False Then
        MsgBox "No file was selected."
    Else
        MsgBox "You selected " & FileName
    End If
End Sub
```

Figure 15-6 shows the dialog box Excel displays when you execute this procedure. In a real application, you would do something more meaningful with the filename. For example, you may want to open it using a statement such as this:

```
Workbooks.Open FileName
```

Notice that the FileName variable is declared as a variant data type. If the user clicks Cancel, that variable contains a Boolean value (False). Otherwise, FileName is a string. Therefore, using a variant data type handles both possibilities.

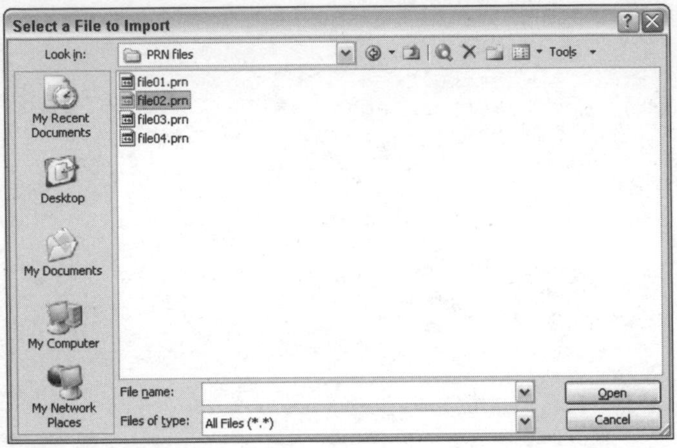

Figure 15-6:
The
GetOpenFile
name
method
displays a
customiz-
able dialog
box and
returns the
selected
file's path
and name. It
does not
open the
file.

Selecting multiple files

If the MultiSelect argument for the GetOpenFilename method is True, the user can select multiple files in the dialog box. In this case, the GetOpenFilename method returns an array of filenames. Your code must loop through the array to identify each selected filename, as the following example demonstrates:

```
Sub GetImportFileName2()
    Dim FileNames As Variant
    Dim Msg As String
    Dim I As Integer
    FileNames =
        Application.GetOpenFilename(MultiSelect:=True)
    If IsArray(FileNames) Then
'       Display full path and name of the files
        Msg = "You selected:" & vbCrLf

        For I = LBound(FileNames) To UBound(FileNames)
            Msg = Msg & FileNames(i) & vbCrLf
        Next i
        MsgBox Msg
    Else
'       Cancel button clicked
        MsgBox "No files were selected."
    End If
End Sub
```

Figure 15-7 shows the result of running this procedure. The message box displays the filenames that were selected.

Figure 15-7:
Select
multiple
filenames
using the
GetOpenFile
name
method.

Notice that I used a named argument for the GetOpenFilename method. I set the MultiSelect argument to True. The other arguments are omitted, so they take on their default values. Using named arguments eliminates the need to specify arguments that aren't used.

The FileNames variable is defined as a variant data type. I use the IsArray function to determine whether FileName contains an array. If so, the code uses the VBA UBound function to determine the array's upper bound and build a message that consists of each array element. If FileNames is not an array, the user clicked the Cancel button. Remember that the FileNames variable contains an array even if only one file is selected.

The GetSaveAsFilename Method

The Excel GetSaveAsFilename method works just like the GetOpenFilename method, but it displays the Excel Save As dialog box instead of its Open dialog box. The GetSaveAsFilename method gets a path and filename from the user but doesn't do anything with it.

The syntax for this method follows:

```
object.GetSaveAsFilename([initialFilename], [fileFilter],
        [filterIndex], [title], [buttonText])
```

The GetSaveAsFilename method takes Table 15-6's arguments, all of which are optional.

Table 15-6	GetSaveAsFilename Method Arguments
Argument	*What It Does*
initialFilename	Specifies a default filename that appears in the File Name box.
fileFilter	Determines the types of files Excel displays in the dialog box (for example, *.TXT). You can specify several different filters from which the user can choose.
filterIndex	Determines which of the file filters Excel displays by default.
title	Defines a caption for the dialog box's title bar.

Displaying Excel's Built-in Dialog Boxes

You can write VBA code that performs the equivalent of selecting an Excel menu command and making choices in the resulting dialog box — although Excel doesn't actually display the dialog box.

For example, the following statement has the same effect as choosing the Edit⇨Go To command, specifying a range named InputRange, and clicking OK:

```
Application.Goto Reference:="InputRange"
```

When you execute this statement, the Go To dialog box does not appear. This is almost always what you want to happen; you don't want dialog boxes flashing across the screen while your macro executes.

In some cases, however, you may want your code to simply display one of Excel's many built-in dialog boxes and let the user make the choices in the dialog box. You can do this by using the Application object's Dialogs property. Here's an example:

```
Result = Application.Dialogs(xlDialogFormulaGoto).Show
```

When executed, this statement displays the Go To dialog box, as shown in Figure 15-8. The user can specify a named range or enter a cell address. This dialog box works exactly as it does when you choose Edit⇨Go To or press F5.

You may think that the value assigned to the Result variable is the range that the user selects in the Go To dialog box. Actually, the value assigned to Result is True if the user clicks OK and False if the user clicks Cancel or presses Escape.

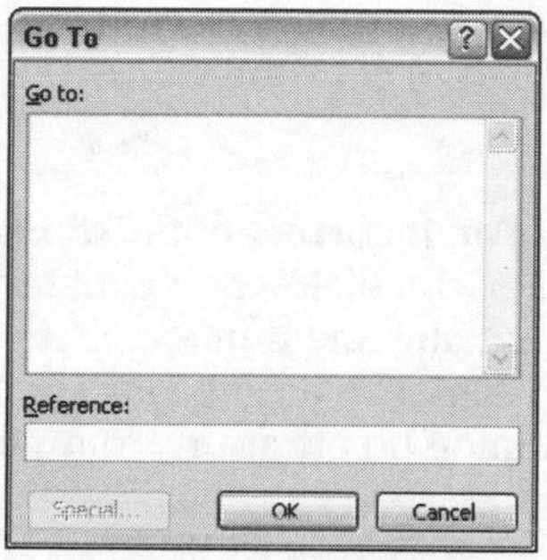

Figure 15-8:
The GoTo
dialog box,
displayed by
using VBA
code.

The preceding example uses the predefined constant xlDialogFormulaGoto. This constant determines which dialog box Excel displays. You can get a list of available dialog box constants by using the Object Browser. Follow these steps:

1. **In the VBE, press F2.**

    The Object Browser appears.

2. **In the Project/Library drop-down list (the one at the upper-left corner of the Object Browser), select Excel.**

3. **In the Search Text drop-down list (just below the Project/Library drop-down list) type** xlDialog.

4. **Click the Search button (the button with the binoculars).**

Figure 15-9 shows the Object Browser displaying a list of the dialog box constants.

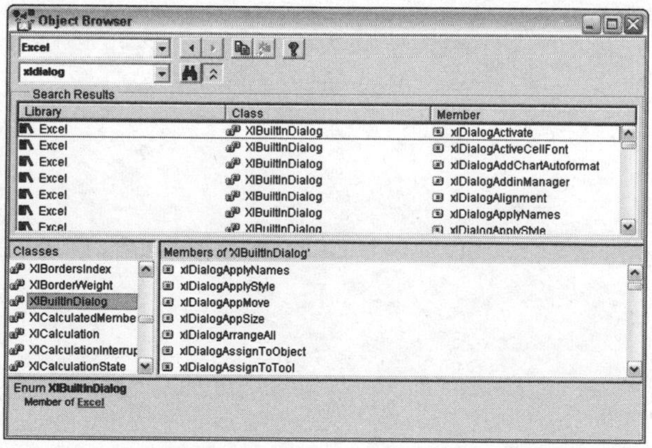

Figure 15-9:
Use the
Object
Browser
to get a
list of the
dialog box
constants.

Unfortunately, these dialog box constants are not documented in the Help system. Therefore, you may need to use a bit of trial and error to figure out which is appropriate for your needs.

If you try to display a built-in dialog box in an incorrect context, Excel displays an error message. For example, one of the dialog box constants is xlDialogAlignment. This dialog box sets text alignment in a cell. If you try to display this dialog box when something other than a range is selected, Excel displays an error message because that dialog box is appropriate only for worksheet cells.

Chapter 16

Custom Dialog Box Basics

A custom dialog box is useful if your VBA macro needs to get information from a user. For example, your macro may have some options that can be specified in a custom dialog box. If only a few pieces of information are required (for example, a Yes/No answer or a text string), the techniques I describe in Chapter 15 may do the job. But if you need to obtain more information, you must create a custom dialog box. In this chapter, you find out what essential skills you need to create and work with custom dialog boxes.

Knowing When to Use a Custom Dialog Box (Also Known as UserForm)

This section describes a situation in which a custom dialog box is useful. The following macro changes the text in each cell in the selection to uppercase letters. It does this by using the VBA built-in UCase function.

```
Sub ChangeCase()
    Dim cell As Range
    If TypeName(Selection) = "Range" Then
        For Each cell In Selection
            cell.Value = UCase(cell.Value)
        Next cell
    End If
End Sub
```

You can make this macro even more useful. For example, it would be nice if the macro could also change the text in the cells to either lowercase or proper case (capitalizing the first letter in each word). One approach is to create two additional macros (one for lowercase and one for proper case). Another approach is to modify the macro to handle the other options. Regardless of the approach, you need some method of asking the user which type of change to make to the cells.

The solution is to display a dialog box like the one shown in Figure 16-1. You create this dialog box on a UserForm in the VBE and display it using a VBA macro. In the next section, I provide step-by-step instructions for creating this dialog box. But before I get into that, I set the stage with some introductory material.

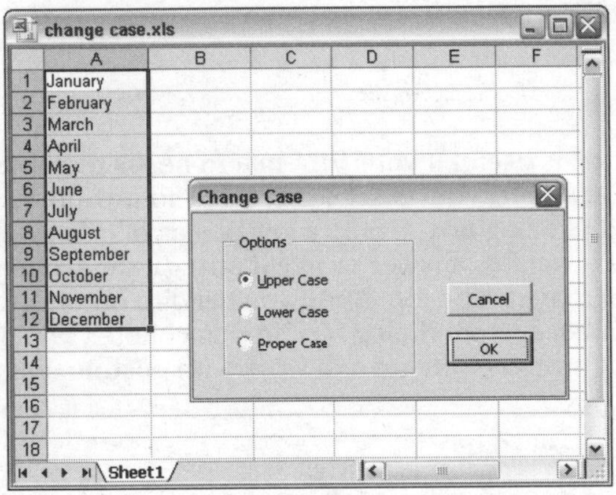

Figure 16-1:
You can get information from the user by displaying a custom dialog box.

In Excel, the official name for a custom dialog box is a UserForm. But a UserForm is really an object that contains what's commonly known as a *dialog box.* This distinction isn't important, so I tend to use these terms interchangeably.

Creating Custom Dialog Boxes: An Overview

To create a custom dialog box, you usually take the following general steps:

1. **Determine how the dialog box will be used and where it will be displayed in your VBA macro.**

2. **Press Alt+F11 to activate the VBE and insert a new UserForm object.**

   A UserForm object holds a single custom dialog box.

3. **Add controls to the UserForm.**

   Controls include items such as text boxes, buttons, check boxes, and list boxes.

4. **Use the Properties window to modify the properties for the controls or for the UserForm itself.**

5. **Write event-handler procedures for the controls (for example, a macro that executes when the user clicks a button in the dialog box).**

   These procedures are stored in the Code window for the UserForm object.

6. **Write a procedure (stored in a VBA module) that displays the dialog box to the user.**

Don't worry if some of these steps seem foreign. I provide more details in the following sections, along with step-by-step instructions for creating a custom dialog box.

Working with UserForms

Each custom dialog box that you create is stored in its own UserForm object — one dialog box per UserForm. You create and access these UserForms in the Visual Basic Editor.

Inserting a new UserForm

Insert a UserForm object with the following steps:

1. **Activate the VBE by pressing Alt+F11.**

2. **Select the workbook in the Project window.**

3. **Choose Insert⇨UserForm.**

   The VBE inserts a new UserForm object, which contains an empty dialog box.

Figure 16-2 shows a UserForm — an empty dialog box.

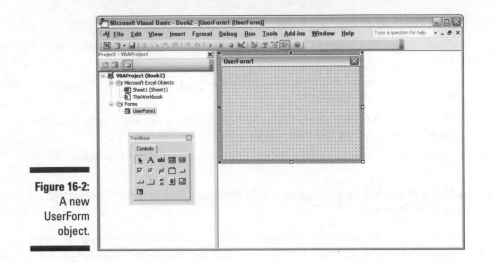

Figure 16-2:
A new
UserForm
object.

Adding controls to a UserForm

When you activate a UserForm, the VBE displays the Toolbox in a floating window, as shown in Figure 16-3. You use the tools in the Toolbox to add controls to your custom dialog box. Just click the desired control in the Toolbox and drag it into the dialog box to create the control. After you add a control, you can move and resize it using standard techniques.

Figure 16-3:
You use the
tools in the
Toolbox to
add controls
to a
UserForm.

Table 16-1 indicates the various tools, as well as their capabilities. To determine which tool is which, hover your mouse button over the control and read the small pop-up description.

Table 16-1	Toolbox Controls
Control	*What It Does*
Label	Stores text
TextBox	Allows the user to enter text
ComboBox	A drop-down list
ListBox	A list of items
CheckBox	Useful for on/off or yes/no options
OptionButton	Used in groups, allows the user to select one of several options
ToggleButton	A button that is either on or off
Framo	Contains other controls
CommandButton	A clickable button
TabStrip	Displays tabs
MultiPage	Tabbed container for other objects
ScrollBar	Draggable bar
SpinButton	Clickable button often used for changing a value
Image	Contains an image
RefEdit	Allows the user to select a range

Changing properties for a UserForm control

Every control you add to a UserForm has a number of properties that determine how the dialog box looks or behaves. You can change these properties with the Properties window, shown in Figure 16-4. The Properties window appears when you press F4, and the properties shown in this window depend on what is selected. If you select a different control, the properties change to those appropriate for that control. To hide the Properties window, click the close button in its title bar.

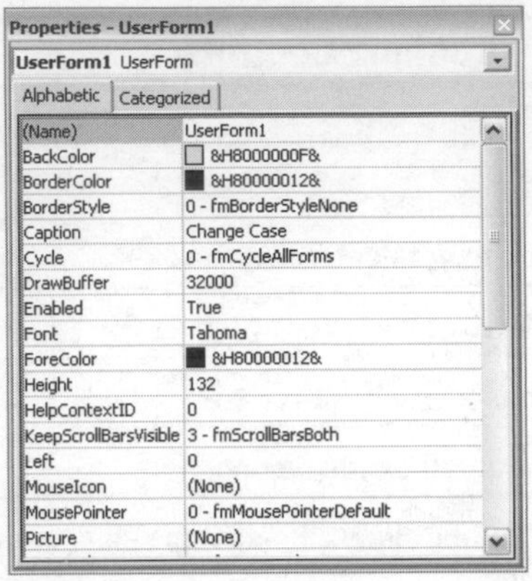

Figure 16-4:
Use the
Properties
windows to
change the
properties
of UserForm
controls.

Properties - UserForm1

UserForm1 UserForm

Alphabetic | Categorized

(Name)	UserForm1
BackColor	&H8000000F&
BorderColor	&H80000012&
BorderStyle	0 - fmBorderStyleNone
Caption	Change Case
Cycle	0 - fmCycleAllForms
DrawBuffer	32000
Enabled	True
Font	Tahoma
ForeColor	&H80000012&
Height	132
HelpContextID	0
KeepScrollBarsVisible	3 - fmScrollBarsBoth
Left	0
MouseIcon	(None)
MousePointer	0 - fmMousePointerDefault
Picture	(None)

Properties for controls include the following:

✔ Name

✔ Width

✔ Height

✔ Value

✔ Caption

Each control has its own set of properties (although many controls have many common properties). The next chapter tells you everything you need to know about working with dialog box controls.

If you select the UserForm itself (not a control on the UserForm), you can use the Properties window to adjust UserForm properties.

Viewing the UserForm Code window

Every UserForm object has a Code window that holds the VBA code (the event-handler procedures) executed when the user works with the dialog box. To view the Code window, press F7. The Code window is empty until you add some procedures. Press Shift+F7 to return to the dialog box.

Another way to switch between the Code window and the UserForm display: Use the View Code and View Object buttons in the Project window's title bar. You find out more about the Code window in Chapter 17.

Displaying a custom dialog box

You can display a custom dialog box by using the UserForm's Show method in a VBA procedure.

The macro that displays the dialog box must be in a VBA module — not in the Code window for the UserForm.

The following procedure displays the dialog box named UserForm1:

```
Sub ShowDialog()
    UserForm1.Show
'    Other statements can go here
End Sub
```

When Excel displays the dialog box, the macro halts until the user closes the dialog box. Then VBA executes any remaining statements in the procedure. Most of the time, you won't have any more code in the procedure. As you later see, you can put your macro code in the Code window for the UserForm.

Using information from a custom dialog box

The VBE provides a name for each control you add to a UserForm. The control's name corresponds to its Name property. Use this name to refer to a particular control in your code. For example, if you add a CheckBox control to a UserForm named UserForm1, the CheckBox control is named CheckBox1 by default. The following statement makes this control appear with a check mark:

```
UserForm1.CheckBox1.Value = True
```

Your VBA code can also check various properties of the controls and take appropriate actions. The following statement executes a macro named PrintReport if the check box (named CheckBox1) is checked:

```
If UserForm1.CheckBox1.Value = True Then Call PrintReport
```

I discuss this topic in detail in the next chapter.

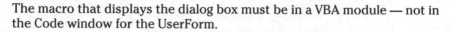

A Custom Dialog Box Example

This section's UserForm example is an enhanced version of the ChangeCase macro from the beginning of the chapter. Recall that the original version of this macro changes the text in the selected cells to uppercase. This modified version uses a custom dialog box to ask the user which type of change to make: uppercase, lowercase, or proper case.

This dialog box needs to obtain one piece of information from the user: the type of change to make to the text. Because the user has three choices, your best bet is a custom dialog box with three OptionButton controls. The dialog box also needs two more buttons: an OK button and a Cancel button. Clicking the OK button runs the code that does the work. Clicking the Cancel button causes the macro to halt without doing anything.

This workbook is available at the book's Web site. However, you get more out of this exercise if you follow the steps provided here and create it yourself.

Creating the custom dialog box

These steps create the custom dialog box. Start with an empty workbook.

1. **Press Alt+F11 to activate the VBE.**

2. **If multiple projects are in the Project window, select the project that corresponds to the workbook you're using.**

3. **Choose Insert⇨UserForm.**

   The VBE inserts a new UserForm object with an empty dialog box.

4. **Press F4 to display the Properties window.**

5. **In the Properties window, change the dialog box's Caption property to** Change Case.

6. **The dialog box is a bit too large, so you may want to click it and use the handles to make it smaller.**

   Step 6 can also be done after you position all the controls in the dialog box.

Adding the CommandButtons

Ready to add two CommandButtons — OK and Cancel — to the dialog box? Follow along:

1. **Make sure the toolbox is displayed. If it isn't, choose View➪Toolbox.**

2. **If the Properties window isn't visible, press F4 to display it.**

3. **In the toolbox, drag a CommandButton into the dialog box to create a button.**

   As you see in the Properties box, the button has a default name and caption: CommandButton1.

4. **Make sure the CommandButton is selected. Then activate the Properties window and change the following properties:**

Property	*Change To*
Name	**OKButton**
Caption	**OK**
Default	**True**

5. **Add a second CommandButton object to the UserForm and change the following properties:**

Property	*Change To*
Name	**CancelButton**
Caption	**Cancel**
Cancel	**True**

6. **Adjust the size and position of the controls so your dialog box looks something like Figure 16-5.**

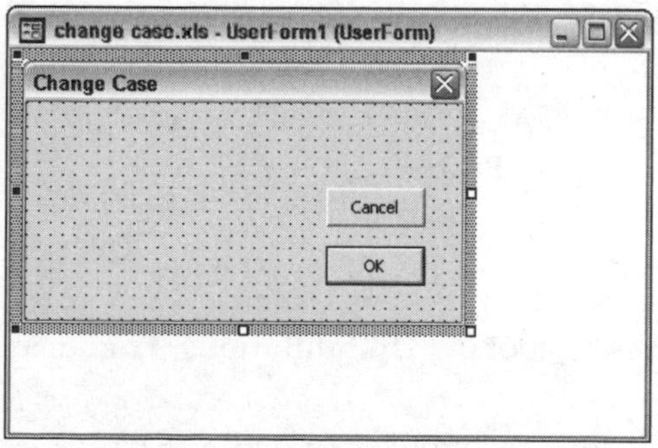

Figure 16-5:
The UserForm with two Command-Button controls.

Adding the OptionButtons

In this section, you add three OptionButtons to the dialog box. Before adding the OptionButtons, you add a Frame object that contains the OptionButtons. The Frame isn't necessary, but it makes the dialog box look better.

1. **In the toolbox, click the Frame tool and drag in the dialog box.**

   This creates a frame to hold the options buttons.

2. **Use the Properties window to change the frame's caption to** Options.

3. **In the Toolbox, click the OptionButton tool and drag in the dialog box (within the Frame).**

   This creates an OptionButton control.

4. **Select the OptionButton and use the Properties window to change the following properties:**

Property	*Change To*
Name	**OptionUpper**
Caption	**Upper Case**
Accelerator	**U**
Value	**True**

   Setting the Value property to True makes this OptionButton the default.

5. **Add another OptionButton and use the Properties window to change the following properties:**

Property	*Change To*
Name	**OptionLower**
Caption	**Lower Case**
Accelerator	**L**

6. **Add a third OptionButton and use the Properties window to change the following properties:**

Property	*Change To*
Name	**OptionProper**
Caption	**Proper Case**
Accelerator	**P**

7. **Adjust the size and position of the OptionButtons, Frame, and dialog box.**

   Your UserForm should look something like Figure 16-6.

The Accelerator property determines which letter in the caption is underlined. For example, you can select the Lower Case option by pressing Alt+L because the L is underlined.

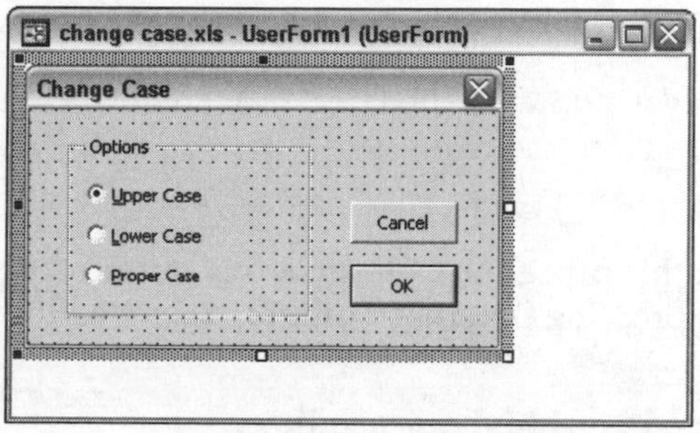

Figure 16-6:
This is the
UserForm
after adding
three Option
Button
controls
inside a
Frame
control.

You may wonder why the OptionButtons have accelerator keys but the CommandButtons go without. Generally, OK and Cancel buttons never have accelerator keys because they can be accessed from the keyboard. Pressing Enter is equivalent to clicking OK because the control's Default property is True. Pressing Esc is equivalent to clicking Cancel, because the control's Cancel property is True.

Adding event-handler procedures

Here's how to add an event-handler procedure for the Cancel and OK buttons:

1. **Double-click the Cancel button.**

   VBE activates the Code window for the UserForm and inserts an empty procedure:

   ```
   Private Sub CancelButton_Click()
   ```

   The procedure named CancelButton_Click is executed when the Cancel button is clicked, but only when the dialog box is displayed. In other words, clicking the Cancel button when you're designing the dialog box won't execute the procedure. Because the Cancel button's Cancel property is set to True, pressing Esc also triggers the CancelButton_Click procedure.

2. **Insert the following statement inside the procedure (before the End Sub statement):**

   ```
   Unload UserForm1
   ```

   This statement simply closes the UserForm when the Cancel button is clicked.

3. **Press Shift+F7 to return to the UserForm.**

4. **Double-click the OK button.**

   VBE activates the code window for the UserForm and inserts an empty Sub procedure called

   ```
   Private Sub OKButton_Click()
   ```

   Clicking OK executes this procedure. Because this button has its Default property set to True, pressing Enter also executes the OKButton_Click procedure.

5. **Enter the following code inside the procedure:**

   ```
   Private Sub OKButton_Click()
       Dim cell As Range
   '   Uppercase
       If OptionUpper Then
           For Each cell In Selection
               cell.Value = UCase(cell.Value)
           Next cell
       End If
   '   Lowercase
       If OptionLower Then
           For Each cell In Selection
               cell.Value = LCase(cell.Value)
           Next cell
       End If
   '   Proper case
       If OptionProper Then
           For Each cell In Selection
               cell.Value = _
                   Application.WorksheetFunction.Proper _
                   (cell.Value)
       Next cell
       End If
   '   Unload the dialog box
       Unload UserForm1
   End Sub
   ```

The preceding code is an enhanced version of the original ChangeCase macro that I presented at the beginning of the chapter. The macro consists of three separate blocks of code. This code uses three If-Then structures; each one has a For Each loop. Only one block is executed, according to which OptionButton the user selects. The last statement *unloads* (closes) the dialog box after the work is finished.

Notice that VBA has a UCase function and an LCase function, but not a function to convert text to proper case. Therefore, I use Excel's PROPER worksheet function (preceded by Application.WorksheetFunction) to do the actual conversion. Another option is to use the VBA StrConv function. (See the Help system for details.) The StrConv function is not available in all Excel versions, so I used the PROPER worksheet function instead.

Creating a macro to display the dialog box

The only thing missing is a way to display the dialog box. Follow these steps to make the procedure that makes the dialog box appear:

1. **In the VBE window, choose Insert➪Module.**

   The VBE adds an empty VBA module (named Module1) to the project.

2. **Enter the following code:**

   ```
   Sub ChangeCase()
   '    Exit if a range is not selected
       If TypeName(Selection) = "Range" Then
   '        Show the dialog box
           UserForm1.Show
       End If
   End Sub
   ```

This procedure is simple. It checks to make sure that a range is selected. If not, the macro ends with no action. If a range is selected, the dialog box is displayed (using the Show method). The user then interacts with the dialog box and the code stored in the UserForm's Code pane is executed.

Making the macro available

At this point, everything should be working properly. But you still need an easy way to execute the macro. Assign a shortcut key (Ctrl+Shift+C) that executes the ChangeCase macro:

1. **Activate the Excel window via Alt+F11.**

2. **Choose Tools➪Macro➪Macros or press Alt+F8.**

3. **In the Macros dialog box, select the ChangeCase macro.**

4. **Click the Options button.**

   Excel displays its Macro Options dialog box.

5. **Enter an uppercase C for the Shortcut key.**

   See Figure 16-7.

6. **Enter a description of the macro in the Description field.**

7. **Click OK.**

8. **Click Cancel when you return to the Macro dialog box.**

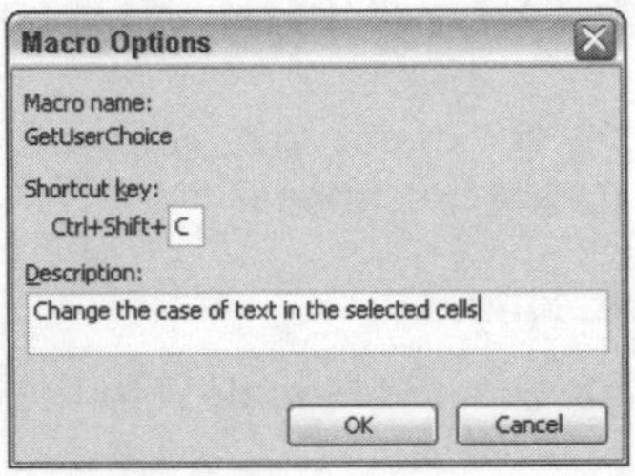

Figure 16-7:
Assign a
shortcut key
to execute
the Change-
Case macro.

After you perform this operation, pressing Ctrl+Shift+C executes the ChangeCase macro, which displays the custom dialog box if a range is selected.

Testing the macro

Finally, you need to test the macro and dialog box to make sure they work properly:

1. **Activate a worksheet (any worksheet in any workbook).**

2. **Select some cells that contain text.**

3. **Press Ctrl+Shift+C.**

   The custom dialog box appears. Figure 16-8 shows how it should look.

4. **Make your choice and click OK.**

   If you did everything correctly, the macro makes the specified change to the text in the selected cells.

Figure 16-9 shows the worksheet after converting the text to uppercase.

As long as the workbook is open, you can execute the macro from any other workbook. If you close the workbook that contains your macro, Ctrl+Shift+C no longer has any function.

If the macro doesn't work properly, double-check the preceding steps to locate and correct the error. Don't be alarmed; debugging is a normal part of developing macros. As a last resort, download the completed workbook from this book's Web site.

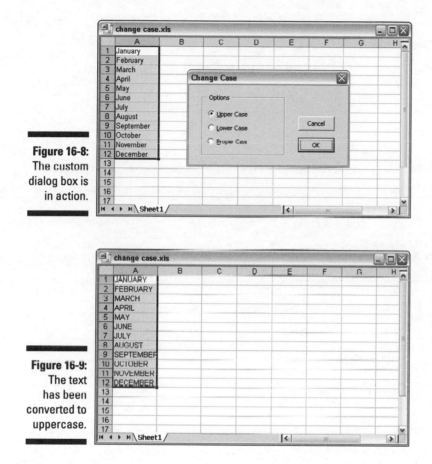

Figure 16-8:
The custom dialog box is in action.

Figure 16-9:
The text has been converted to uppercase.

Chapter 17

Using Dialog Box Controls

A user responds to a custom dialog box (also known as a *UserForm*) by using the various controls (buttons, edit boxes, option buttons, and so on) that the dialog box contains. Your VBA code then makes use of these responses to determine which actions to take. You have lots of controls at your disposal, and this chapter tells you about them.

If you worked through the hands-on example in Chapter 16, you already have some experience with UserForm controls. This chapter fills in the gaps.

Getting Started with Dialog Box Controls

In this section, I tell you how to add controls to a UserForm, give them meaningful names, and adjust some of their properties.

Before you can do any of these things, you must have a UserForm, which you get by choosing Insert⇨UserForm in the VBE. When you add a UserForm, make sure that the correct project is selected in the Project window (if more than one project is available).

Adding controls

Oddly enough, the VBE doesn't have menu commands that let you add controls to a dialog box. You must use the Toolbox, which I describe in the preceding chapter, to add controls. Normally, the Toolbox pops up automatically when you activate a UserForm in the VBE. If it doesn't, you can display the Toolbox by choosing View⇨Toolbox.

Follow along to add a control to the UserForm:

1. **Click the Toolbox tool that corresponds to the control you want to add.**

2. **Click in the UserForm.**

3. **Drag the control into position.**

   Alternatively, you can simply drag a control from the Toolbox to the UserForm to create a control with the default dimensions. Figure 17-1 shows a UserForm that contains a few controls.

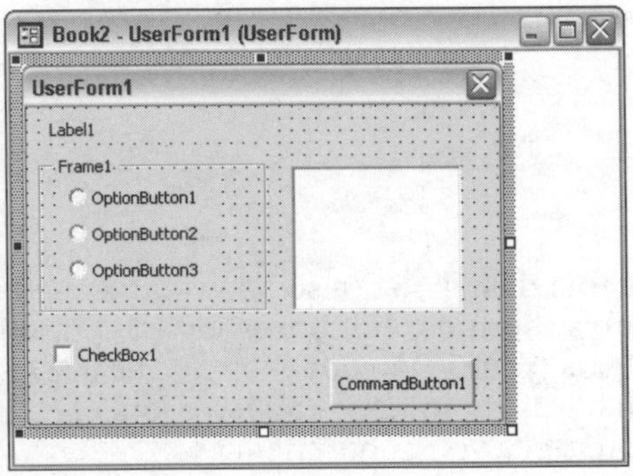

Figure 17-1:
A UserForm with a few controls added.

A UserForm may contain vertical and horizontal grid lines, which help align the controls you add. When you add or move a control, it *snaps* to the grid. If you don't like this feature, you can turn off the grids:

1. **Choose Tools⇨Options in the VBE.**

2. **In the Options dialog box, select the General tab.**

3. **Set your desired options in the Form Grid Settings section.**

Introducing control properties

Every control that you add to a UserForm has properties that determine how the control looks and behaves. You can change a control's properties at these two times:

- ✔ At design time — when you're designing the UserForm. You do so manually, using the Properties window.

- ✔ At run time — while your program is running. You do so by writing VBA code.

When you add a control to a UserForm, you almost always need to make some design-time adjustments to its properties. You make these changes in the

Properties window. (To display the Properties window, press F4.) Figure 17-2 shows the Properties window, which displays properties for the object selected in the UserForm.

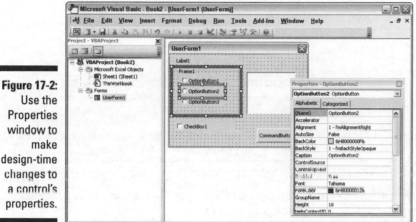

Figure 17-2:
Use the
Properties
window to
make
design-time
changes to
a control's
properties.

To change a control's properties at run time you must write VBA code. For example, you may want to hide a particular control when a check box is checked by the user. In such a case, you would write code to change the control's Visible property.

Each control has its own set of properties. All controls, however, share some common properties, such as Name, Width, and Value. Table 17-1 lists some of the common properties available for most controls.

Table 17-1	Common Control Properties
Property	*What It Does*
Accelerator	The letter underlined in the control's caption. The user presses this key in conjunction with the Alt key to select the control.
AutoSize	If True, the control resizes itself automatically based on the text in its caption.
BackColor	The control's background color.
BackStyle	The background style (transparent or opaque).
Caption	The text that appears on the control.
Value	The control's value.

(continued)

Table 17-1 (continued)

Property	What It Does
Left and Top	Values that determine the control's position.
Width and Height	Values that determine the control's width and height.
Visible	If False, the control is hidden.
Name	The control's name. By default, a control's name is based on the control type. You can change the name to any valid name, but each control's name must be unique within the dialog box.
Picture	A graphics image to display. The image must be contained in a file; it can't be copied from the Clipboard.

When you select a control, that control's properties appear in the Properties window. To change a property, just select it in the Properties window and make the change. Some properties give you some help. For example, if you need to change the TextAlign property, the Properties window displays a drop-down list that contains all valid property values as shown in Figure 17-3.

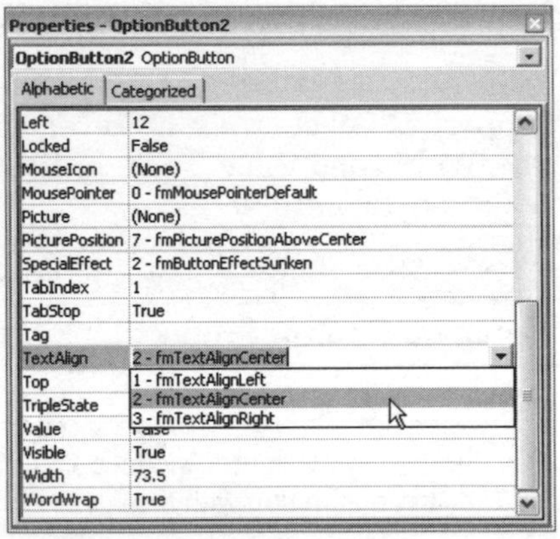

Figure 17-3: Change properties by selecting from a drop-down list of valid property values.

Dialog Box Controls — the Details

In the following sections I introduce you to each type of control you can use in custom dialog boxes and discuss some of the more useful properties. I don't discuss every property for every control because that would take up too much space (and would be very boring).

The Help system for controls and properties is thorough. To find complete details for a particular property, select the property in the Properties window and press F1. Figure 17-4 shows part of the online help for the ControlSource property.

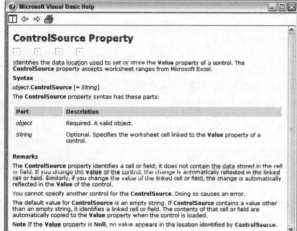

Figure 17-4:
The Help system provides lots of information for each property and control.

All of the sample files in this section are available at this book's Web site.

CheckBox control

A CheckBox control is useful for getting a binary choice: yes or no, true or false, on or off, and so on. Figure 17-5 shows some examples of CheckBox controls.

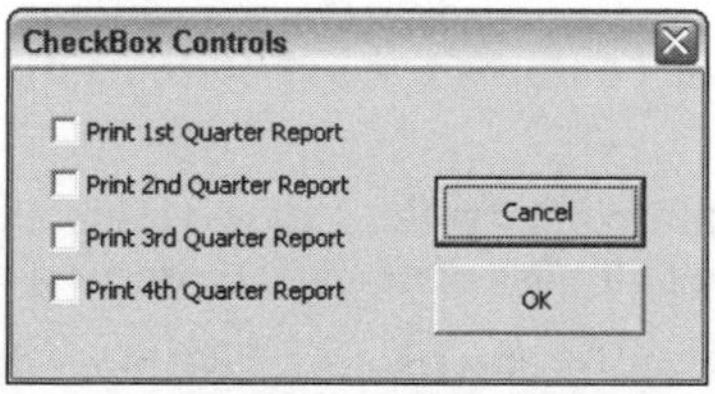

Figure 17-5:
CheckBox controls.

The following is a description of a CheckBox control's most useful properties:

✔ **Accelerator:** A letter that lets the user change the value of the control by using the keyboard. For example, if the accelerator is A, pressing Alt+A changes the value of the CheckBox control (from checked to unchecked, or from unchecked to checked).

> ✔ **ControlSource:** The address of a worksheet cell that's linked to the CheckBox. The cell displays TRUE if the control is checked or FALSE if the control is not checked.
>
> ✔ **Value:** If True, the CheckBox has a checkmark. If False, it does not have a checkmark.

ComboBox control

A ComboBox control is similar to a ListBox control (described later, in this chapter's "ListBox control" section). A ComboBox, however, is a drop-down box and displays only one item at a time. Another difference is that the user may be allowed to enter a value that does not appear in the list of items. Figure 17-6 shows two ComboBox controls.

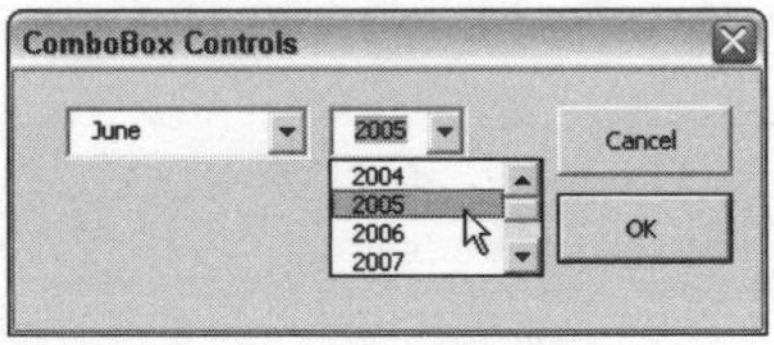

Figure 17-6: ComboBox controls.

The following is a description of some useful ComboBox control properties:

> ✔ **BoundColumn:** If the list contains multiple columns, this property determines which column contains the returned value.
>
> ✔ **ColumnCount:** The number of columns in the list.
>
> ✔ **ControlSource:** A cell that stores the value selected in the ComboBox.
>
> ✔ **ListRows:** The number of items to display when the list drops down.
>
> ✔ **ListStyle:** The appearance of the list items.
>
> ✔ **RowSource:** A range address that contains the list of items displayed in the ComboBox.
>
> ✔ **Style:** Determines whether the control acts like a drop-down list or a combo box. A drop-down list doesn't allow the user to enter a new value.
>
> ✔ **Value:** The text of the item selected by the user and displayed in the ComboBox.

If your list of items is not in a worksheet, you can add items to a ComboBox control by using the AddItem method. More information on this method is provided in Chapter 18.

CommandButton control

CommandButton is simply a clickable button. It is of no use unless you provide an event-handler procedure to execute when the button is clicked. Figure 17-7 shows a dialog box with a few CommandButtons. One of these buttons features a picture (specified using the Picture property).

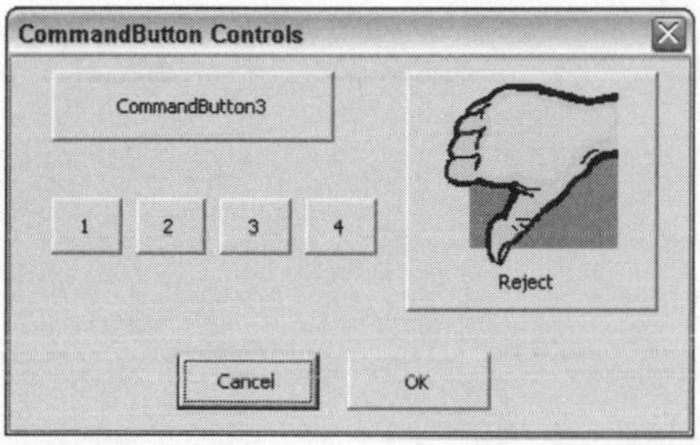

Figure 17-7: Command Button controls.

When a CommandButton is clicked, it executes a macro with a name that consists of the CommandButton's name, an underscore, and the word *Click*. For example, if a command button is named MyButton, clicking it executes the macro named MyButton_Click. This macro is stored in the Code window for the UserForm.

The following is a description of some useful CommandButton control properties:

   ✔ **Cancel:** If True, pressing Esc executes the macro attached to the button.

   ✔ **Default:** If True, pressing Enter executes the macro attached to the button.

Frame control

A Frame control encloses other controls. You do so either for aesthetic purposes or to logically group a set of controls. A frame is particularly useful when the dialog box contains more than one set of OptionButton controls. (See "OptionButton control," later in this chapter.)

The following list describes some useful Frame control properties:

   ✔ **BorderStyle:** The frame's appearance.

   ✔ **Caption:** The text displayed at the top of the frame. The caption can be an empty string if you don't want the control to display a caption.

Image control

An Image control displays an image. You may want to use an Image control to display your company's logo in a dialog box. Figure 17-8 shows a dialog box with an Image control that displays a photo of a famous Excel book author.

Figure 17-8: An Image control displays a photo.

The following list describes the most useful Image control properties:

- **Picture:** The graphics image that is displayed.
- **PictureSizeMode:** How the picture is displayed if the control size does not match the image size.

When you click the Picture property, you are prompted for a filename. However, the graphics image is stored in the workbook. That way, if you distribute your workbook to someone else, you don't have to include a copy of the graphics file.

Here's an easy way to set the Picture property: Copy the image to the Clipboard, select the Image property in the Properties box, and press Ctrl+V to paste the copied image.

Some graphics images are very large and can make your workbook size increase dramatically. For best results, use an image that's as small as possible.

Label control

A Label control simply displays text in your dialog box. Figure 17-9 shows a few Label controls. As you can see, you have a great deal of influence over the formatting of a Label control.

Figure 17-9:
Label
controls
are easily
molded.

ListBox control

The ListBox control presents a list of items from which the user can choose
one or more. Figure 17-10 shows a dialog box with two ListBox controls.

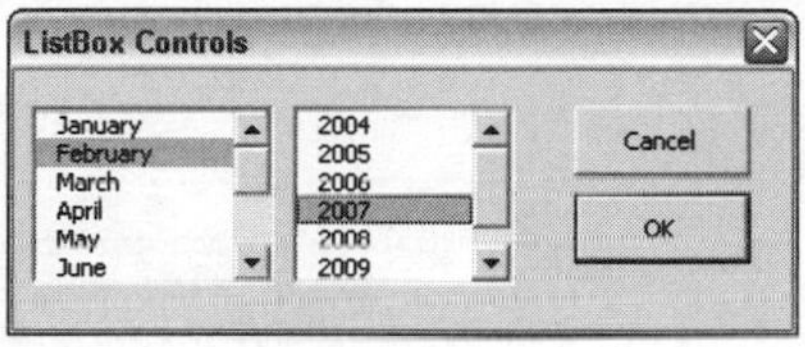

Figure 17-10:
ListBox
controls.

ListBox controls are very flexible. For example, you can specify a worksheet
range that holds the ListBox items, and the range can consist of multiple
columns. Or you can fill the ListBox with items by using VBA code.

The following is a description of the most useful ListBox control properties:

- **BoundColumn:** If the list contains multiple columns, this property deter-
  mines which column contains the returned value.
- **ColumnCount:** The number of columns in the list.
- **ControlSource:** A cell that stores the value selected in the ListBox.
- **IntegralHeight:** This is True if the ListBox height adjusts automatically
  to display full lines of text when the list is scrolled vertically. If False, the
  ListBox may display partial lines of text when it is scrolled vertically.
- **ListStyle:** The appearance of the list items.
- **MultiSelect:** Determines whether the user can select multiple items from
  the list.
- **RowSource:** A range address that contains the list of items displayed in
  the ListBox.
- **Value:** The text of the selected item in the ListBox.

If the ListBox has its MultiSelect property set to 1 or 2, then the user can select multiple items in the ListBox. In such a case, you cannot specify a ControlSource; you need to write a macro that determines which items are selected. Chapter 18 demonstrates how to do so.

MultiPage control

A MultiPage control lets you create tabbed dialog boxes, like the one that appears when you choose the Tools⇨Options command. Figure 17-11 shows an example of a custom dialog box that uses a MultiPage control. This particular control has three pages, or tabs.

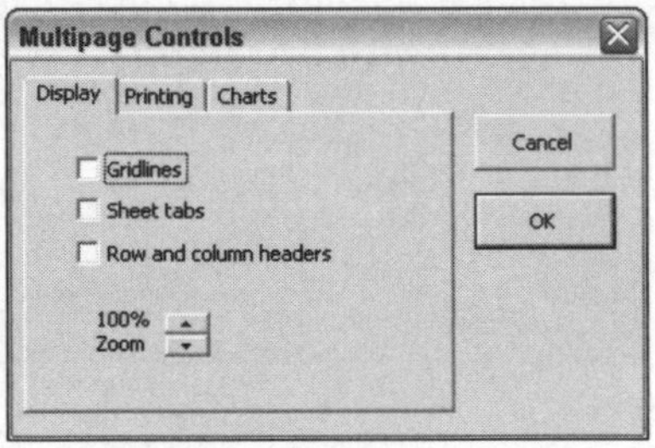

Figure 17-11:
Use a
MultiPage
control to
create a
tabbed
dialog box.

Descriptions of the most useful MultiPage control properties follow:

- ✔ **Style:** Determines the appearance of the control. The tabs can appear normally (on the top), on the left, as buttons, or hidden (no tabs — your VBA code determines which page is displayed).

- ✔ **Value:** Determines which page or tab is displayed. A Value of 0 displays the first page, a Value of 1 displays the second page, and so on.

By default, a MultiPage control has two pages. To add pages, right-click a tab and select New Page from the resulting Context menu.

OptionButton control

OptionButtons are useful when the user needs to select from a small number of items. OptionButtons are always used in groups of at least two. Figure 17-12 shows two sets of OptionButtons (Report Destination and Layout). One set uses graphics images (set with the Picture property).

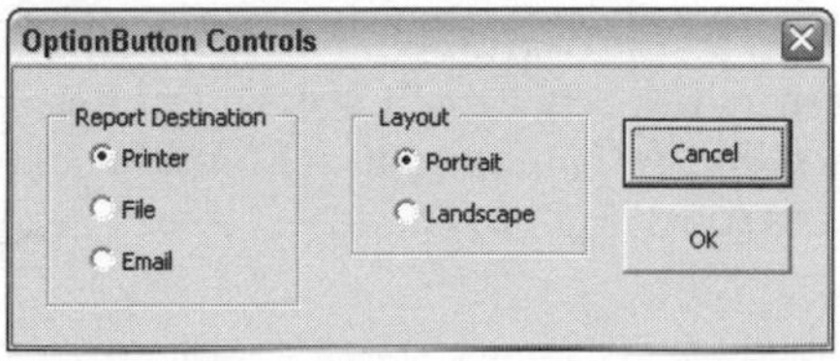

Figure 17-12:
Two sets of
Option
Button
controls,
each
contained in
a Frame
control.

The following is a description of the most useful OptionButton control properties:

- **Accelerator:** A letter that lets the user select the option by using the keyboard. For example, if the accelerator for an option button is C, then pressing Alt+C selects the control.

- **GroupName:** A name that identifies an option button as being associated with other option buttons with the same GroupName property.

- **ControlSource:** The worksheet cell that's linked to the option button. The cell displays TRUE if the control is selected or FALSE if the control is not selected.

- **Value:** If True, the OptionButton is selected. If False, the OptionButton is not selected.

REMEMBER

If your dialog box contains more than one set of OptionButtons, you *must* change the GroupName property for all OptionButtons in a particular set. Otherwise, all OptionButtons become part of the same set. Alternatively, you can enclose each set of OptionButtons in a Frame control, which automatically groups the OptionButtons in the frame.

RefEdit control

The RefEdit control is used when you need to let the user select a range in a worksheet. Figure 17-13 shows a custom dialog box with two RefEdit controls. Its Value property holds the address of the selected range.

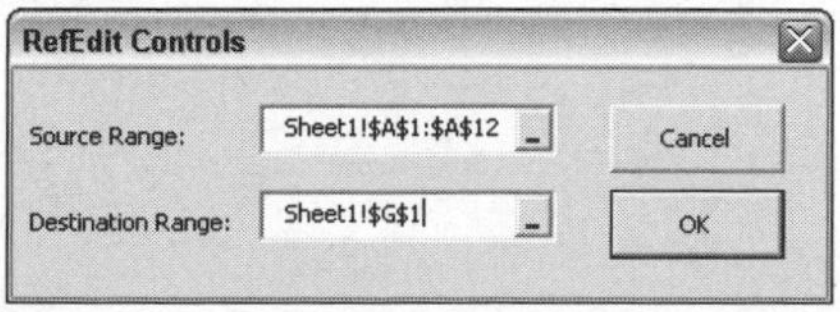

Figure 17-13:
Two RefEdit
controls.

ScrollBar control

The ScrollBar control is similar to a SpinButton control (described later). The difference is that the user can drag the ScrollBar's button to change the control's value in larger increments. Figure 17-14 shows a ScrollBar control. Its Value is displayed in a Label control.

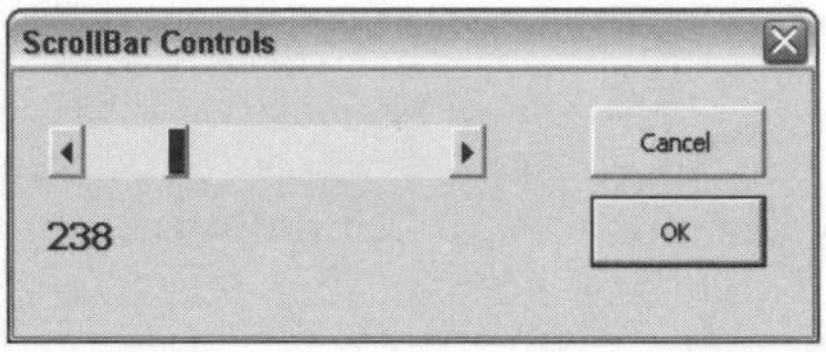

Figure 17-14:
A ScrollBar control, with a Label control below it.

The following is a description of the most useful properties of a ScrollBar control:

- **Value:** The control's current value.
- **Min:** The control's minimum value.
- **Max:** The control's maximum value.
- **ControlSource:** The worksheet cell that displays the control's value.
- **SmallChange:** The amount that the control's value is changed by a click.
- **LargeChange:** The amount that the control's value is changed by clicking either side of the button.

The ScrollBar control is most useful for specifying a value that extends across a wide range of possible values.

SpinButton control

The SpinButton control lets the user select a value by clicking the control, which has two arrows (one to increase the value and the other to decrease the value). Figure 17-15 shows a dialog box that uses two SpinButton controls. Each control is linked to the Label control on the right (by using VBA procedures).

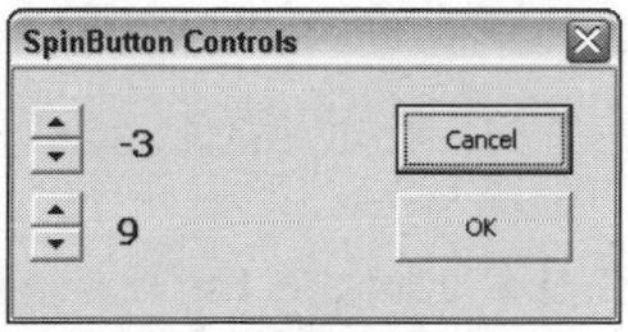

Figure 17-15:
SpinButton
controls.

SpinButton Controls

-3   Cancel

9   OK

The following descriptions explain the most useful properties of a SpinButton control:

- ✔ **Value:** The control's current value.
- ✔ **Min:** The control's minimum value.
- ✔ **Max:** The control's maximum value.
- ✔ **ControlSource:** The worksheet cell that displays the control's value.
- ✔ **SmallChange:** The amount that the control's value is changed by a click. Usually this property is set to 1, but you can make it any value.

If you use a ControlSource for a SpinButton, you should understand that the worksheet is recalculated every time the control's value is changed. Therefore, if the user changes the value from 0 to 12, the worksheet is calculated 12 times. If your worksheet takes a long time to calculate, you may want to avoid using a ControlSource to store the value.

TabStrip control

A TabStrip control is similar to a MultiPage control, but it's not as easy to use. In fact, I'm not sure why this control is even included. You can pretty much ignore it and use the MultiPage control instead.

TextBox control

A TextBox control lets the user enter text. Figure 17-16 shows a dialog box with two TextBox controls.

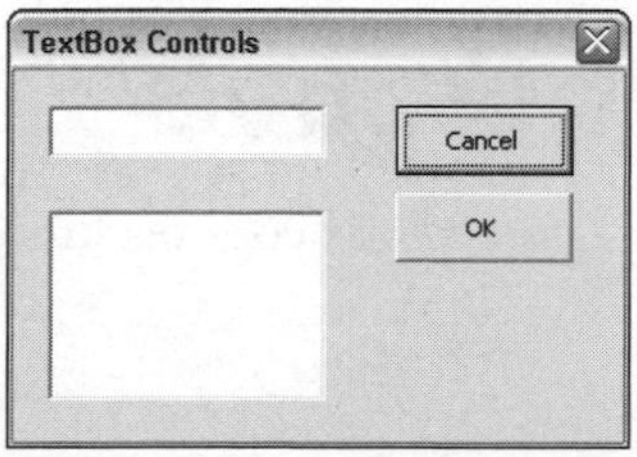

Figure 17-16:
TextBox
controls.

TextBox Controls

Cancel

OK

The following is a description of the most useful TextBox control properties:

- **AutoSize:** If True, the control adjusts its size automatically, depending on the amount of text.
- **ControlSource:** The address of a cell that contains the text in the TextBox.
- **IntegralHeight:** If True, the TextBox height adjusts automatically to display full lines of text when the list is scrolled vertically. If False, the TextBox may display partial lines of text when it is scrolled vertically.
- **MaxLength:** The maximum number of characters allowed in the TextBox. If 0, the number of characters is unlimited.
- **MultiLine:** If True, the TextBox can display more than one line of text.
- **TextAlign:** Determines how the text is aligned in the TextBox.
- **WordWrap:** Determines whether the control allows word wrap.
- **ScrollBars:** Determines the type of scroll bars for the control: horizontal, vertical, both, or none.

ToggleButton control

A ToggleButton control has two states: on and off. Clicking the button toggles between these two states, and the button changes its appearance when clicked. Its value is either True (pressed) or False (not pressed). You can sometimes use a toggle button in place of a CheckBox control. Figure 17-17 shows a dialog box with some ToggleButton controls.

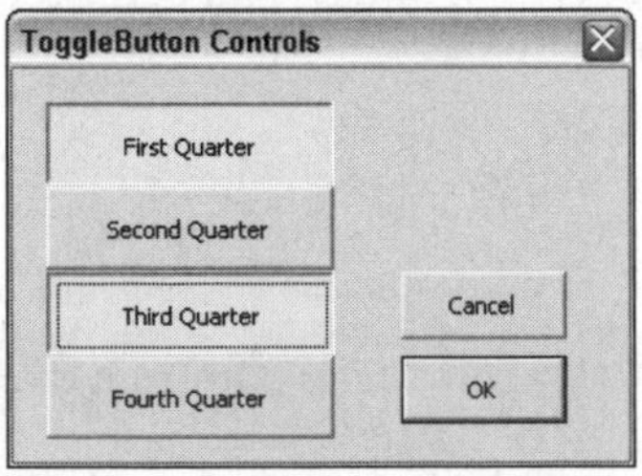

Figure 17-17: Toggle Button controls.

Working with Dialog Box Controls

In this section, I discuss how to work with dialog box controls in a UserForm object.

Moving and resizing controls

After you place a control in a dialog box, you can move it and resize it by using standard mouse techniques. Or for precise control, you can use the Properties window to enter a value for the control's Height, Width, Left, or Top property.

You can select multiple controls by Ctrl+clicking the controls. Or you can click and drag to "lasso" a group of controls. When multiple controls are selected, the Properties window displays only the properties common to all selected controls.

A control can hide another control; in other words, you can stack one control on top of another. Unless you have a good reason for doing so, make sure that you do not overlap controls.

Aligning and spacing controls

The Format menu in the VBE window provides several commands to help you precisely align and space the controls in a dialog box. Before you use these commands, select the controls you want to work with. These commands work just as you would expect, so I don't explain them here. Figure 17-18 shows a dialog box with several CheckBox controls about to be aligned.

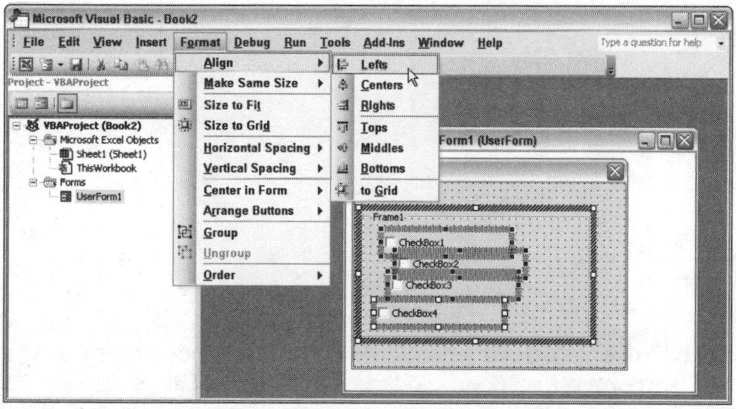

Figure 17-18: Use the Format⇔ Align command to change the alignment of UserForm controls.

When you select multiple controls, the last selected control appears with white handles rather than the normal black handles. The control with the white handles is the basis for aligning or resizing the other selected controls when you use the Format menu.

Accommodating keyboard users

Many users (including me) prefer to navigate through a dialog box by using the keyboard: Pressing Tab and Shift+Tab cycles through the controls, while pressing a hot key instantly activates a particular control.

To make sure that your dialog box works properly for keyboard users, you must be mindful of two issues:

- ✔ Tab order
- ✔ Accelerator keys

Changing the tab order

The tab order determines the order in which the controls are activated when the user presses Tab or Shift+Tab. It also determines which control has the initial *focus* — that is, which control is the active control when the dialog box first appears. For example, if a user is entering text into a TextBox, the TextBox has the focus. If the user clicks an OptionButton, the OptionButton has the focus. The first control in the tab order has the focus when Excel first displays a dialog box.

To set the control tab order, choose View⇨Tab Order. You can also right-click the dialog box and choose Tab Order from the shortcut menu. In either case, Excel displays the Tab Order dialog box shown in Figure 17-19.

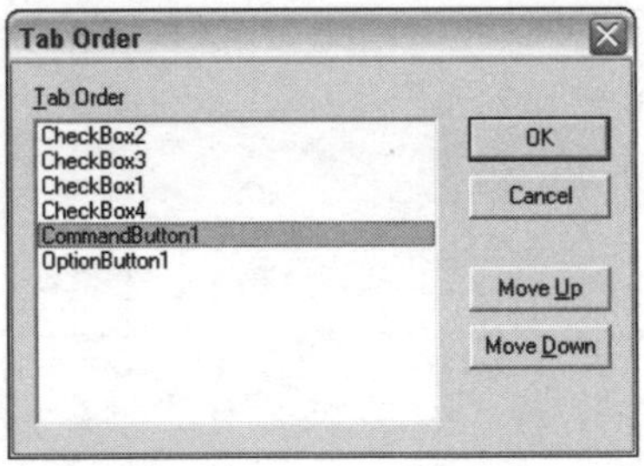

Figure 17-19:
The Tab Order dialog box.

The Tab Order dialog box lists all the controls in the UserForm. The tab order in the UserForm corresponds to the order of the items in the list. To move a control, select it and then click the arrow buttons up or down. You can choose more than one control (click while pressing Shift or Ctrl) and move them all at one time.

Rather than use the Tab Order dialog box, you can set a control's position in the tab order by using the Properties window. The first control in the tab order has a TabIndex property of 0. If you want to remove a control from the tab order, set its TabStop property to False.

Some controls (such as Frame or MultiPage controls) act as containers for other controls. The controls inside a container control have their own tab order. To set the tab order for a group of OptionButtons inside a Frame control, select the Frame control before you choose the View➪Tab Order command.

Setting hot keys

Normally, you want to assign an accelerator key, or *hot key,* to dialog box controls. You do so by entering a letter for the Accelerator property in the Properties window. If a control doesn't have an Accelerator property (a TextBox, for example), you can still allow direct keyboard access to it by using a Label control. That is, assign an accelerator key to the Label and put the Label directly before the TextBox in the tab order.

Figure 17-20 shows several TextBoxes. The Labels that describe the TextBoxes have accelerator keys, and each Label precedes its corresponding TextBox in the tab order. Pressing Alt+D, for example, activates the TextBox next to the Department Label.

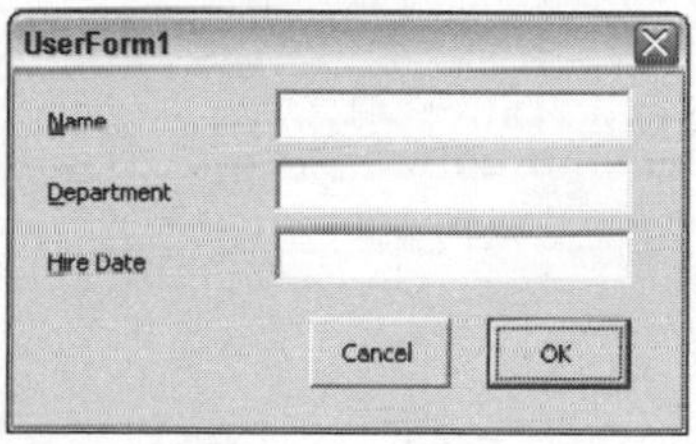

Figure 17-20:
Use Labels
to provide
direct
access to
controls that
don't have
accelerator
keys.

Testing a UserForm

The VBE offers three ways to test a UserForm without calling it from a VBA procedure:

- ✔ Choose the Run➪Run Sub/UserForm command.
- ✔ Press F5.
- ✔ Click the Run Sub/UserForm button on the Standard toolbar.

When a dialog box is displayed in this test mode, you can try out the tab order and the accelerator keys.

Dialog Box Aesthetics

Dialog boxes can look good, bad, or somewhere in between. A good-looking dialog box is easy on the eye, has nicely sized and aligned controls, and makes its function perfectly clear to the user. Bad-looking dialog boxes confuse the user, have misaligned controls, and give the impression that the developer didn't have a plan (or a clue).

A good rule to follow is to try to make your dialog boxes look like the Excel built-in dialog boxes. As you gain more experience with dialog box construction, you can duplicate almost all the features of the Excel dialog boxes.

Chapter 18

UserForm Techniques and Tricks

· ·

· ·

*T*he previous chapters show you how to insert a UserForm (which contains a custom dialog box), add controls to the UserForm, and adjust some of the control's properties. These skills, however, won't do you much good unless you understand how to make use of custom dialog boxes in your VBA code. This chapter provides these missing details and presents some useful techniques and tricks in the process.

Using Dialog Boxes

When you use a custom dialog box in your application, you normally write VBA code that does the following:

✔ Initializes the UserForm controls. For example, you may write code that sets the default values for the controls.

✔ Displays the dialog box by using the UserForm object's Show method.

✔ Writes event-handler procedures for the various controls.

✔ Validates the information provided by the user (if the user did not cancel the dialog box). This step is optional.

✔ Takes some action with the information provided by the user (if the information is valid).

A UserForm Example

This example demonstrates the five points I describe in the preceding section. (In Chapter 16, I present a different, simple hands-on dialog box example.) You use a dialog box to get two pieces of information: a person's name and sex. The dialog box uses a TextBox control to get the name and three OptionButtons to get the sex (Male, Female, or Unknown). The information collected in the dialog box is then sent to the next blank row in a worksheet.

Creating the dialog box

Figure 18-1 shows the finished custom dialog box for this example. For best results, start with a new workbook with only one worksheet in it. Then follow these steps:

1. **Press Alt+F11 to activate the VBE.**

2. **In the Project window, select the empty workbook and choose Insert⇨UserForm.**

   An empty UserForm is added to the project.

3. **Change the UserForm's Caption property to** Get Name and Sex.

   If the Properties window isn't visible, press F4.

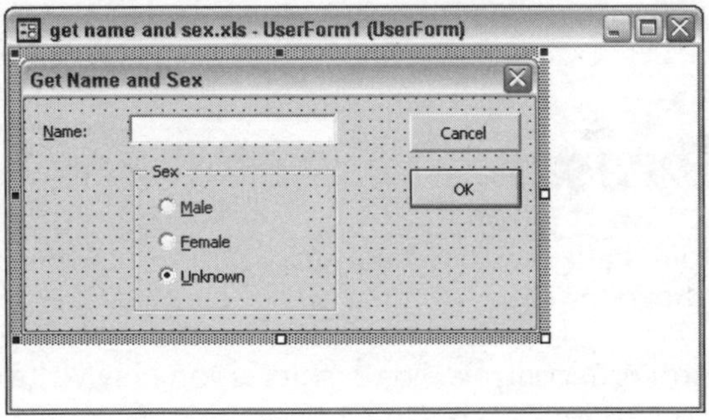

Figure 18-1:
This dialog box asks the user to enter a name and a sex.

This dialog box has eight controls:

✓ **A Label.** I modified the following properties for this control:

Property	Value
Accelerator	N
Caption	Name
TabIndex	0

✓ **A TextBox.** I modified the following properties for this control:

Property	Value
Name	TextName
TabIndex	1

✔ **A Frame object.** I modified the following properties for this control:

Property	Value
Caption	Sex
TabIndex	2

✔ **An OptionButton.** I modified the following properties for this control:

Property	Value
Accelerator	M
Caption	Male
Name	OptionMale
TabIndex	0

✔ **Another OptionButton.** I modified the following properties for this control:

Property	Value
Accelerator	F
Caption	Female
Name	OptionFemale
TabIndex	1

✔ **Another OptionButton.** I modified the following properties for this control:

Property	Value
Accelerator	U
Caption	Unknown
Name	OptionUnknown
TabIndex	2
Value	True

✔ **A CommandButton.** I modified the following properties for this button:

Property	Value
Caption	OK
Default	True
Name	OKButton
TabIndex	3

✔ **Another CommandButton.** I modified the following properties for this button:

Property	Value
Caption	Cancel
Cancel	True
Name	CancelButton
TabIndex	4

If you're following along on your computer (and you should be), take a few minutes to create this UserForm using the preceding information. Make sure to create the Frame object before adding the OptionButtons to it.

In some cases, you may find copying an existing control easier than creating a new one. To copy a control, press Ctrl while you drag the control.

If you prefer to cut to the chase, you can download the example from this book's Web site.

Writing code to display the dialog box

After you've added the controls to the UserForm, your next step is to develop some VBA code to display this dialog box:

1. **In the VBE window, choose Insert⇨Module to insert a VBA module.**

2. **Enter the following macro:**

```
Sub GetData()
    UserForm1.Show
End Sub
```

This short procedure uses the UserForm object's Show method to display the dialog box.

Making the macro available

The next set of steps makes executing this procedure an easy task:

1. **Activate Excel.**

2. **Right-click a toolbar and select Forms from the shortcut menu.**

Excel displays its Forms toolbar.

3. **Use the Forms toolbar to add a button to the worksheet: Click the Button tool and drag in the worksheet to create the button.**

   The Assign Macro dialog box appears.

4. **Assign the GetData macro to the button.**

5. **Edit the button's caption so that it reads** Data Entry.

Trying out your dialog box

Follow these steps to test your dialog box.

1. **Click the Data Entry button on the worksheet.**

   The dialog box appears, as shown in Figure 18-2.

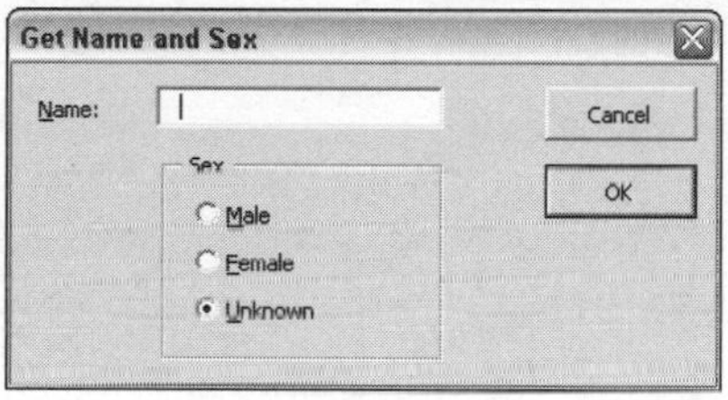

Figure 18-2: Executing the GetData procedure displays the dialog box.

2. **Enter some text into the edit box.**

3. **Click OK or Cancel.**

   Nothing happens — which is understandable because you haven't created any procedures yet.

4. **Click the Close button in the dialog box's title bar to get rid of the dialog box.**

Adding event-handler procedures

In this section, I explain how to write the procedures that handle the events that occur when the dialog box is displayed.

1. **Press Alt+F11 to activate the VBE.**

2. **Make sure the UserForm is displayed; double-click the Cancel button.**

   The VBE activates the Code window for the UserForm and provides an empty procedure named CancelButton_Click.

3. **Modify the procedure as follows:**

```
Private Sub CancelButton_Click()
    Unload UserForm1
End Sub
```

This procedure, which is executed when the user clicks the Cancel button, simply unloads the dialog box.

4. **Press Shift+F7 to redisplay UserForm1.**

5. **Double-click the OK button and enter the following procedure:**

```
Private Sub OKButton_Click()
    Dim NextRow As Long

'   Make sure Sheet1 is active
    Sheets("Sheet1").Activate

'   Determine the next empty row
    NextRow = Application.WorksheetFunction. _
        CountA(Range("A:A")) + 1

'   Transfer the name
    Cells(NextRow, 1) = TextName.Text

'   Transfer the sex
    If OptionMale Then Cells(NextRow, 2) = "Male"
    If OptionFemale Then Cells(NextRow, 2) = "Female"
    If OptionUnknown Then Cells(NextRow, 2) = "Unknown"

'   Clear the controls for the next entry
    TextName.Text = ""
    OptionUnknown = True
    TextName.SetFocus
End Sub
```

6. **Now activate Excel and run the procedure again by clicking the Data Entry button.**

The dialog box works just fine. Figure 18-3 shows how this looks in action.

Here's how it works:

✔ First, the procedure makes sure that the proper worksheet (Sheet1) is active.

✔ It then uses the Excel COUNTA function to count the number of entries in column A and to determine the next blank cell in the column.

✔ Next, the procedure transfers the text from the TextBox to Column A.

✔ It then uses a series of If statements to determine which OptionButton was selected and writes the appropriate text (Male, Female, or Unknown) to column B.

✔ Finally, the dialog box is reset to make it ready for the next entry. Notice that clicking OK doesn't close the dialog box. To end data entry, click the Cancel button.

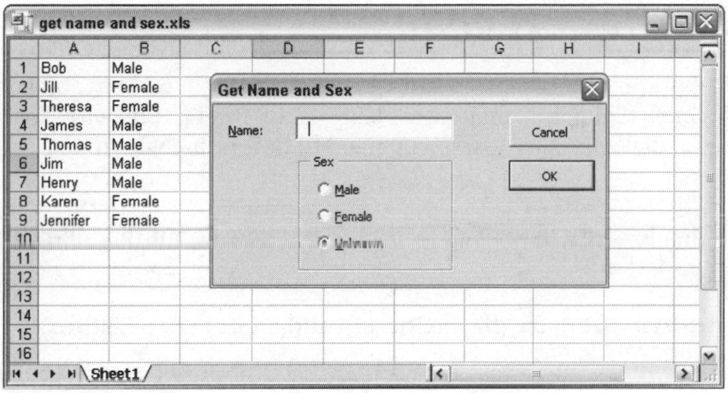

Figure 18-3: Use the custom dialog box for data entry.

Validating the data

Play around with this routine some more and you find that the macro has a small problem: It doesn't ensure that the user actually enters a name into the TextBox. The following code — which is inserted in the OKButton_Click procedure before the text is transferred to the worksheet — ensures that the user enters some text in the TextBox. If the TextBox is empty, a message appears and the routine stops.

```
'   Make sure a name is entered
    If TextName.Text = "" Then
        MsgBox "You must enter a name."
        Exit Sub
    End If
```

Now the dialog box works

After making these modifications, you find that the dialog box works flawlessly. In real life, you'd probably need to collect more information than just name and sex. However, the same basic principles apply. You just have to deal with more UserForm controls.

More UserForm Examples

I could probably fill an entire book with interesting and useful tips for working with custom dialog boxes. Unfortunately, this book has a limited number of pages, so I wrap it up with a few more examples.

A ListBox example

ListBoxes are useful controls, but working with them can be a bit tricky. Before displaying a dialog box that uses a ListBox, fill the ListBox with items. Then, when the dialog box is closed, you need to determine which item(s) the user selected.

When dealing with list boxes, you need to know about the following properties and methods:

- ✔ **AddItem:** You use this method to add an item to a ListBox.
- ✔ **ListCount:** This property returns the number of items in the ListBox.
- ✔ **ListIndex:** This property returns the index number of the selected item or sets the item that's selected (single selections only). The first item has a ListIndex of 0 (not 1).
- ✔ **MultiSelect:** This property determines whether the user can select more than one item from the ListBox.
- ✔ **RemoveAllItems:** Use this method to remove all items from a ListBox.
- ✔ **Selected:** This property returns an array indicating selected items (applicable only when multiple selections are allowed).
- ✔ **Value:** This property returns the selected item in a ListBox.

Most of the methods and properties that work with ListBoxes also work with ComboBoxes. Thus, after you have figured out how to handle ListBoxes, you can transfer that knowledge to your work with ComboBoxes.

Filling a list box

For best results, start with an empty workbook. The example in this section assumes the following:

- ✔ You've added a UserForm.
- ✔ The UserForm contains a ListBox control named ListBox1.
- ✔ The UserForm has a CommandButton named OKButton.

✔ The UserForm has a CommandButton named CancelButton, which has the following event-handler procedure:

```
Private Sub CancelButton_Click()
    Unload UserForm1
End Sub
```

The following procedure is stored in the Initialize procedure for the UserForm:

1. **Select your UserForm and press F7 to find this predefined procedure.**

   The VBE displays the Code window for your form and stands ready for you to input the code for the Click event. (The procedure is UserForm_Click.)

2. **Using the Procedure drop-down list at the top of the Code window, choose Initialize.**

3. **Add the initialization code for the form:**

```
Sub UserForm_Initialize()
'    Fill the list box
    With ListBox1
        .AddItem "January"
        .AddItem "February"
        .AddItem "March"
        .AddItem "April"
        .AddItem "May"
         AddItem "June"
        .AddItem "July"
        .AddItem "August"
        .AddItem "September"
        .AddItem "October"
        .AddItem "November"
        .AddItem "December"
    End With

'    Select the first list item
    ListBox1.ListIndex = 0
End Sub
```

This initialization routine runs automatically whenever your UserForm is loaded. Thus, when you use the Show method for the UserForm, the code is automatically run and your list is populated with 12 items, each added via the AddItem method.

4. **Create a VBA module with a small Sub procedure to simply display the dialog box:**

```
Sub ShowList()
    UserForm1.Show
End Sub
```

It is not mandatory to use the Initialize event procedure to populate your lists. You could do so in a regular VBA procedure. Using an Initialize event procedure just seems like a natural place to take care of such a mundane (though important) step, however.

Determining the selected item

The preceding code merely displays a dialog box with a ListBox filled with month names. What's missing is a procedure to determine which item in the ListBox is selected.

Add the following to the OKButton_Click procedure:

```
Private Sub OKButton_Click()
    Dim Msg As String
    Msg = "You selected item # "
    Msg = Msg & ListBox1.ListIndex
    Msg = Msg & vbNewLine
    Msg = Msg & ListBox1.Value
    MsgBox Msg
    Unload UserForm1
End Sub
```

This procedure displays a message box with the selected item number and the selected item. Figure 18-4 shows how this looks.

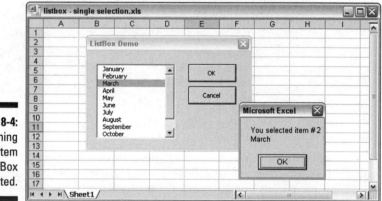

Figure 18-4: Determining which item in a ListBox is selected.

The first item in a ListBox has a ListIndex of 0, not 1 (as you may expect). This is always the case, even if you use an Option Base 1 statement to change the default lower bound for arrays.

This example is available at this book's Web site.

Determining multiple selections

If your ListBox is set up so the user can select more than one item, you find that the ListIndex property returns only the *last* item selected. To determine all selected items, you need to use the Selected property, which contains an array.

To allow multiple selections in a ListBox, set the MultiSelect property to either 1 or 2. You can do so at design time by using the Properties window or at run time by using a VBA statement such as this:

```
UserForm1.ListBox1.MultiSelect = 1
```

The MultiSelect property has three possible settings. The meaning of each is shown in Table 18-1.

Table 18-1	Settings for the MultiSelect Property	
Value	*VBA Constant*	*Meaning*
0	fmMultiSelectSingle	Only a single item can be selected.
1	fmMultiSelectMulti	Clicking an item or pressing the space-bar selects or deselects an item in the list.
2	fmMultiSelectExtended	Items are added to or removed from the selection set in the traditional manner: holding down the Shift or Ctrl key as you click items.

The following procedure displays a message box that lists all selected items in a ListBox. Figure 18-5 shows an example.

```
Private Sub OKButton_Click()
    Dim Msg As String
    Dim i As Integer
    Msg = "You selected" & vbNewLine
    For i = 0 To ListBox1.ListCount - 1
        If ListBox1.Selected(i) Then
            Msg = Msg & ListBox1.List(i) & vbNewLine
        End If
    Next i
    MsgBox Msg
    Unload UserForm1
End Sub
```

This routine uses a For-Next loop to cycle though each item in the ListBox. Notice that the loop starts with item 0 (the first item) and ends with the last item (determined by the value of the ListCount property minus 1). If an item's Selected property is True, it means that the list item was selected.

This example is available at this book's Web site.

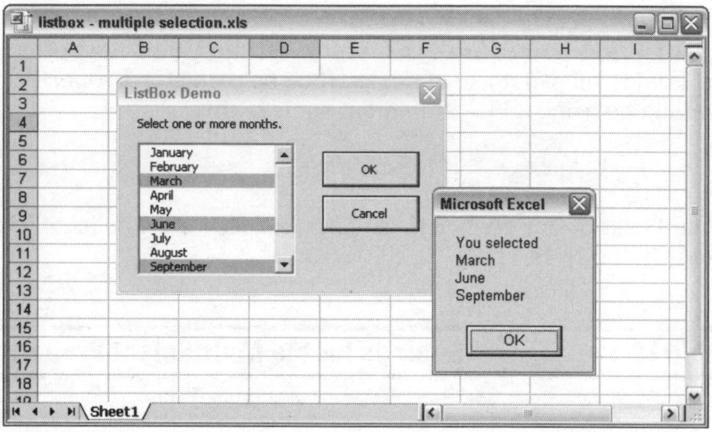

Figure 18-5:
Determining the selected items in a ListBox allows multiple selections.

Selecting a range

In some cases, you may want the user to select a range while a dialog box is displayed. An example of this choice occurs in the second step of the Excel Chart Wizard. The Chart Wizard guesses the range to be charted, but the user is free to change it from the dialog box.

To allow a range selection in your dialog box, add a RefEdit control. The following example displays a dialog box with the current region's range address displayed in a RefEdit control, as shown in Figure 18-6. The current region is the block of nonempty cells that contains the active cell. The user can accept or change this range. When the user clicks OK, the procedure makes the range bold.

This example assumes the following:

- You have a UserForm named UserForm1.
- The UserForm contains a CommandButton control named OKButton.
- The UserForm contains a CommandButton control named CancelButton.
- The UserForm contains a RefEdit control named RefEdit1.

The code is stored in a VBA module and shown here. This code does two things: initializes the dialog box by assigning the current region's address to the RefEdit control and displays the UserForm.

```
Sub BoldCells()
'    Exit if worksheet is not active
     If TypeName(ActiveSheet) <> "Worksheet" Then Exit Sub

'    Select the current region
     ActiveCell.CurrentRegion.Select

'    Initialize RefEdit control
     UserForm1.RefEdit1.Text = Selection.Address

'    Show dialog
     UserForm1.Show
End Sub
```

The following procedure is executed when the OK button is clicked. This procedure does some simple error checking to make sure that the range specified in the RefEdit control is valid.

```
Private Sub OKButton_Click()
     On Error GoTo BadRange
     Range(RefEdit1.Text).Font.Bold = True
     Unload UserForm1
     Exit Sub
BadRange:
     MsgBox "The specified range is not valid."
End Sub
```

If an error occurs (most likely an invalid range specification in the RefEdit control), the code jumps to the BadRange label and a message box is displayed. The dialog box remains open so the user can select another range.

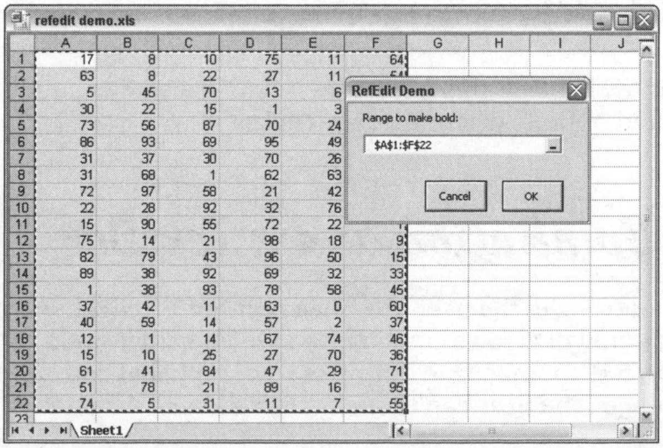

Figure 18-6:
This dialog box lets the user select a range.

Using multiple sets of OptionButtons

Figure 18-7 shows a custom dialog box with three sets of OptionButtons. If your UserForm contains more than one OptionButtons set, make sure that each set of OptionButtons works as a set. You can do so in either of two ways:

✔ Enclose each set of OptionButtons in a Frame control. This approach is the best and also makes the dialog box look better. It's easier to add the Frame before adding the OptionButtons. You can, however, also drag existing OptionButtons into a Frame.

✔ Make sure that each set of OptionButtons has a unique GroupName property. If the OptionButtons are in a Frame, you don't have to be concerned with the GroupName property.

Figure 18-7:
This dialog box contains three sets of Option Button controls.

OptionButtons Demo	☒
Favorite Music Genre	
⦿ Blues ○ Jazz	
○ Folk ○ Other	
Favorite Ice Cream	
⦿ Vanilla ○ Chocolate	
○ Other	
	Cancel
Favorite Spreadsheet	
⦿ Excel ○ Other	OK

Only one OptionButton in a group can have a value of True. To specify a default option for a set of OptionButtons, just set the Value property for the default item to True. You can do this directly in the Properties box or do it using VBA code:

```
UserForm1.OptionButton1.Value = True
```

This example is available at this book's Web site. It also has code that displays the selected options when the user clicks OK.

Using a SpinButton and a TextBox

A SpinButton control lets the user specify a number by clicking arrows. This control consists only of arrows (no text), so you usually want a method to display the selected number. One option is to use a Label control, but this has a disadvantage: The user can't type text in a Label. A better choice is to use a TextBox.

A SpinButton control and TextBox control form a natural pair. Excel uses them frequently. (Check out the Print dialog box for a few examples.) Ideally, the SpinButton and its TextBox should be in sync: If the user clicks the SpinButton, the SpinButton's value should appear in the TextBox. And if the user enters a value directly into the TextBox, the SpinButton should take on that value. Figure 18-8 shows a custom dialog box with a SpinButton and a TextBox.

Figure 18-8:
A UserForm with a SpinButton and a companion TextBox.

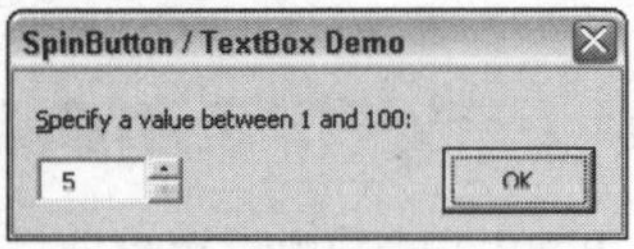

This UserForm contains the following controls:

- A SpinButton named SpinButton1, with its Min property set to 1 and its Max property set to 100

- A TextBox named TextBox1

- A CommandButton named OKButton

The event-handler procedure for the SpinButton follows. This procedure handles the Change event, which is triggered whenever the SpinButton value is changed. When the SpinButton's value changes (when it's clicked), this procedure assigns the SpinButton's value to the TextBox. To create this procedure, double-click the SpinButton to activate the Code window for the UserForm.

```
Private Sub SpinButton1_Change()
    TextBox1.Text = SpinButton1.Value
End Sub
```

The event-handler for the TextBox, which is listed next, is a bit more complicated. To create this procedure, double-click the TextBox to activate the Code window for the UserForm. This procedure is executed whenever the user changes the text in the TextBox.

```
Private Sub TextBox1_Change()
    Dim NewVal As Integer

    NewVal = Val(TextBox1.Text)
    If NewVal >= SpinButton1.Min And _
        NewVal <= SpinButton1.Max Then _
        SpinButton1.Value = NewVal
End Sub
```

This procedure uses a variable, which stores the text in the TextBox (converted to a value with the Val function). It then checks to ensure that the value is within the proper range. If so, the SpinButton is set to the value in the TextBox. The net effect is that the SpinButton's value is always equal to the value in the TextBox (assuming that the SpinButton's value is in the proper range).

This example is available at this book's Web site. It also has a few other bells and whistles that you may find useful.

Using a UserForm as a progress indicator

One of the most common Excel programming questions I hear is "How can I make a UserForm display the progress of a lengthy macro?"

Use Excel's custom dialog box to easily create an attractive progress indicator, as shown in Figure 18-9. Such a use of dialog boxes does, however, require a few tricks — which I'm about to show you.

Figure 18-9:
This UserForm functions as a progress indicator for a lengthy macro.

Progress	✕
Entering random numbers...	
┌ 28% ────────	

Creating the progress indicator dialog box

The first step is to create your UserForm. In this example, the dialog box displays the progress while a macro inserts random numbers into 25 columns and 100 rows of the active worksheet. To create the dialog box, follow these steps:

1. **Activate the VBE and insert a new UserForm.**

2. **Change the UserForm's caption to** Progress.

3. **Add a Frame object and set the following properties:**

Property	Value
Caption	**0%**
Name	**FrameProgress**

SpecialEffect	**2 — fmSpecialEffectSunken**
Width	**204**
Height	**28**

4. **Add a Label object inside the Frame and set the following properties:**

Property	*Value*
Name	**LabelProgress**
BackColor	**&H000000FF& (red)**
Caption	(no caption)
SpecialEffect	**1 — fmSpecialEffectRaised**
Width	**20**
Height	**13**
Top	**5**
Left	**2**

5. **Add another Label above the frame and change its caption to** Entering random numbers. . . .

The UserForm should resemble Figure 18-10.

Figure 18-10:
The progress indicator UserForm.

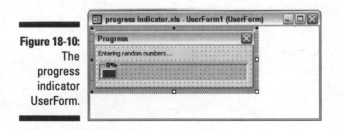

The procedures

This example uses four procedures.

✔ **Start.** Located in a VBA module, Start is the entry procedure that is executed to get things going:

```
Sub Start()
'    The UserForm1_Activate sub calls Main
    UserForm1.LabelProgress.Width = 0
    UserForm1.Show
End Sub
```

✔ **UserForm_Activate.** This procedure, located in the Code window for the UserForm object, is executed when the UserForm is displayed. This procedure simply calls another procedure called Main:

```
Private Sub UserForm_Activate()
    Call Main
End Sub
```

✔ **Main.** It does all the work and is executed when the UserForm is shown. Notice that it calls the UpdateProgress procedure, which updates the progress indicator in the dialog box:

```
Sub Main()
'    Inserts random numbers on the active worksheet
    Dim Counter As Integer
    Dim RowMax As Integer, ColMax As Integer
    Dim r As Integer, c As Integer
    Dim PctDone As Single

    If TypeName(ActiveSheet) <> "Worksheet" Then
        Unload UserForm1
        Exit Sub
    End If    Cells.Clear
    Counter = 1
    RowMax = 100
    ColMax = 25
    For r = 1 To RowMax
        For c = 1 To ColMax
            Cells(r, c) = Int(Rnd * 1000)
            Counter = Counter + 1
        Next c
        PctDone = Counter / (RowMax * ColMax)
        Call UpdateProgress(PctDone)
    Next r
    Unload UserForm1
End Sub
```

✔ **UpdateProgress.** This procedure accepts one argument and updates the progress indicator in the dialog box:

```
Sub UpdateProgress(pct)
    With UserForm1
        .FrameProgress.Caption = Format(pct, "0%")
        .LabelProgress.Width = pct * (.FrameProgress _
        .Width - 10)
    End With
'    The DoEvents statement is responsible for the
'    form updating
    DoEvents
End Sub
```

How this example works

When the Start procedure is executed, it sets the width of the LabelProgress label to 0 and then shows the UserForm, which triggers an Activate event for the UserForm. The UserForm_Activate( ) procedure is executed, which in turn executes the Main procedure.

The Main procedure checks the active sheet. If it's not a worksheet, the UserForm is closed and the procedure ends with no action. If the active sheet is a worksheet, the procedure does the following:

1. Erases all cells on the active worksheet.

2. Loops through the rows and columns (specified by the RowMax and ColMax variables) and inserts a random number.

3. Increments the Counter variable and calculates the percentage completed (which is stored in the PctDone variable).

4. Calls the UpdateProgress procedure, which displays the percentage completed by changing the width of the LabelProgress label.

5. Unloads the UserForm.

If you adapt this technique for your own use, you need to figure out how to determine the macro's progress, which varies, depending on your macro. Then call the UpdateProgress procedure at periodic intervals while your macro is executing.

This example is available at this book's Web site.

Creating a tabbed dialog box

Tabbed dialog boxes are useful because they let you present information in small, organized chunks. The Excel Options dialog box (which is displayed when you choose Tools➪Options) is a good example. This dialog box uses a whopping 13 tabs to add some organization to an overwhelming number of options.

Creating your own tabbed dialog boxes is relatively easy, thanks to the MultiPage control. Figure 18-11 shows a custom dialog box that uses a MultiPage control with three *pages,* or *tabs.* When the user clicks a tab, a new page is activated and only the controls on that page are displayed.

Keep the following points in mind when using the MultiPage control to create a tabbed dialog box:

- Use only one MultiPage control per dialog box.

- Make sure to use the MultiPage control, not the TabStrip control. The TabStrip control is more difficult to use.

✔ Make some controls (such as OK and Cancel buttons) visible at all times. Place these controls outside the MultiPage control.

✔ Right-click a tab on the MultiPage control to display a shortcut menu that lets you add, remove, rename, or move a tab.

✔ At design time, click a tab to activate the page. After it is activated, add other controls to the page using normal procedures.

✔ To select the MultiPage control itself (rather than a page on the control), click the border of the MultiPage control. Keep your eye on the Properties window, which displays the name and type of the selected control. You can also select the MultiPage control by selecting its name from the drop-down list in the Properties window.

✔ You can change the look of the MultiPage control by changing the Style and TabOrientation properties.

✔ The Value property of a MultiPage control determines which page is displayed. For example, if you write code to set the Value property to 0, the first page of the MultiPage control is displayed.

This example is available at this book's Web site.

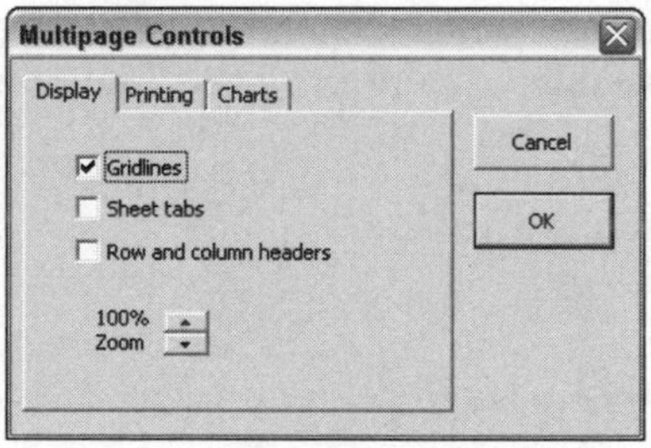

Figure 18-11:
This dialog box uses a MultiPage control.

> **Multipage Controls**
>
> Display | Printing | Charts
>
> ☑ Gridlines
> ☐ Sheet tabs
> ☐ Row and column headers
>
> 100% Zoom
>
> Cancel
> OK

Displaying a chart in a dialog box

If you need to display a chart in a UserForm, you find that Excel doesn't provide any direct way to do so. Therefore, you need to get creative. This section describes a technique that lets you display one or more charts in a UserForm.

The UserForm has an Image control. The trick is to use VBA code to save the chart as a GIF file and then specify that file as the Image control's Picture property.

Figure 18-12 shows an example, which displays three charts. The Previous and Next buttons switch the displayed chart.

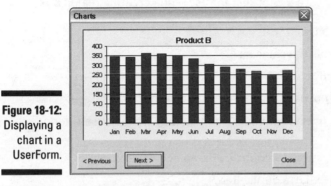

Figure 18-12:
Displaying a
chart in a
UserForm.

In this example, which is also available on this book's Web site, the three charts are on a sheet named Charts. The Previous and Next buttons determine which chart to display, and this chart number is stored as a Public variable named ChartNum, which is accessible to all procedures. A procedure named UpdateChart, which is listed here, does the actual work.

```
Private Sub UpdateChart()
    Dim CurrentChart As Chart
    Dim Fname As String

    Set CurrentChart = _
      Sheets("Charts").ChartObjects(ChartNum).Chart
    CurrentChart.Parent.Width = 300
    CurrentChart.Parent.Height = 150

'   Save chart as GIF
    Fname = ThisWorkbook.Path & "\temp.gif"
    CurrentChart.Export FileName:=Fname, FilterName:="GIF"

'   Show the chart
    Image1.Picture = LoadPicture(Fname)
End Sub
```

This procedure determines a name for the saved chart and then uses the Export method to export the GIF file. Finally, it uses the VBA LoadPicture function to specify the Picture property of the Image object.

A Dialog Box Checklist

I wrap up this chapter with a checklist for use when creating dialog boxes:

❑ Are the controls aligned with each other?

❑ Are similar controls the same size?

❑ Are controls evenly spaced?

❑ Does the dialog box have an appropriate caption?

❑ Is the dialog box overwhelming? If so, you may want to use a series of dialog boxes.

❑ Can the user access every control with an accelerator key?

❑ Are any accelerator keys duplicated?

❑ Are the controls grouped logically, by function?

❑ Is the tab order set correctly? The user should be able to tab through the dialog box and access the controls sequentially.

❑ If you plan to store the dialog box in an add-in (which I discuss in Chapter 22), did you test it thoroughly after creating the add-in? Remember that an add-in is never the active workbook.

❑ Will your VBA code take appropriate action if the user cancels the dialog box or presses Esc?

❑ Does the text contain any misspellings? Unfortunately, the Excel spell checker doesn't work with UserForms, so you're on your own when it comes to spelling.

❑ Will your dialog box fit on the screen in the lowest resolution to be used (usually 800×600 mode)? In other words, if you develop your dialog box by using a high-resolution video mode, your dialog box may be too big to fit on a screen in lower resolution.

❑ Do all TextBox controls have the appropriate validation setting?

❑ Do all ScrollBars and SpinButtons allow valid values only?

❑ Do all ListBoxes have their MultiSelect property set properly?

The best way to master custom dialog boxes is by creating dialog boxes — lots of them. Start simply and experiment with the controls and their properties. And don't forget about the Help system; it's your best source for details about every control and property.

Part V
Creating Custom Toolbars and Menus

The 5th Wave   By Rich Tennant

"WELL, SHOOT! THIS EGGPLANT CHART IS JUST AS CONFUSING AS THE BUTTERNUT SQUASH CHART AND THE GOURD CHART. CAN'T YOU JUST MAKE A PIE CHART LIKE EVERYONE ELSE?"

In this part . . .

This part consists of only two chapters, both of which deal with customizing the Excel user interface. Chapter 19 focuses on toolbars. In Chapter 20, I discuss the types of modifications you can make to the Excel menus.

Chapter 19

Customizing the Excel Toolbars

*E*xcel is definitely *not* a toolbar-challenged product. It comes with dozens of built-in toolbars, and constructing new toolbars is very easy. This chapter shows you how to manipulate toolbars with VBA.

Introducing CommandBars

When programming in Excel, a toolbar is technically known as a *CommandBar object*. In fact, a toolbar is just one of the three types of CommandBar objects:

> ✔ **Toolbar.** A floating bar with one or more clickable controls. This chapter focuses on this type of CommandBar.
>
> ✔ **Menu bar.** The two built-in menu bars are the Worksheet menu bar and the Chart menu bar. See Chapter 20.
>
> ✔ **Shortcut menu.** These menus pop up when you right-click an object. See Chapter 20.

Customizing Toolbars

The following list summarizes the ways you can customize toolbars. (I discuss these topics in detail later in this chapter.)

✔ **Remove toolbar controls from built-in toolbars.** You can get rid of toolbar controls that you never use, reduce screen clutter, and free up a few pixels of screen space, to boot.

✔ **Add toolbar controls to built-in toolbars.** You can add as many toolbar controls as you want to any toolbar. The controls can be custom buttons or buttons copied from other toolbars, or they can come from the stock of toolbar controls that Excel provides for you. And, of course, you can attach your VBA macros to these buttons.

✔ **Create new toolbars.** You can create as many new toolbars as you like, with toolbar buttons (or other types of controls) from any source.

✔ **Change the functionality of built-in toolbar controls.** You do this by attaching your own macro to a built-in toolbar button.

✔ **Change the image that appears on any toolbar button.** Excel includes a rudimentary but functional toolbar button editor. You can also change a toolbar's image by using several other techniques.

Don't be afraid to experiment with toolbars. If you mess up a built-in toolbar, you can easily reset it to its default state:

1. **Choose View➪Toolbars➪Customize.**

2. **Select the toolbar in the list.**

3. **Click the Reset button.**

How Excel handles toolbars

When you start Excel, it displays the same toolbar configuration that was in effect the last time you used the program. Did you ever wonder how Excel keeps track of this information?

When you exit Excel, it updates a file called EXCEL11.XLB. The exact location (and even the name) of this file varies, but you can use Windows' Find File feature to locate the file. (Search for *.XLB.) This file stores all of your custom toolbars, as well as information about the on-screen location of each toolbar and which toolbars are visible.

If you need to restore the toolbars to their previous configuration, choose File➪Open and open your XLB file. This restores your toolbar configuration to the way it was when you started the current session of Excel. You also can make a copy of the XLB file and give it a different name. Doing so lets you store multiple toolbar configurations that you can load any time. And if you've made lots of toolbar changes and want to return to Excel's original toolbar state, just delete your XLB file and restart Excel. It creates a new one for you.

Working with Toolbars

As you probably know, you can display as many toolbars as you like. A toolbar can be either docked or floating. A *docked* toolbar is fixed in place at the top, bottom, left, or right edge of Excel's workspace. *Floating* toolbars appear in an *always-on-top* window, which means that they are never obscured by other windows. You can change the dimensions of a floating toolbar by dragging a border.

As shown in Figure 19-1, right-clicking any toolbar or toolbar button displays a shortcut menu that lets you hide or display a toolbar. This shortcut menu, however, does not display the names of *all* toolbars. For a complete list of toolbars, use the Customize dialog box. This dialog box lets you hide or display toolbars (among other things).

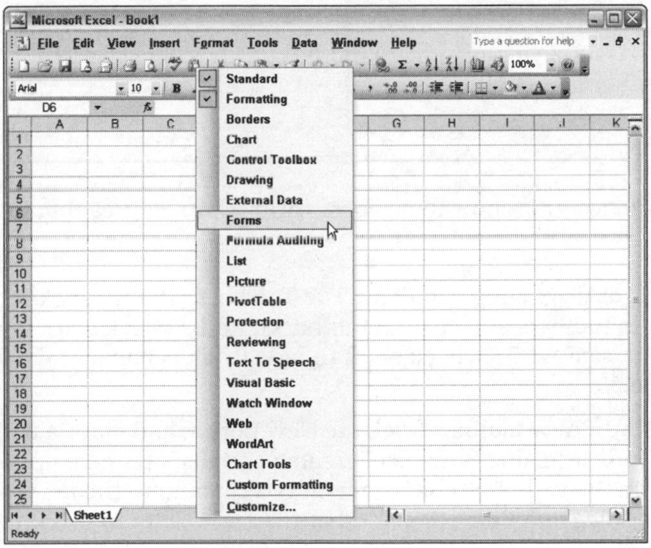

Figure 19-1:
Right-clicking a toolbar or a toolbar button displays this shortcut menu.

You can access the Customize dialog box in two ways:

- Choose View⇨Toolbars⇨Customize.
- Right-click a toolbar and choose Customize from the shortcut menu.

The Toolbars tab

The Customize dialog box's Toolbars tab, shown in Figure 19-2, lists all the available toolbars, including toolbars you have created. This dialog box also lists the two menu bars (Worksheet and Chart), which are similar to toolbars.

Figure 19-2:
The Toolbars tab is in the Customize dialog box.

This section describes how to perform various procedures that involve toolbars.

✔ **Hiding or displaying a toolbar:** The Toolbars tab displays every toolbar (built-in toolbars and custom toolbars). Add a check mark to display a toolbar; remove the check mark to hide it. The changes take effect immediately.

✔ **Creating a new toolbar:** Click the New button and enter a name in the New Toolbar dialog box. Excel creates and displays an empty toolbar. You can then add buttons (or menu commands) to the new toolbar. See "Adding and Removing Toolbar Controls" later in this chapter.

Figure 19-3 shows a custom toolbar that I created. This toolbar, called Custom Formatting, contains the formatting tools that I use most frequently. Notice that this toolbar includes drop-down menus as well as standard toolbar buttons.

✔ **Renaming a custom toolbar:** Select the custom toolbar from the list and click the Rename button. In the Rename Toolbar dialog box, enter a new name. You can't rename a built-in toolbar.

✔ **Deleting a custom toolbar:** Select the custom toolbar from the list and click the Delete button. You can't delete a built-in toolbar.

Deleting a toolbar is one of the few actions in Excel that cannot be undone.

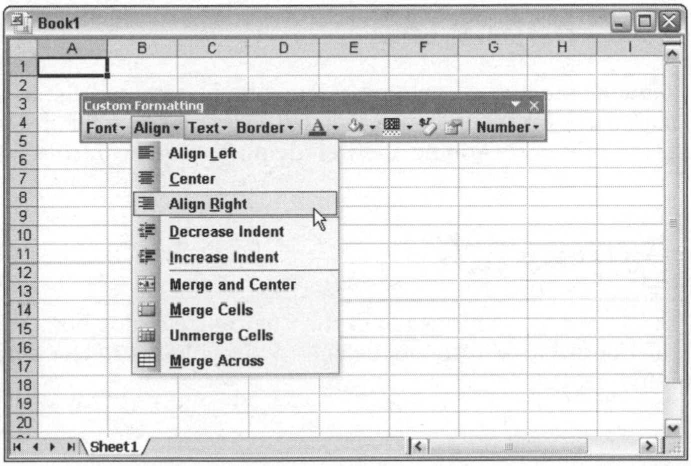

Figure 19-3:
A custom
toolbar.

> ✔ **Resetting a built-in toolbar:** Select a built-in toolbar from the list and click the Reset button. The toolbar is restored to its default state. Any added custom tools are removed. Any removed default tools are restored. The Reset button is not available when a custom toolbar is selected.
>
> ✔ **Attaching a toolbar to a workbook:** You can share a custom toolbar by attaching it to a workbook. Click the Attach button and you get a new dialog box that lets you select toolbars to attach to a workbook. You can attach any number of toolbars to a workbook — but remember, attaching toolbars increases the size of your workbook. For more about this, see "Distributing Toolbars," later in this chapter.

Toolbar autosensing

Normally, Excel displays a particular toolbar automatically when you change contexts. This is called *autosensing*. For example, when you activate a chart, the Chart toolbar appears. When you activate a sheet that contains a pivot table, the PivotTable toolbar appears.

You can easily defeat autosensing by hiding the toolbar: Click its Close button. After you do so, Excel no longer displays that toolbar when you

switch to its former context. You can restore this automatic behavior by displaying the appropriate toolbar when you're in the appropriate context. Thereafter, Excel reverts to its normal automatic toolbar display when you switch to that context.

You can simulate this type of behavior by writing VBA code. Refer to "Displaying a toolbar when a worksheet is activated," later in this chapter.

The Commands tab

The Commands tab of the Customize dialog box contains a list of every available tool. Use this tab when you customize a toolbar. This feature is described later in this chapter in "Adding and Removing Toolbar Controls."

The Options tab

Figure 19-4 shows the Options tab of the Customize dialog box. The options on this tab control how both menus and toolbars behave. The options that affect toolbars are as follows:

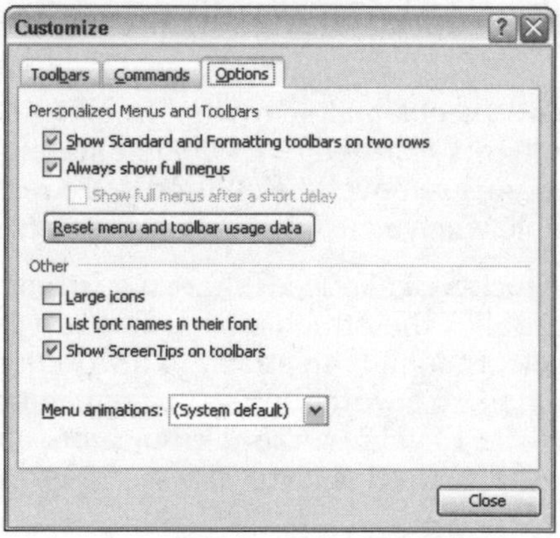

Figure 19-4:
The Options
tab of the
Customize
dialog box.

✔ **Using one row for two toolbars:** You can save a little bit of valuable screen space by removing the checkmark from the Show Standard and Formatting Toolbars on Two Rows check box to force Excel to stuff both toolbars on a single row. Go ahead with this if you're running your system at a high screen resolution; you can get more on the screen horizontally. However, you may not want to choose this option if you're running in a lower screen resolution.

✔ **Showing full menus:** Perhaps one of Microsoft's dumbest ideas is *adaptive menus*. In other words, the software hides menu items that are not used frequently. I've never met anyone who likes this. If you find that your menus seem to be missing some commands, select the Always Show Full Menus check box.

✔ **Changing the icon size:** To change the size of the icons used in toolbars, select or deselect the Large Icons check box. This option affects only the images in buttons. Buttons that contain only text (such as buttons in a menu) are not changed.

✔ **Display fancy font names:** Some people like the feature for which the drop-down Font list on the Formatting toolbar shows names using the actual font; others despise it. The List Font Names In Their Font check box controls whether Excel does this. Personally, I think using the fonts slows down Excel if you're working with a lot of fonts.

✔ **Toggling the ScreenTips display:** ScreenTips are the pop-up messages that display the button names when you pause the mouse pointer over a button. If you find the ScreenTips distracting, deselect the Show ScreenTips on Toolbars check box.

✔ **Changing the menu animations:** When you select a menu, Excel animates its menu display. Choose whichever animation style you prefer.

Adding and Removing Toolbar Controls

When the Customize dialog box is displayed, Excel is in a special customization mode. You have access to all the commands and options in the Customize dialog box. In addition, you can perform the following actions:

✔ Reposition a control on a toolbar

✔ Move a control to a different toolbar

✔ Copy a control from one toolbar to another

✔ Add new controls to a toolbar using the Commands tab of the Customize dialog box

✔ Change lots of toolbar control attributes

Moving and copying controls

When the Customize dialog box is displayed, you can copy and move toolbar controls freely among any visible toolbars. To move a control, drag it to its new location. The new location can be within the current toolbar or on a different toolbar.

To copy a control, press Ctrl while dragging the control to another toolbar. You can copy a toolbar control within the same toolbar, but you've no reason to have multiple copies of a button on the same toolbar.

Inserting a new control

To add a new control to a toolbar, use the Customize dialog box's Commands tab shown in Figure 19-5.

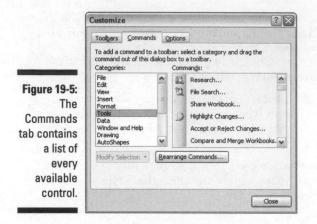

Figure 19-5:
The
Commands
tab contains
a list of
every
available
control.

The controls are arranged in 17 categories. When you select a category, the controls in that category appear to the right. Previous versions of Excel had a Description button that, when clicked, described the selected control's function. For reasons known only to Microsoft, that Description button was removed in Excel 2003.

To add a control to a toolbar, locate it in the Commands tab, click it, and drag it to the toolbar.

Using other toolbar button operations

When Excel is in customization mode (that is, when the Customize dialog box is displayed), you can right-click a toolbar control to display a shortcut menu of additional actions. Figure 19-6 shows the shortcut menu that appears when you right-click a button in customization mode.

These commands are described in the following list. (Note that some of these commands are unavailable for certain toolbar controls.)

- **Reset:** Resets the control to its original state.
- **Delete:** Deletes the control.
- **Name:** Lets you change the control's name.
- **Copy Button Image:** Copies the control's image and places it on the Clipboard.
- **Paste Button Image:** Pastes the image from the Clipboard to the control.
- **Reset Button Image:** Restores the control's original image.
- **Edit Button Image:** Lets you edit the control's image using the Excel button editor.

✔ **Change Button Image:** Lets you change the image by selecting from a list of different button images.

✔ **Default Style:** Displays the control using its default style. (For buttons, the default is image only. For menu items, the default is both image and text.)

✔ **Text Only (Always):** Always displays text (no image) for the control.

✔ **Text Only (In Menus):** Displays text (no image) if the control is in a menu bar.

✔ **Image and Text:** Displays the control's image and text.

✔ **Begin a Group:** Inserts a divider in the toolbar. In a drop-down menu, a separator bar appears as a horizontal line between commands. In a toolbar, a separator bar appears as a vertical line.

✔ **Assign a Hyperlink:** Lets you assign a hyperlink that activates when the control is clicked.

✔ **Assign a Macro:** Lets you assign a macro that executes when the control is clicked.

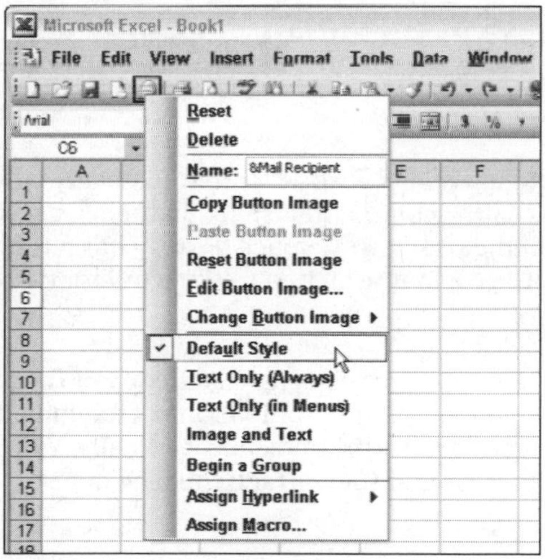

Figure 19-6:
In customiza-tion mode, right-clicking a toolbar control displays this shortcut menu.

Distributing Toolbars

If you want to distribute a custom toolbar to other users, store it in a workbook. To store a toolbar in a workbook file, follow these steps:

1. **Create the custom toolbar and test it to make sure it works correctly.**

2. **Activate the workbook that will store the new toolbar.**

3. **Choose View➪Toolbars➪Customize.**

4. **In the Customize dialog box, click the Toolbars tab.**

5. **Click the Attach button.**

   Excel displays the Attach Toolbars dialog box shown in Figure 19-7. This dialog box lists all custom toolbars stored on your system.

6. **To attach a toolbar, select it and click the Copy button.**

   When a toolbar in the Toolbars in Workbook list (right side of the dialog box) is selected, the Copy button changes to a Delete button. You can click the Delete button to remove the selected toolbar from the workbook.

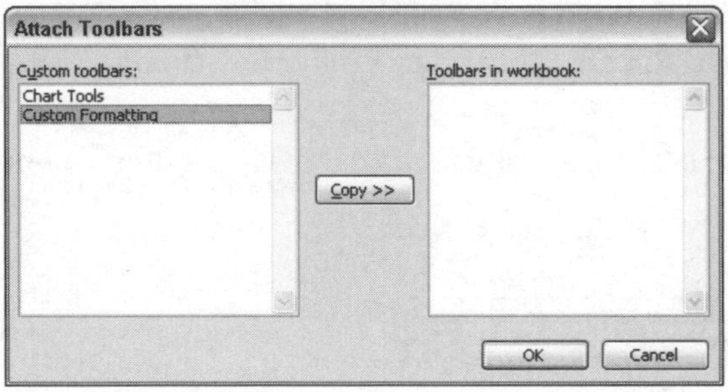

Figure 19-7:
The Attach
Toolbars
dialog box
lets you
attach one
or more
toolbars to a
workbook.

Attach Toolbars	✕
Custom toolbars:	Toolbars in workbook:
Chart Tools	
Custom Formatting	
	Copy >>
	OK Cancel

A toolbar that's attached to a workbook appears automatically when the workbook is opened, and that toolbar is then saved in the user's XLB file when Excel closes down. If the user's workspace already has a toolbar by the same name, however, the toolbar attached to the workbook does *not* replace the existing one.

The toolbar that's stored in the workbook is an exact copy of the toolbar at the time you attach it. If you modify the toolbar after attaching it, the changed version is not stored in the workbook automatically. You must manually remove the old toolbar and then attach the new one.

Using VBA to Manipulate Toolbars

As you may expect, you can write VBA code to do things with toolbars. In this section, I provide some background information that you simply must know before you start mucking around with toolbars.

Commanding the CommandBars collection

You manipulate Excel toolbars (and menus, for that matter) by using objects located in the CommandBars collection. The CommandBars collection consists of

- ✔ All Excel built-in toolbars
- ✔ Any other custom toolbars that you create
- ✔ A built-in menu bar named Worksheet menu bar, which appears when a worksheet is active
- ✔ A built-in menu bar named Chart menu bar, which appears when a chart sheet is active
- ✔ Any other custom menu bars that you create
- ✔ All built-in shortcut menus

As I mention at the beginning of this chapter, the three types of CommandBar are differentiated by their Type properties. The Type property can be any of these three values:

- ✔ **msoBarTypeNormal:** A toolbar (Type = 0)
- ✔ **msoBarTypeMenuBar:** A menu bar (Type = 1)
- ✔ **msoBarTypePopUp:** A shortcut menu (Type = 2)

Listing all CommandBar objects

If you're curious about the objects in the CommandBars collection, enter and execute the following macro. The result is a list of all CommandBar objects in the CommandBars collection, plus any custom menu bars or toolbars. For each CommandBar, the procedure lists its Index, Name, and Type. (The Type can be 0, 1, or 2).

```
Sub ShowCommandBarNames()
    Dim Row As Long
    Dim cbar As CommandBar
    Row = 1
    For Each cbar In Application.CommandBars
        Cells(Row, 1) = cbar.Index
        Cells(Row, 2) = cbar.Name
        Cells(Row, 3) = cbar.Type
        Row = Row + 1
    Next cbar
End Sub
```

Figure 19-8 shows a portion of the result of running this procedure, which is available at this book's Web site. As you can see, Excel has a lot of CommandBars.

	A	B	C	D	E
1	1	Worksheet Menu Bar	1		
2	2	Chart Menu Bar	1		
3	3	Standard	0		
4	4	Formatting	0		
5	5	PivotTable	0		
6	6	Chart	0		
7	7	Reviewing	0		
8	8	Forms	0		
9	9	Stop Recording	0		
10	10	External Data	0		
11	11	Formula Auditing	0		
12	12	Full Screen	0		
13	13	Circular Reference	0		
14	14	Visual Basic	0		
15	15	Web	0		
16	16	Control Toolbox	0		
17	17	Exit Design Mode	0		
18	18	Refresh	0		
19	19	Watch Window	0		
20	20	PivotTable Field List	0		
21	21	Borders	0		
22	22	Protection	0		

Figure 19-8: A VBA macro produced this list of all CommandBar objects.

Referring to CommandBars

You can refer to a particular CommandBar by its Index or by its Name. For example, the Standard toolbar has an Index of 3, so you can refer to the toolbar one of two ways:

```
Application.CommandBars(3)
```

or

```
Application.CommandBars("Standard")
```

For some reason, Microsoft isn't consistent with CommandBar index numbers across versions of Excel. Therefore, it's better to refer to a CommandBar by its Name, rather than by its Index.

Referring to controls in a CommandBar

A CommandBar object contains Control objects, which are buttons, menus, or menu items. The following procedure displays the Caption property for the first Control in the Standard toolbar:

```
Sub ShowCaption()
    MsgBox Application.CommandBars("Standard"). _
        Controls(1).Caption
End Sub
```

When you execute this procedure, you see the message box shown in Figure 19-9.

Figure 19-9:
Displaying
the Caption
property for
a control.

In some cases, these Control objects can contain other Control objects. For example, the first control on the Drawing toolbar contains other controls. (This also demonstrates that you can include menu items on a toolbar.) The concept of Controls within Controls becomes clearer in Chapter 20, when I discuss menus.

Properties of CommandBar controls

CommandBar controls have a number of properties that determine how the controls look and work. This list contains some of the more useful properties for CommandBar controls:

- ✔ **Caption:** The text displayed for the control. If the control shows only an image, the Caption appears when you move the mouse over the control.

- ✔ **FaceID:** A number that represents a graphics image displayed next to the control's text.

- ✔ **BeginGroup:** True if a separator bar appears before the control.

- ✔ **OnAction:** The name of a VBA macro that executes when the user clicks the control.

- ✔ **BuiltIn:** True if the control is an Excel built-in control.

- ✔ **Enabled:** True if the control can be clicked.

- ✔ **ToolTipText:** Text that appears when the user moves the mouse pointer over the control.

When you work with toolbars, you can turn on the macro recorder to see what's happening in terms of VBA code. Unless you're editing button images, the steps you take while customizing toolbars generate VBA code. By examining this code, you can discover how Excel arranges the object model for toolbars. The model is pretty simple.

VBA Examples

This section contains a few examples of using VBA to manipulate the Excel toolbars. These examples give you an idea of the types of things you can do, and they can all be modified to suit your needs.

Resetting all built-in toolbars

The following procedure resets all built-in toolbars to their original state:

```
Sub ResetAll()
    Dim cbar As CommandBar
    For Each cbar In Application.CommandBars
        If cbar.Type = msoBarTypeNormal Then
            cbar.Reset
        End If
    Next cbar
End Sub
```

Using the Reset method on a custom toolbar has no effect (and does not generate an error).

Be careful with the preceding routine. Executing it erases all of your customizations to all built-in toolbars. The toolbars will be just as they were when you first installed Excel.

Displaying a toolbar when a worksheet is activated

Assume that you have a workbook (named Budget) that holds your budget information. In addition, assume that you've developed a custom toolbar (named Budget Tools) that you use with this workbook. The toolbar should be visible when you work on the Budget sheet; otherwise, it should remain hidden and out of the way.

The following procedures, which are stored in the code window for the ThisWorkbook object, display the Budget Tools toolbar when the Budget workbook is active and hide the toolbar when the Budget workbook is deactivated:

```
Private Sub Workbook_WindowActivate(ByVal Wn As _
    Excel.Window)
    Application.CommandBars("Budget Tools").Visible = True
End Sub

Private Sub Workbook_WindowDeactivate(ByVal Wn As _
    Excel.Window)
    Application.CommandBars("Budget Tools").Visible = False
End Sub
```

For this example go to this book's Web site. For more information about using automatic procedures, go to Chapter 11.

Ensuring that an attached toolbar is displayed

As I explained earlier in this chapter, you can attach any number of toolbars to a workbook. But I also noted that the attached toolbar won't replace an existing toolbar that has the same name.

In some cases, the failure to display a toolbar can present a problem. For example, assume that you distribute a workbook to your coworkers, and this workbook has an attached toolbar that executes your macros. Later, you update the workbook and add some new controls to your attached toolbar. When you distribute this new workbook, the updated toolbar doesn't display because the old toolbar already exists!

One solution is to simply use a new toolbar name for the updated application. Perhaps a better solution is to write VBA code to delete the toolbar when the workbook closes. That way, the toolbar isn't stored on the user's system and you're assured that the latest copy of your toolbar is always displayed when the workbook opens.

The following procedure, which is stored in the code window for the ThisWorkbook object, displays the toolbar named Budget Tools when the workbook is opened. The Budget Tools toolbar is attached to the workbook.

```
Private Sub Workbook_Open()
    Application.CommandBars("Budget Tools").Visible = True
End Sub
```

The next procedure, which is also stored in the code window for the ThisWorkbook object, deletes the toolbar named Budget Tools when the workbook is closed:

```
Private Sub Workbook_BeforeClose(Cancel As Boolean)
    On Error Resume Next
    Application.CommandBars("Budget Tools").Delete
End Sub
```

Notice that I use an On Error Resume Next statement to avoid the error message that appears if the toolbar has already been deleted.

Hiding and restoring toolbars

In some cases, you may want to remove all the toolbars when a workbook is opened. It's only polite, however, to restore the toolbars when your application closes. In this section I present two procedures, both stored in the code window of the ThisWorkbook object.

The Workbook_Open procedure, available at this book's Web site, is executed when the workbook is opened. This procedure saves the names of all visible toolbars in column A of Sheet1 and then hides all the toolbars:

```
Private Sub Workbook_Open()
    Dim TBarCount As Integer
    Dim cbar As CommandBar
    Sheets("Sheet1").Range("A:A").ClearContents
    TBarCount = 0
    For Each cbar In Application.CommandBars
        If cbar.Type = msoBarTypeNormal Then
            If cbar.Visible Then
                TBarCount = TBarCount + 1
                Sheets("Sheet1").Cells(TBarCount, 1) = _
                    cbar.Name
                cbar.Visible = False
            End If
        End If
    Next cbar
End Sub
```

The following procedure is executed before the workbook is closed. This routine loops through the toolbar names stored on Sheet1 and changes their Visible property to True:

```
Private Sub Workbook_BeforeClose(Cancel As Boolean)
    Dim Row As Long
    Dim TBar As String
    Row = 1
    TBar = Sheets("Sheet1").Cells(Row, 1)
    Do While TBar <> ""
        Application.CommandBars(TBar).Visible = True
        Row = Row + 1
        TBar = Sheets("Sheet1").Cells(Row, 1)
    Loop
End Sub
```

Notice that the Workbook_Open routine saves the toolbar names in a worksheet range rather than in an array, ensuring that the toolbar names are still available when the Workbook_BeforeClose routine is executed. Values stored in an array may be lost between the time the Workbook_Open procedure is executed and the Workbook_BeforeClose procedure is executed.

Chapter 20

When the Normal Excel Menus Aren't Good Enough

In This Chapter

▶ Knowing menu terminology

▶ Understanding the types of menu modifications you can make

▶ Understanding the object model

▶ Modifying menus with VBA

*Y*ou may not realize it, but you can change almost every aspect of Excel's menus. Typical Excel users get by just fine with the standard menus. Because you're reading this book, however, you're probably not the typical Excel user. In this chapter I describe how to make changes to the Excel menu system.

Most of the Excel applications you develop get along just fine with the standard menu system. In some cases, however, you may want to add a new menu to make it easier to run your VBA macros. In other cases, you may want to remove some menu items to prevent users from accessing certain features. If these sorts of changes seem useful, you should read this chapter. Otherwise, you can safely skip it until the need arises.

Defining Menu Lingo

Before I get too far into this section, I need to discuss terminology. At first, menu terminology confuses people because many of the terms are similar. The following list describes official Excel menu terminology, which I use throughout this chapter and the rest of the book:

- ✔ **Menu bar:** The row of words that appears directly below the application's title bar. Excel has two menu bars that appear automatically, depending on the context. The menu bar displayed when a worksheet is active differs from the menu bar displayed when a chart sheet is active.

- ✔ **Menu:** A single, top-level element of a menu bar. For example, both of Excel's menu bars have a menu called File.

- ✔ **Menu item:** An element that appears in the drop-down list when you select a menu. For example, the first menu item under the File menu is New. Menu items also appear in submenus and shortcut menus.

- ✔ **Separator bar:** A horizontal line that appears between two menu items. The separator bar groups similar menu items.

- ✔ **Submenu:** A menu that is under some menus. For example, the Edit menu has a submenu called Clear.

- ✔ **Submenu item:** A menu item that appears in the list when you select a submenu. For example, the Edit⇨Clear submenu contains the following submenu items: All, Formats, Contents, and Comments.

- ✔ **Shortcut menu:** The floating list of menu items that appears when you right-click a selection or an object. In Excel, you can right-click just about anything and get a shortcut menu.

- ✔ **Enabled:** A menu item that can be used. If a menu item isn't enabled, its text appears grayed out and it can't be used.

- ✔ **Checked:** A menu item can display a graphical box that is checked or unchecked. The View⇨Status Bar menu item is an example.

How Excel Handles Menus

Excel provides you with two ways to change the menu system:

- ✔ Use the View⇨Toolbars⇨Customize command. This displays the Customize dialog box, which lets you change menus (and toolbars).

- ✔ Write VBA code to modify the menu system.

When you close Excel, it saves any changes that you've made to the menu system, and these changes appear the next time you open Excel. The information about menu modifications is stored in a file with an XLB extension. In most cases, you won't want your menu modifications to be saved between sessions. Generally, you need to write VBA code to change the menus while a particular workbook is open and then change them back when the workbook closes.

Customizing Menus Directly

Because a menu bar is actually a toolbar in disguise, you can modify a menu bar using the View⇨Toolbars⇨Customize command. To demonstrate how easy it is to change the Excel menu, try this:

If you've already modified your menu, *don't* perform the following steps. Doing so involves resetting your menu bar, which wipes out all of your menu modifications.

1. **Choose View⇨Toolbars⇨Customize.**

2. **Click the Help menu (in the menu bar) and drag it away.**

3. **Click Close to close the Customize dialog box.**

You've just wiped out your Help menu (see Figure 20-1). Exit Excel and then restart it. Although you may expect the menu bar to be restored when you restart Excel, it's not! The Help menu is still missing. Follow these steps to get things back to normal:

1. **Choose View⇨Toolbars⇨Customize.**

   The Customize dialog box appears.

2. **Click the Toolbars tab.**

3. **Select the Worksheet Menu Bar item in the Toolbars list.**

4. **Click Reset to restore the Worksheet menu bar to its default state.**

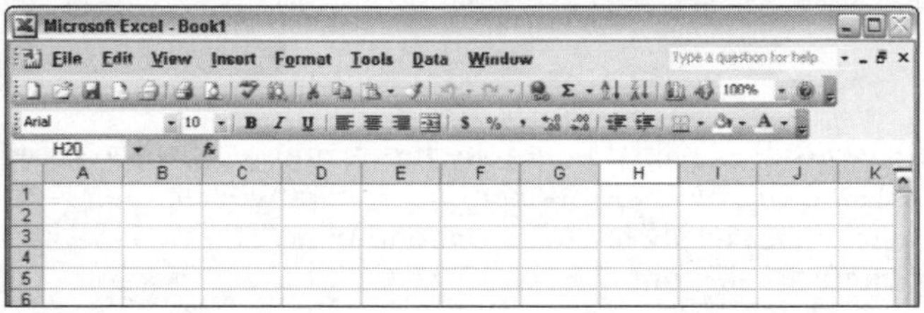

Figure 20-1:
The worksheet menu bar after zapping the Help menu.

I think Microsoft made it far too easy to mess up your menus. My advice? Don't use the View⇨Toolbars⇨Customize command to change menus. In almost every case, you want your menu modifications to be in effect only when a particular workbook is open. To do that, you need to use VBA to make your menu changes — which is the topic of this chapter.

Refer to Chapter 19 for details regarding the Customize dialog box. The procedures that I describe for toolbars also work for menu bars.

Looking Out for the CommandBar Object

For an introduction to the CommandBar object, refer to Chapter 19. There I explain that a menu bar is one of three types of CommandBars.

Referring to CommandBars

Because this chapter deals with menus, you're interested in the two CommandBar objects that are built-in menu bars. The Worksheet Menu Bar is the first object in the CommandBars collection, so you can refer to it as one of the following:

```
CommandBars(1)
```

or

```
CommandBars("Worksheet Menu Bar")
```

Similarly, you can refer to the Chart Menu Bar object using either one of these:

```
CommandBars(2)
```

or

```
CommandBars("Chart Menu Bar")
```

 In Chapter 19, I advise against using the index numbers when referring to toolbars, because the toolbar index numbers change from version to version. That warning doesn't apply to the two menu bars. The two menu bars always have index numbers of 1 and 2.

Referring to Controls in a CommandBar

A CommandBar object contains Control objects, and these Control objects can contain other Control objects. When you choose File⇨Open, you're actually manipulating a Control (a menu item with a Caption of Open) that's contained in another Control (a menu with a Caption of File) that's contained in a CommandBar (the Worksheet menu bar).

Confused? Here's an example that may help clear things up. The following macro displays the Caption property for the first Control contained in the first Control of the first CommandBar object. When you execute this procedure, you see the message box shown in Figure 20-2.

```
Sub ShowCaption()
    MsgBox CommandBars(1).Controls(1).Controls(1).Caption
End Sub
```

Figure 20-2:
Displaying
the Caption
property for
a control.

Rather than use index numbers, you can also use the captions, which makes things a bit clearer. The next procedure has the same result as the preceding procedure:

```
Sub ShowCaption2()
    MsgBox CommandBars("Worksheet Menu Bar") _
        .Controls("File").Controls("New...").Caption
End Sub
```

If you refer to a control by using its caption, the caption must exactly match the text displayed in the menu. In the preceding procedure, I had to use ellipses (three dots) after the word *New* because that's how it appears in the menu. You can mix and match index numbers with captions, if you like.

You might find the next procedure instructive. It loops through all the Controls (menus) in the Worksheet menu bar. For each of these menus, it loops through the Controls (menu items) within the menu. For each of these menu items, it loops through the Controls (submenu items). The result is a listing of all menus, menu items, and submenu items in the Worksheet menu bar.

```
Sub ListMenuStuff()
    Dim Row As Long
    Dim Menu As CommandBarControl
    Dim MenuItem As CommandBarControl
    Dim SubMenuItem As CommandBarControl
    Row = 1
    On Error Resume Next
```

```
For Each Menu In CommandBars(1).Controls
    For Each MenuItem In Menu.Controls
        For Each SubMenuItem In MenuItem.Controls
            Cells(Row, 1) = Menu.Caption
            Cells(Row, 2) = MenuItem.Caption
            Cells(Row, 3) = SubMenuItem.Caption
            Row = Row + 1
        Next SubMenuItem
    Next MenuItem
Next Menu
End Sub
```

Notice that I use On Error Resume Next to ignore the error that occurs if a menu item doesn't have any submenu items. Figure 20-3 shows part of the output from this procedure. This code is available on this book's Web site.

	A	B	C	D	E	F	G
	list menu stuff.xls						
1	&File	&New...					
2	&File	&Open...					
3	&File	&Close					
4	&File	&Save					
5	&File	Save &As...					
6	&File	Save as Web Pa&ge...					
7	&File	Save &Workspace...					
8	&File	File Searc&h...					
9	&File	Per&mission...					
10	&File	Per&mission	Unrestricted Access				
11	&File	Per&mission	Do Not Distribute...				
12	&File	Per&mission					
13	&File	Per&mission					
14	&File	Per&mission					
15	&File	Per&mission					
16	&File	Per&mission					
17	&File	Per&mission					
18	&File	Per&mission					
19	&File	Per&mission					
20	&File	Per&mission					
21	&File	Per&mission					
22	&File	Per&mission					
23	&File	Per&mission					

Sheet1

Figure 20-3: List all menus, menu items, and submenu items in the Worksheet menu bar.

Properties of CommandBar Controls

CommandBar controls have a number of properties that determine how they look and work. This list contains some of the more useful CommandBar control properties:

✔ **Caption:** The text displayed for the control.

✔ **FaceID:** A number that represents a graphics image displayed next to the control's text.

- ✔ **BeginGroup:** True if a separator bar appears before the control.

- ✔ **OnAction:** The name of a VBA macro to execute when the user clicks the control.

- ✔ **BuiltIn:** True if the control is an Excel built-in control.

- ✔ **Enabled:** True if the control can be clicked.

- ✔ **ToolTipText:** Text that appears when the user moves the mouse pointer over the control.

Placing your menu code

Most of the time you want your menu changes to be in effect only when a particular workbook is open. Therefore, you need VBA code to modify the menu when the workbook is opened and more VBA code to return the menus to normal when the workbook is closed. A good place for your menu-manipulating code: in the code window for the ThisWorkbook object. More specifically, you use the following two event-handler procedures, which you can find out more about in Chapter 11:

- ✔ Sub Workbook_Open( )

- ✔ Sub Workbook_BeforeClose(Cancel As Boolean)

 If you would like to set things up so that a particular menu modification appears only when a specific workbook is active, store your menu manipulation procedures in the Workbook_Activate and Workbook_Deactivate procedures. Refer to Chapter 19 for an example that uses toolbars.

Would You Like to See Our Menu Examples?

In this section I present some practical examples of VBA code that manipulates Excel's menus. Adapt these examples for your own use.

Creating a menu

When you create a menu, you add a new word to a menu bar. The control that you add is of the Popup type because the menu always contains menu items.

The following procedure adds a new menu (Budgeting) between the Window menu and the Help menu on the Worksheet menu bar:

```
Sub AddNewMenu()
    Dim HelpIndex As Integer
    Dim NewMenu As CommandBarPopup

'   Get Index of Help menu
    HelpIndex = CommandBars(1).Controls("Help").Index

'   Create the control
    Set NewMenu = CommandBars(1) _
        .Controls.Add(Type:=msoControlPopup, _
        Before:=HelpIndex, Temporary:=True)
'   Add a caption
    NewMenu.Caption = "&Budgeting"
End Sub
```

Notice that this procedure creates an essentially worthless menu — it has no menu items. See the next section, "Adding a menu item," for an example of adding a menu item to a menu. Figure 20-4 shows the Worksheet menu bar after executing this procedure.

This example is available on this book's Web site.

Adding the menu is a two-step process:

1. **Create an object variable that refers to the new Control.**

   In this case, the object variable is named NewMenu, and its type is CommandBarPopup.

2. **Adjust the new Control's properties.**

   In this case, I changed only one property: Caption.

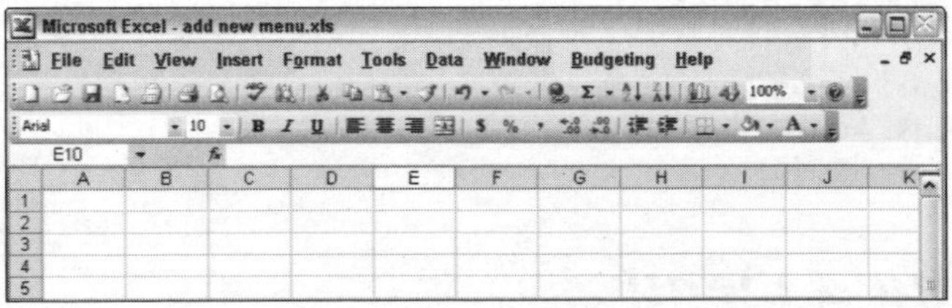

Figure 20-4:
A new menu, called Budgeting, was added to this menu bar.

[Screenshot: Microsoft Excel - add new menu.xls with menu bar showing File, Edit, View, Insert, Format, Tools, Data, Window, Budgeting, Help]

The preceding procedure uses the Add method, with three named arguments:

- ✔ **Type:** Identifies the type of control. (msoControlPopup is a built-in constant.)
- ✔ **Before:** Identifies the position on the menu bar. I determined the position of the Help menu and assigned it to the variable HelpIndex.
- ✔ **Temporary:** This argument is True, so the menu change is not permanent. In other words, the Budgeting menu doesn't appear when you restart Excel.

Adding a menu item

The example in the preceding section demonstrates how to create a new menu. The following example adds a menu item to the Excel Format menu. This menu item, when clicked, executes a macro named ToggleWordWrap. The ToggleWordWrap procedure changes the WrapText property of the selected cells.

After creating the menu item, I change the Caption, OnAction, and BeginGroup properties. Setting BeginGroup to True displays a separator bar before the new menu item. Figure 20-5 shows the modified Format menu.

```
Sub AddMenuItem()
    Set Item = CommandBars(1).Controls("Format") _
        .Controls.Add
    Item.Caption = "&Toggle Word Wrap"
    Item.OnAction = "ToggleWordWrap"
    Item.BeginGroup = True
End Sub
```

Figure 20-5: The Format menu has a new menu item: Toggle Word Wrap.

The ToggleWordWrap procedure, available on this book's Web site, is shown next:

```
Sub ToggleWordWrap()
    If TypeName(Selection) = "Range" Then
        Selection.WrapText = Not ActiveCell.WrapText
    End If
End Sub
```

Deleting a menu

In some cases, you may want to delete one or more Excel built-in menus while a particular workbook is open, or delete a custom menu that you added.

The following statements delete the Help menu for the Worksheet menu bar and the Chart menu bar:

```
Application.CommandBars(1).Controls("Help").Delete
Application.CommandBars(2).Controls("Help").Delete
```

You get an error message if the Help menu doesn't exist. Therefore, you might want to precede the statements with the following statement, which causes Excel to ignore any errors:

```
On Error Resume Next
```

You can restore in one of two ways built-in menu items that you deleted:

- ✔ Reset the entire menu bar.
- ✔ Use the Add method to add the built-in menu and then add all the menu items. You may want to record your actions while you use the Customize dialog box to restore a menu.

The following statements reset the Worksheet menu bar and the Chart menu bar:

```
Application.CommandBars(1).Reset
Application.CommandBars(2).Reset
```

Resetting a menu bar destroys any customization you may have performed. For example, if you added a new menu item to the Tools menu, that menu item is removed when the menu bar is reset.

Deleting a menu item

Use the Delete method to delete custom or built-in menu items. The following statement deletes the Exit menu item from the File menu on the Worksheet menu bar:

```
CommandBars(1).Controls("File").Controls("Exit").Delete
```

To get this menu item back, use the Add method:

```
CommandBars(1).Controls("File").Controls.Add _
   Type:=msoControlButton, Id:=752
```

Notice that I have to supply the Id for the Control that I add. The Id for the Exit menu item is 752. How did I figure that out? Before deleting the File menu, I typed the following statement in the Immediate window of the VBE (followed by pressing Enter to see the result):

```
? CommandBars(1).Controls("File").Controls("Exit").Id
```

Changing menu captions

You can change the text displayed (the Caption) for both custom and built-in menus and menu items. You do so by changing the Caption property. This example changes the Help menu in the Worksheet menu bar so that it displays Assistance:

```
Sub ChangeHelp()
    CommandBars(1).Controls("Help") _
      .Caption = "&Assistance"
End Sub
```

The following example, available on this book's Web site, changes the text of all the menus, menu items, and submenu items to uppercase letters — probably not something you'd want to do, but it *does* give Excel a new look:

```
Sub UpperCaseMenus()
   On Error Resume Next
   For Each Menu In CommandBars(1).Controls
       Menu.Caption = UCase(Menu.Caption)
       For Each MenuItem In Menu.Controls
           MenuItem.Caption = UCase(MenuItem.Caption)
           For Each SubMenu In MenuItem.Controls
               SubMenu.Caption = UCase(SubMenu.Caption)
           Next SubMenu
       Next MenuItem
   Next Menu
End Sub
```

Figure 20-6 shows how the menus look after you execute this routine. To return things to normal, see the "So you messed up your menus, eh?" sidebar in this chapter.

So you messed up your menus, eh?

As you work your way through this chapter, I hope you try out various examples and write your own code to change the Excel menus. In the process, your menus might get messed up. Mine did as I was writing this chapter. Don't fret. It's easy to restore the menu bar to its factory-fresh, out-of-the box state:

1. **Choose View ➪ Toolbars ➪ Customize.**

   The Customize dialog box appears.

2. **Click the Toolbars tab.**

3. **Select the Worksheet Menu Bar item (or the Chart Menu Bar item if you've messed up that menu).**

4. **Click Reset.**

Or you can just execute this VBA statement to reset the Worksheet Menu Bar:

```
Application.CommandBars(1).Reset
```

Using either method, the menu bar is restored to its default state.

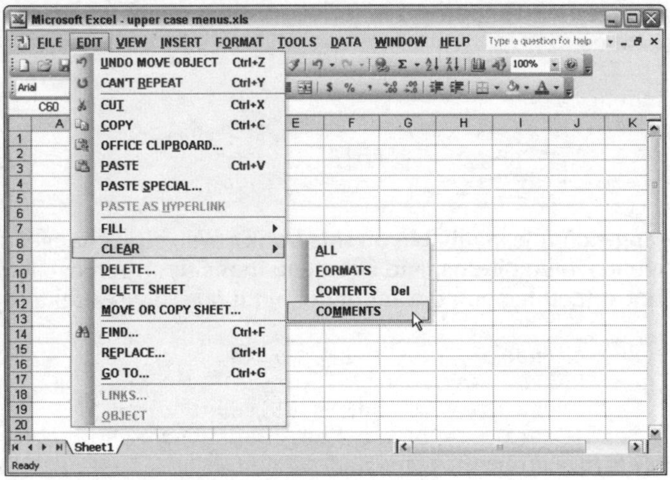

Figure 20-6:
Excel's menus look like this after being converted to uppercase.

Adding a menu item to the Tools menu

A common task is to add a new item to the Tools menu (or any other menu, for that matter). The best approach is to write your own VBA code to do so. Or you can simply use the code that follows. No charge.

The two macros are stored in the code window for the ThisWorkbook object. The procedures are event handlers that respond to the Workbook Open event and the Workbook BeforeClose event. They include some simple error-handling

code to handle the case in which there is no Tools menu (or if it has a different name).

```
Const MenuItemName As String = "Run Budget Macro"
Const MenuItemMacro As String = "UpdateBudget"

Private Sub Workbook_Open()
'    Adds a menu item to the Tools menu
     Dim NewItem As CommandBarControl
     Dim Msg As String

'    Delete the existing item just in case
     On Error Resume Next
     Application.CommandBars(1). _
         Controls("Tools").Controls(MenuItemName).Delete

'   Set up error trapping
    On Error GoTo NoCanDo

'   Create the new menu item
    Set NewItem = Application.CommandBars(1). _
        Controls("Tools").Controls.Add

'   Specify the Caption and OnAction properties
    NewItem.Caption = MenuItemName
    NewItem.OnAction = MenuItemMacro

'   Add a separator bar before the menu item
    NewItem.BeginGroup = True
    Exit Sub

'   Error handler
NoCanDo:
    Msg = "An error occurred." & vbNewLine
    Msg = Msg & "Attempting to add an item to the Tools
            menu."
    MsgBox Msg, vbCritical
End Sub

Private Sub Workbook_BeforeClose(Cancel As Boolean)
'    Delete the new menu item
     On Error Resume Next
     Application.CommandBars(1). _
     Controls("Tools").Controls(MenuItemName).Delete
End Sub
```

The example adds a new menu item (Run Budget Macro) to the Tools menu
when the workbook is opened. This menu item, when clicked, runs a macro
named UpdateBudget. When the workbook is closed, the menu item is
removed from the Tools menu.

To use this code in your own application, enter the code into the code window for the ThisWorkbook object; then change the values for the MenuItemName and MenuItemMacro constants.

This example is available on this book's Web site.

Working with Shortcut Menus

You can't use the Customize dialog box to remove or modify shortcut menus. The only way to customize shortcut menus is to use VBA.

A shortcut menu appears when you right-click an object. Excel has lots of shortcut menus. You can pretty much right-click anything and get a shortcut menu. To work with a shortcut menu, you need to know the shortcut menu's Caption or Index. This information isn't available in the Help system, but you can use the following procedure to generate a list of all shortcut menus and the Index and Caption for each:

```
Sub ListShortCutMenus()
    Dim Row As Long
    Dim Col As Long
    Dim cbar As CommandBar
    Row = 1
    For Each cbar In CommandBars
        If cbar.Type = msoBarTypePopup Then
            Cells(Row, 1) = cbar.Index
            Cells(Row, 2) = cbar.Name
            For Col = 1 To cbar.Controls.Count
                Cells(Row, Col + 2) = _
                cbar.Controls(col).Caption
            Next Col
            Row = Row + 1
        End If
    Next cbar
End Sub
```

This example, available on this book's Web site, produces something like that shown in Figure 20-7.

Be careful when you modify shortcut menus. Like normal menus, changes to shortcut menus are saved between sessions. Therefore, you probably want to reset the shortcut menus when your application ends.

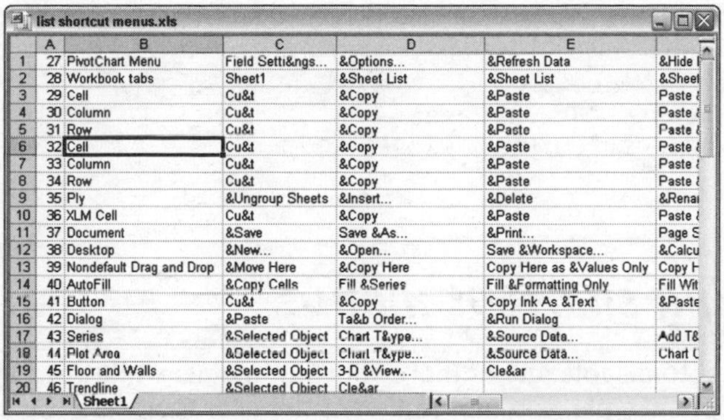

list shortcut menus.xls

	A	B	C	D	E	
1	27	PivotChart Menu	Field Setti&ngs...	&Options...	&Refresh Data	&Hide
2	28	Workbook tabs	Sheet1	&Sheet List	&Sheet List	&Sheet
3	29	Cell	Cu&t	&Copy	&Paste	Paste
4	30	Column	Cu&t	&Copy	&Paste	Paste
5	31	Row	Cu&t	&Copy	&Paste	Paste
6	32	Cell	Cu&t	&Copy	&Paste	Paste
7	33	Column	Cu&t	&Copy	&Paste	Paste
8	34	Row	Cu&t	&Copy	&Paste	Paste
9	35	Ply	&Ungroup Sheets	&Insert...	&Delete	&Renai
10	36	XLM Cell	Cu&t	&Copy	&Paste	Paste
11	37	Document	&Save	Save &As...	&Print...	Page S
12	38	Desktop	&New...	&Open...	Save &Workspace...	&Calcu
13	39	Nondefault Drag and Drop	&Move Here	&Copy Here	Copy Here as &Values Only	Copy H
14	40	AutoFill	&Copy Cells	Fill &Series	Fill &Formatting Only	Fill Wit
15	41	Button	Cu&t	&Copy	Copy Ink As &Text	&Paste
16	42	Dialog	&Paste	Ta&b Order...	&Run Dialog	
17	43	Series	&Selected Object	Chart T&ype...	&Source Data...	Add T&
18	44	Plot Area	&Selected Object	Chart T&ype...	&Source Data...	Chart
19	45	Floor and Walls	&Selected Object	3-D &View...	Cle&ar	
20	46	Trendline	&Selected Object	Cle&ar		

Sheet1

Figure 20-7: A listing of all shortcut menus, plus the menu items in each.

Adding menu items to a shortcut menu

Adding a menu item to a shortcut menu works just like adding a menu item to a regular menu. You need to know the Index or the Caption for the shortcut menu. See the preceding section to find out how to get a list of all shortcut menus.

The following example demonstrates how to add a menu item to the shortcut menu that appears when you right-click a cell. The Caption for this shortcut menu is Cell. This menu item is added to the end of the shortcut menu.

```
Sub AddItemToShortcut()
    Dim NewItem As CommandBarControl
    Set NewItem = CommandBars("Cell").Controls.Add
    NewItem.Caption = "Toggle Word Wrap"
    NewItem.OnAction = "ToggleWordWrap"
    NewItem.BeginGroup = True
End Sub
```

Selecting the new menu item executes the ToggleWordWrap procedure.

Deleting menu items from a shortcut menu

The following routine removes the Hide menu item from two shortcut menus: the menus that appear when you right-click a row header or a column header.

```
Sub RemoveHideMenuItem()
    CommandBars("Row").Controls("Hide").Delete
    CommandBars("Column").Controls("Hide").Delete
End Sub
```

To restore these shortcut menus, use this procedure:

```
Sub ResetHideMenuItem()
    CommandBars("Row").Reset
    CommandBars("Column").Reset
End Sub
```

Disabling shortcut menus

You may want to disable one or more shortcut menus while your application is running. For example, you may not want the user to access the commands by right-clicking a cell. If you want to disable all shortcut menus, use the following procedure, also available on this book's Web site:

```
Sub DisableShortcuts()
    Dim cbar As CommandBar
    For Each cbar In Application.CommandBars
        If cbar.Type = msoBarTypePopup Then
            cbar.Enabled = False
        End If
    Next cbar
End Sub
```

Disabling the shortcut menus remains between sessions. Therefore, you probably want to restore the shortcut menus before closing Excel. To restore the shortcut menus, modify the preceding procedure by setting Enabled to True.

Finding Out More

This chapter introduces the concept of menu modifications made with VBA and presents several examples that you can adapt to your own needs. A good way to find out more about using VBA to modify menus is to record your actions while you make menu changes using the View➪Toolbars➪ Customize command. And, of course, the online Help system contains all the details you need.

Part VI
Putting It All Together

The 5th Wave — By Rich Tennant

"The top line represents our revenue, the middle line is our inventory, and the bottom line shows the rate of my hair loss over the same period."

In this part . . .

The preceding 20 chapters cover quite a bit of material. At this point, you may still feel a bit disjointed about all the VBA stuff. The chapters in this part fill in the gaps and tie everything together. I discuss custom worksheet functions (a very useful feature), describe add-ins, provide more programming examples, and wrap up with a discussion of user-oriented applications.

Chapter 21

Creating Worksheet Functions — and Living to Tell about It

*F*or many people, VBA's main attraction is the capability to create custom worksheet functions — functions that look, work, and feel just like those that Microsoft built into Excel. A *custom function* offers the added advantage of working exactly how you want it to. I introduce custom functions in Chapter 5. In this chapter, I get down to the nitty-gritty and describe some tricks of the trade.

Why Create Custom Functions?

You are undoubtedly familiar with Excel's worksheet functions — even Excel novices know how to use common worksheet functions such as SUM, AVERAGE, and IF. By my count, Excel contains more than 300 predefined worksheet functions, not counting those available through add-ins, such as the Analysis ToolPak (which is included with Excel). And if that's not enough, you can create functions by using VBA.

With all the functions available in Excel and VBA, you may wonder why you would ever need to create functions. The answer: to simplify your work. With a bit of planning, custom functions are very useful in worksheet formulas and VBA procedures. Often, for example, you can significantly shorten a formula by creating a custom function. After all, shorter formulas are more readable and easier to work with.

> ## What custom worksheet functions can't do
>
> As you develop custom functions for use in your worksheet formulas, it's important that you understand a key point. VBA worksheet Function procedures are essentially *passive*. For example, code within a Function procedure cannot manipulate ranges, change formatting, or do many of the other things that are possible with a Sub procedure. An example may help.
>
> It might be useful to create a function that changes the color of text in a cell based on the cell's value. Try as you might, however, you can't write such a function. It always returns an error value.
>
> Just remember this: A function used in a worksheet formula returns a value — it does not perform actions with objects.

Understanding VBA Function Basics

A VBA *function* is a procedure that's stored in a VBA module. You can use these functions in other VBA procedures or in your worksheet formulas.

A module can contain any number of functions. You can use a custom function in a formula just as if it were a built-in function. If the function is defined in a different workbook, however, you must precede the function name with the workbook name. For example, assume you developed a function called DiscountPrice (which takes one argument), and the function is stored in a workbook named PRICING.XLS.

To use this function in the PRICING.XLS workbook, enter a formula such as this:

```
=DiscountPrice(A1)
```

If you want to use this function in a *different* workbook, enter a formula such as this:

```
=pricing.xls!discountprice(A1)
```

If the custom function is stored in an add-in, you don't need to precede the function name with the workbook name. I discuss add-ins in Chapter 22.

Custom functions appear in the Insert Function dialog box, in the User Defined category. The easiest way to enter a custom function into a formula is to use the Insert⇨Function command or click the Insert Function button on the Standard toolbar. Both of these methods display the Insert Function dialog box.

Writing Functions

Remember that a function's name acts like a variable. The final value of this variable is the value returned by the function. To demonstrate, examine the following function, which returns the user's first name:

```
Function FirstName()
    Dim FullName As String
    Dim FirstSpace As Integer
    FullName = Application.UserName
    FirstSpace = InStr(FullName, " ")
    If FirstSpace = 0 Then
        FirstName = FullName
    Else
        FirstName = Left(FullName, FirstSpace - 1)
    End If
End Function
```

This function starts by assigning the UserName property of the Application object to a variable named FullName. Next, it uses the VBA InStr function to locate the first space in the name. If there is no space, FirstSpace is equal to 0 and FirstName is equal to the entire name. If FullName *does* have a space, the Left function extracts the text to the left of the space and assigns it to FirstName.

Notice that FirstName is the name of the function and is also used as a variable name *in* the function. The final value of FirstName is the value that's returned by the function. Several intermediate calculations may be going on in the function, but the function always returns the last value assigned to the variable that is the same as the function's name.

All of the examples in this chapter are available at this book's Web site.

Working with Function Arguments

To work with functions, you need to understand how to work with arguments. The following points apply to the arguments for Excel worksheet functions and custom VBA functions:

- ✔ *Arguments* can be cell references, variables (including arrays), constants, literal values, or expressions.
- ✔ Some functions have no arguments.
- ✔ Some functions have a fixed number of required arguments (from 1 to 60).
- ✔ Some functions have a combination of required and optional arguments.

Function Examples

The examples in this section demonstrate how to work with various types of arguments.

A function with no argument

Like Sub procedures, Function procedures need not have arguments. For example, Excel has a few built-in worksheet functions that don't use arguments, including RAND, TODAY, and NOW.

Here's a simple example of a function with no arguments. The following function returns the UserName property of the Application object. This name appears in the Options dialog box (General tab). This simple but useful example shows the only way you can get the user's name to appear in a worksheet formula:

```
Function User()
'   Returns the name of the current user
    User = Application.UserName
End Function
```

When you enter the following formula into a worksheet cell, the cell displays the current user's name:

```
=User()
```

As with the Excel built-in functions, you must include a set of empty parentheses when using a function with no arguments.

A function with one argument

A single-argument function is designed for sales managers who need to calculate the commissions earned by their salespeople. The commission rate depends on the monthly sales volume; those who sell more earn a higher commission rate. The function returns the commission amount based on the monthly sales (which is the function's only argument — a required argument). The calculations in this example are based on Table 21-1.

Table 21-1	Commission Rates by Sales
Monthly Sales	*Commission Rate*
$0–$9,999	8.0%
$10,000–$19,999	10.5%
$20,000–$39,999	12.0%
$40,000+	14.0%

You can use several approaches to calculate commissions for sales amounts entered into a worksheet. You *could* write a lengthy worksheet formula such as this:

```
=IF(AND(A1>=0,A1<=9999.99),A1*0.08,IF(AND(A1>=10000,A1<=19999
     .99),A1*0.105,IF(AND(A1>=20000,A1<=39999.99),A1*0.
     12,IF(A1>=40000,A1*0.14,0))))
```

A couple reasons make this a bad approach. First, the formula is overly complex. Second, the values are hard-coded into the formula, making the formula difficult to modify if the commission structure changes.

A better approach is to create a table of commission values and use a LOOKUP table function to compute the commissions:

```
=VLOOKUP(A1,Table,2)*A1
```

Another approach, which doesn't require a table of commissions, is to create a custom function:

```
Function Commission(Sales)
'    Calculates sales commissions
     Dim Tier1 As Double, Tier2 As Double
     Dim Tier3 As Double, Tier4 As Double
     Tier1 = 0.08
     Tier2 = 0.105
     Tier3 = 0.12
     Tier4 = 0.14
     Select Case Sales
         Case 0 To 9999.99: Commission = Sales * Tier1
         Case 10000 To 19999.99: Commission = Sales * Tier2
         Case 20000 To 39999.99: Commission = Sales * Tier3
         Case Is >= 40000: Commission = Sales * Tier4
     End Select
     Commission = Round(Commission, 2)
End Function
```

After you define this function in a VBA module, you can use it in a worksheet formula. Entering the following formula into a cell produces a result of 3,000. The amount of 25000 qualifies for a commission rate of 12 percent:

```
=Commission(25000)
```

Figure 21-1 shows a worksheet that uses this new function.

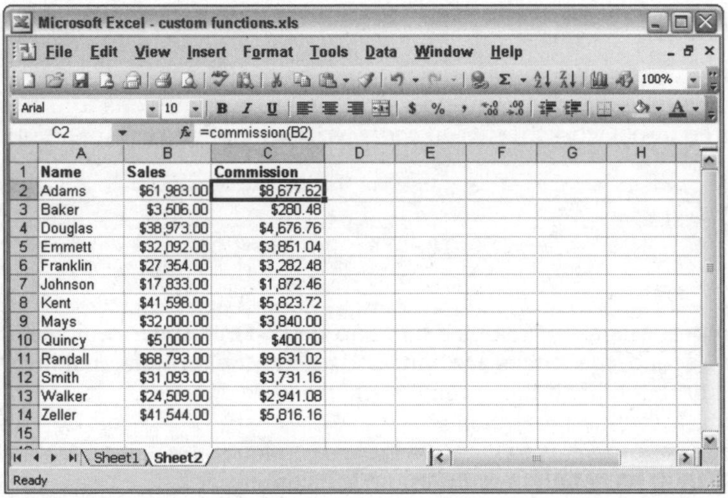

	A	B	C
1	Name	Sales	Commission
2	Adams	$61,983.00	$8,677.62
3	Baker	$3,506.00	$280.48
4	Douglas	$38,973.00	$4,676.76
5	Emmett	$32,092.00	$3,851.04
6	Franklin	$27,354.00	$3,282.48
7	Johnson	$17,833.00	$1,872.46
8	Kent	$41,598.00	$5,823.72
9	Mays	$32,000.00	$3,840.00
10	Quincy	$5,000.00	$400.00
11	Randall	$68,793.00	$9,631.02
12	Smith	$31,093.00	$3,731.16
13	Walker	$24,509.00	$2,941.08
14	Zeller	$41,544.00	$5,816.16
15			

Figure 21-1: Using the Commission function in a worksheet.

A function with two arguments

The next example builds on the preceding one. Imagine that the sales manager implements a new policy: The total commission paid increases by 1 percent for every year the salesperson has been with the company.

I modified the custom Commission function (defined in the preceding section) so that it takes two arguments, both of which are required arguments. Call this new function *Commission2:*

```
Function Commission2(Sales, Years)
'   Calculates sales commissions based on years in service
    Dim Tier1 As Double, Tier2 As Double
    Dim Tier3 As Double, Tier4 As Double
    Tier1 = 0.08
    Tier2 = 0.105
    Tier3 = 0.12
    Tier4 = 0.14
    Select Case Sales
        Case 0 To 9999.99: Commission2 = Sales * Tier1
        Case 10000 To 19999.99: Commission2 = Sales * Tier2
```

```
        Case 20000 To 39999.99: Commission2 = Sales * Tier3
        Case Is >= 40000: Commission2 = Sales * Tier4
    End Select
    Commission2 = Commission2 + (Commission2 * Years / 100)
    Commission2 = Round(Commission2, 2)
End Function
```

I simply added the second argument (Years) to the Function statement and included an additional computation that adjusts the commission before exiting the function. This additional computation multiplies the original commission by the number of years in services, divides by 100, and then adds the result to the original computation.

Here's an example of how you can write a formula by using this function. (It assumes that the sales amount is in cell A1; cell B1 specifies the number of years the salesperson has worked.)

```
=Commission2(A1,B1)
```

A function with a range argument

Using a worksheet range as an argument is not at all tricky; Excel takes care of the behind-the-scenes details.

Assume that you want to calculate the average of the five largest values in a range named Data. Excel doesn't have a function that can do this, so you would probably write a formula:

```
=(LARGE(Data,1)+LARGE(Data,2)+LARGE(Data,3)+LARGE(Data,4)+LAR
        GE(Data,5))/5
```

This formula uses Excel's LARGE function, which returns the nth largest value in a range. The formula adds the five largest values in the range named Data and then divides the result by 5. The formula works fine, but it's rather unwieldy. And what if you decide that you need to compute the average of the top six values? You would need to rewrite the formula — and make sure that you update all copies of the formula.

Wouldn't this be easier if Excel had a function named TopAvg? Then you could compute the average by using the following (nonexistent) function:

```
=TopAvg(Data,5)
```

This example shows a case in which a custom function can make things much easier for you. The following custom VBA function, named TopAvg, returns the average of the N largest values in a range:

```
Function TopAvg(InRange, N)
'    Returns the average of the highest N values in InRange
    Dim Sum As Double
    Dim I As Long
    Sum = 0
    For i = 1 To N
        Sum = Sum + _
            Application.WorksheetFunction.LARGE(InRange, i)
    Next i
    TopAvg = Sum / N
End Function
```

This function takes two arguments: InRange (which is a worksheet range) and N (the number of values to average). It starts by initializing the Sum variable to 0. It then uses a For-Next loop to calculate the sum of the *N* largest values in the range. Note that I use the Excel LARGE function within the loop. Finally, TopAvg is assigned the value of Sum divided by N.

You can use all Excel worksheet functions in your VBA procedures *except* those that have equivalents in VBA. For example, VBA has a Rnd function that returns a random number. Therefore, you can't use the Excel RAND function in a VBA procedure.

A function with an optional argument

Many Excel built-in worksheet functions use optional arguments. An example is the LEFT function, which returns characters from the left side of a string. Its official syntax follows:

```
LEFT(text[,num_chars])
```

The first argument is required, but the second is optional. If you omit the optional argument, Excel assumes a value of 1. Therefore, the following formulas return the same result:

```
=LEFT(A1,1)
=LEFT(A1)
```

The custom functions you develop in VBA also can have optional arguments. You specify an optional argument by preceding the argument's name with the keyword Optional, followed by an equal sign and the default value. If the optional argument is missing, the code uses the default value.

Debugging custom functions

Debugging a Function procedure can be a bit more challenging than debugging a Sub procedure. If you develop a function for use in worksheet formulas, you find that an error in the Function procedure simply results in an error display in the formula cell (usually #VALUE!). In other words, you don't receive the normal runtime error message that helps you locate the offending statement.

You can choose among three methods for debugging custom functions:

✔ Place MsgBox functions at strategic locations to monitor the value of specific variables. Fortunately, message boxes in Function procedures pop up when you execute the procedure. Make sure that only one formula in the worksheet uses your function, or the message boxes appear for each formula that's evaluated — which could get very annoying.

✔ Test the procedure by calling it from a Sub procedure. Run-time errors appear normally in a pop-up window, and you can either correct the problem (if you know it) or jump right into the debugger.

✔ Set a breakpoint in the function and then use the Excel debugger to step through the function. You can then access all of the usual debugging tools. Refer to Chapter 13 to find out about the debugger.

The following example shows a custom function using an optional argument:

```
Function DrawOne(InRange, Optional Recalc = 0)
'    Chooses one cell at random from a range

'    Make function volatile if Recalc is 1
     If Recalc = 1 Then Application.Volatile True

'    Determine a random cell
     DrawOne = InRange(Int((InRange.Count) * Rnd + 1))
End Function
```

This function randomly chooses one cell from an input range. The range passed as an argument is actually an array, and the function selects one item from the array at random. If the second argument is 1, the selected value changes whenever the worksheet is recalculated. (The function is made *volatile*.) If the second argument is 0 (or is omitted), the function is not recalculated unless one of the cells in the input range is modified.

You can use this function for choosing lottery numbers, selecting a winner from a list of names, and so on.

A function with an indefinite number of arguments

Some Excel worksheet functions take an indefinite number of arguments. A familiar example is the SUM function, which has the following syntax:

```
SUM(number1,number2...)
```

The first argument is required, but you can have as many as 29 additional arguments. Here's an example of a SUM function with four range arguments:

```
=SUM(A1:A5,C1:C5,E1:E5,G1:G5)
```

Here's a function that can have any number of single-value arguments. This function doesn't work with multicell range arguments.

```
Function Concat(string1, ParamArray string2())
'    Demonstrates indefinite number of function arguments
     Dim Args As Variant

'    Process the first argument
     Concat = string1

'    Process additional arguments (if any)
     If UBound(string2) <> -1 Then
         For Args = LBound(string2) To UBound(string2)
             Concat = Concat & " " & string2(Args)
         Next Args
     End If
End Function
```

This function is similar to the Excel CONCATENATE function, which combines text arguments into a single string. The difference is that this custom function inserts a space between each pair of concatenated strings.

The second argument, string2(), is an array preceded by the ParamArray keyword. If the second argument is empty, the UBound function returns –1 and the function ends. If the second argument is not empty, the procedure loops through the elements of the string2 array and processes each additional argument. The LBound and UBound functions determine the beginning and ending elements of the array. The beginning element is normally 0 unless you either declare it as something else or use an Option Base 1 statement at the beginning of your module.

ParamArray can apply to only the *last* argument in the procedure. It is always a variant data type, and it is always an optional argument (although you don't use the Optional keyword). Figure 21-2 shows this function in use. Examine the figure to see how the results differ from those produced by the Excel Concatenate function, which doesn't insert a space between the concatenated items.

Figure 21-2: Using the Concat function.

ParamArray can apply to only the *last* argument in the procedure. It is always a variant data type, and it is always an optional argument (although you don't use the Optional keyword). Figure 21-2 shows this function in use. Examine the figure to see how the results differ from those produced by the Excel Concatenate function, which doesn't insert a space between the concatenated items.

(screenshot: Microsoft Excel - custom functions.xls. Cell D2 formula bar shows `=concat(A2,B2,C2)`)

	A	B	C	D
1	Title	First	Last	
2	Mr.	Jim	Smith	Mr. Jim Smith
3	Dr.	Tina	Peterson	Dr. Tina Peterson
4	Ms.	Jane	Doe	Ms. Jane Doe
5	Mr.	Frank	Franklin	Mr. Frank Franklin
6	Mr.	Willie	Nielson	Mr. Willie Nielson
7	Mrs.	Steve	Marks	Mrs. Steve Marks

Using the Insert Function Dialog Box

The Excel Insert Function dialog box is a handy tool that lets you choose a worksheet function from a list and prompts you for the function's arguments. And, as I note earlier in this chapter, your custom worksheet functions also appear in the Insert Function dialog box. Custom functions appear in the User Defined category.

Function procedures defined with the Private keyword do not appear in the Insert Function dialog box. Therefore, if you write a Function procedure that's designed to be used only by other VBA procedures (but not in formulas), you should declare the function as Private.

Displaying the function's description

The Insert Function dialog box displays a description of each built-in function. But, as you can see in Figure 21-3, a custom function displays the following text as its description: No help available.

Figure 21-3:
By default,
the Insert
Function
dialog box
does not
provide a
description
for custom
functions.

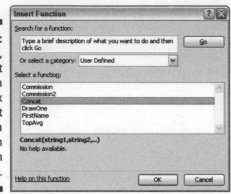

To display a meaningful description of your custom function in the Paste Function dialog box, perform a few additional, (nonintuitive) steps:

1. **Activate a worksheet in the workbook that contains the custom function.**

2. **Choose Tools⇨Macro⇨Macros (or press Alt+F8).**

   The Macro dialog box appears.

3. **In the Macro Name field, type the function's name.**

   Note that the function does not appear in the list of macros; you must type the name in.

4. **Click the Options button.**

   The Macro Options dialog box appears.

5. **In the Description field, type a description for the function.**

6. **Click OK.**

7. **Click Cancel.**

Now the Paste Function dialog box displays the description for your function; see Figure 21-4.

Function categories

Custom functions are always listed under the User Defined category. You cannot directly create a new function category for your custom functions.

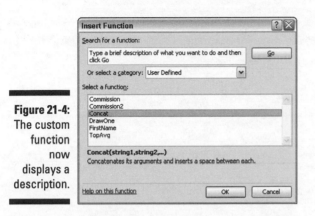

Figure 21-4:
The custom
function
now
displays a
description.

Argument descriptions

When you access a built-in function from the Insert Function dialog box, the
Function Arguments dialog box displays a description of each argument. (See
Figure 21-5.) Unfortunately, you can't provide such descriptions for custom
functions. You can, however, make your argument names descriptive —
which is a good idea.

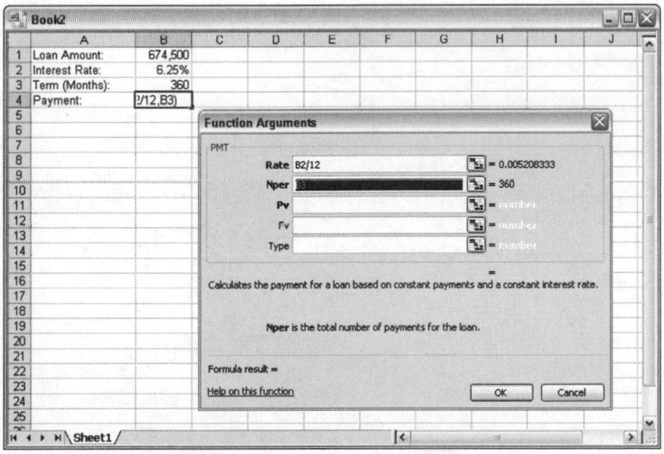

Figure 21-5:
The
Function
Arguments
dialog box
displays
function
argument
descriptions
for built-in
functions
only.

This chapter provides lots of information about creating custom worksheet
functions. Use these examples as models when you create functions for your
own work. As usual, the online help provides additional details. See the next
chapter if you want to find out how to make your custom functions more
accessible by storing them in an add-in.

Chapter 22

Creating Excel Add-Ins

In This Chapter

▶ Using add-ins: What a concept!

▶ Knowing why you might want to create your own add-ins

▶ Creating custom add-ins

*O*ne of the slickest features of Excel — at least in *my* mind — is the capability to create add-ins. In this chapter, I explain why this feature is so slick and show you how to create add-ins by using only the tools built into Excel.

Okay . . . So What's an Add-In?

What's an add-in? Glad you asked. An Excel *add-in* is something you add to enhance Excel's functionality. Some add-ins provide new worksheet functions you can use in formulas; other add-ins provide new commands or utilities. If the add-in is designed properly, the new features blend in well with the original interface, so they appear to be part of the program.

Excel ships with several add-ins. Some of the more popular include the Analysis ToolPak, Conditional Sum Wizard, and Solver. You can also get Excel add-ins from third-party suppliers or as shareware; my Power Utility Pak is an example.

Any knowledgeable user can create add-ins (but VBA programming skills are required). An Excel add-in is basically a different form of an XLS workbook file. More specifically, an add-in is a normal XLS workbook with the following differences:

- ✔ The IsAddin property of the Workbook is True.
- ✔ The workbook window is hidden and can't be unhidden using the Window⇨Unhide command.
- ✔ The workbook is not a member of the Workbooks collection.

You can convert any XLS file into an add-in. Because add-ins are always hidden, you can't display worksheets or chart sheets contained in an add-in. However, you can access an add-in's VBA Sub and Function procedures and display dialog boxes contained on UserForms.

Excel add-ins usually have an XLA file extension to distinguish them from XLS worksheet files. However, this is not a strict requirement. An add-in can have any extension that you want.

Why Create Add-Ins?

You might decide to convert your XLS application into an add-in for any of the following reasons:

- ✔ **Make it more difficult to access your code.** When you distribute an application as an add-in (and you protect it), casual users can't view the sheets in the workbook. If you use proprietary techniques in your VBA code, you can make it more difficult for others to copy the code. Excel's protection features aren't perfect, and password-cracking utilities are available.

- ✔ **Avoid confusion.** If a user loads your application as an add-in, the file is invisible and therefore less likely to confuse novice users or get in the way. Unlike a hidden XLS workbook, an add-in can't be revealed.

- ✔ **Simplify access to worksheet functions.** Custom worksheet functions that you store in an add-in don't require the workbook name qualifier. For example, if you store a custom function named MOVAVG in a workbook named NEWFUNC.XLS, you must use syntax like the following to use this function in a different workbook:

```
=NEWFUNC.XLS!MOVAVG(A1:A50)
```

But if this function is stored in an add-in file that's open, you can use much simpler syntax because you don't need to include the file reference:

```
=MOVAVG(A1:A50)
```

- ✔ **Provide easier access for users.** After you identify the location of your add-in, it appears in the Add-Ins dialog box, with a friendly name and a description of what it does.

- ✔ **Gain better control over loading.** Add-ins can be opened automatically when Excel starts, regardless of the directory in which they are stored.

- ✔ **Avoid displaying prompts when unloading.** When an add-in is closed, the user never sees the Save change in...? prompt.

Working with Add-Ins

The most efficient way to load and unload add-ins is by choosing Tools⇨ Add-Ins. This command displays the Add-Ins dialog box shown in Figure 22-1. The list box contains the names of all add-ins that Excel knows about. In this list, check marks identify any currently open add-ins. You can open and close add-ins from the Add-Ins dialog box by selecting or deselecting the check boxes.

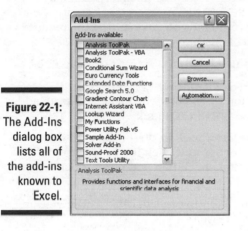

Figure 22-1: The Add-Ins dialog box lists all of the add-ins known to Excel.

You can open most add-in files also by choosing the File⇨Open command. However, you can't close an open add-in by choosing File⇨Close. You can remove the add-in only by exiting and restarting Excel or by writing a macro to close the add-in.

When you open an add-in, you may or may not notice anything different. In many cases, however, the menu changes in some way — Excel displays either a new menu or one or more new items on an existing menu. For example, when opening the Analysis ToolPak add-in gives you a new menu item on the Tools menu: Data Analysis. If the add-in contains only custom worksheet functions, the new functions appears in the Insert Function dialog box.

Add-in Basics

Although you can convert any workbook to an add-in, not all workbooks benefit from this conversion. Workbooks that consist only of worksheets (and no macros) become unusable because the add-ins are hidden; you are unable to access the worksheets.

In fact, the only types of workbooks that benefit from being converted to an add-in are those with macros. For example, a workbook that consists of general-purpose macros (Sub and Function procedures) makes an ideal add-in.

Creating an add-in is simple. Use the following steps to create an add-in from a normal workbook file:

1. **Develop your application and make sure that everything works properly.**

   Don't forget to include a method for executing the macro or macros. You might want to add a new menu item to the Tools menu or create a custom toolbar. See Chapter 20 for details on customizing the menus and Chapter 19 for a discussion of custom toolbars.

2. **Test the application by executing it when a *different* workbook is active.**

   Doing so simulates the application's behavior when it's used as an add-in because an add-in is never the active workbook.

3. **Activate the VBE and select the workbook in the Project window; choose Tools⇨*VBAProject* Properties and click the Protection tab; select the Lock Project for Viewing check box and enter a password (twice); click OK.**

   This step is necessary only if you want to prevent others from viewing or modifying your macros or UserForms.

4. **In Excel, choose File⇨Properties.**

5. **Click the Summary tab.**

6. **Enter a brief descriptive title in the Title field and a longer description in the Comments field. Click OK.**

   Steps 4 through 6 are not required but make the add-in easier to use.

7. **Choose Excel's File⇨Save As.**

8. **In the Save As dialog box, select Microsoft Office Excel add-in (*.xla) from the Save as Type drop-down list.**

9. **Specify the folder that will store the add-in.**

   Excel proposes a folder named AddIns, but you can save the file in any folder you like.

10. **Click Save.**

You've just created an add-in! A copy of your workbook is converted to an add-in and saved with an XLA extension. Your original workbook remains open.

An Add-in Example

In this section I discuss the basic steps involved in creating a useful add-in. The example uses the ChangeCase text conversion utility that I describe in Chapter 16.

The XLS version of this example is available at this book's Web site. You can create an add-in from this workbook.

Setting up the workbook

The workbook consists of one blank worksheet, a VBA module, and a UserForm. In addition, I added code to the ThisWorkbook object that creates a new menu item on the Tools menu.

ThisWorkbook object

The following code, located in the Code window for the ThisWorkbook object, is executed when the workbook (soon to be an add-in) is opened. This procedure creates a new menu item (Change Case of Text) on the Tools menu. (See Chapter 20 for details on working with menus.) This menu item executes the ChangeCase macro, which is listed in the next section.

```
Const MenuItemName = "Change Case of Te&xt..."
Const MenuItemMacro = "ChangeCase"

Private Sub Workbook_Open()
'    Adds a menu item to the Tools menu
     Dim NewItem As CommandBarControl
     Dim Msg As String
'    Delete existing item just in case
     On Error Resume Next
     Application.CommandBars(1) _
         .Controls("Tools").Controls(MenuItemName).Delete

'    Set up error trapping
     On Error GoTo NoCanDo

'    Create the new menu item
     Set NewItem = Application.CommandBars(1) _
         .Controls("Tools").Controls.Add

'    Specify the Caption and OnAction properties
     NewItem.Caption = MenuItemName
     NewItem.OnAction = MenuItemMacro
```

```
'    Add a separator bar before the menu item
     NewItem.BeginGroup = True
     Exit Sub

'    Error handler
NoCanDo:
     Msg = "An error occurred." & vbCrLf
     Msg = Msg & MenuItemName
     Msg = Msg & " was added to the Tools menu."
     MsgBox Msg, vbCritical
End Sub
```

The following procedure is executed before the workbook is closed. This procedure removes the menu item from the Tools menu.

```
Private Sub Workbook_BeforeClose(Cancel As Boolean)
'    Delete the menu item
     On Error Resume Next
     Application.CommandBars(1). _
     Controls("Tools").Controls(MenuItemName).Delete
End Sub
```

Module 1 module

The VBA module contains a short macro named ChangeCase that serves as the entry point. This procedure makes sure that a range is selected. If so, the UserForm is displayed.

```
Sub ChangeCase()
'    Exit if a range is not selected
     If TypeName(Selection) <> "Range" Then Exit Sub
'    Display the dialog box
     UserForm1.Show
End Sub
```

UserForm

Figure 22-2 shows UserForm1. It consists of three OptionButtons, named OptionUpper, OptionLower, and OptionProper. These OptionButtons are inside a Frame control. In addition, the UserForm has a Cancel button (named CancelButton) and an OK button (named OKButton).

The code executed when the Cancel button is clicked shows up next. This procedure simply unloads the UserForm with no action:

```
Private Sub CancelButton_Click()
     Unload UserForm1
End Sub
```

The code executed when the OK button is clicked follows. This code does all
the work:

```
Private Sub OKButton_Click()
    Dim TextCells As Range
    Dim cell As Range

'   Create an object with just text constants
    On Error Resume Next
    Set TextCells = Selection.SpecialCells(xlConstants, _
        xlTextValues)

'   Turn off screen updating
    Application.ScreenUpdating = False

'   Uppercase
    If OptionUpper Then
        For Each cell In TextCells
            cell.Value = UCase(cell.Value)
        Next cell
    End If
'   Lowercase
    If OptionLower Then
        For Each cell In TextCells
            cell.Value = LCase(cell.Value)
        Next cell
    End If
'   Proper case
    If OptionProper Then
        For Each cell In TextCells
            cell.Value = _

            Application.WorksheetFunction.Proper(cell.Value)
        Next cell
    End If

'   Unload the dialog box
    Unload UserForm1
End Sub
```

This version of ChangeCase differs from the version in Chapter 16. For this example, I use the SpecialCells method to create an object variable consisting of only those cells in the selection that contain constants (not formulas) or text. This makes the routine run a bit faster if the selection contains lots of formula cells. See Chapter 14 for more information on this technique.

Testing the workbook

Test the add-in before converting this workbook. To simulate what happens when the workbook is an add-in, you should test the workbook when a different workbook is active. Remember, an add-in is never the active sheet, so testing it when a different workbook is open may help you identify some potential errors. Because this workbook has a Workbook_Open procedure (to add a menu item), save the workbook as an XLS file, close it, and then reopen it to ensure that this procedure is working correctly.

1. **Open a new workbook and enter information into some cells.**

   For testing purposes, enter various types of information, including text, values, and formulas. Or just open an existing workbook and use it for your tests.

2. **Select one or more cells (or entire rows and columns).**

3. **Execute the ChangeCase macro by choosing the new Tools➪Change Case of Text command.**

   I find that this method works just fine.

If the Change Case of Text command doesn't appear on your Tools menu, the most likely reason is that you did not enable macros when you opened the change case.xls workbook. Close the workbook and then reopen it — and make sure that you enable macros.

Adding descriptive information

I recommend entering a description of your add-in, but this isn't required.

1. **Activate the change case.xls workbook.**

2. **Choose the File➪Properties command.**

   The Properties dialog box opens.

3. **Click the Summary tab, as shown in Figure 22-3.**

4. **Enter a title for the add-in in the Title field.**

   This text appears in the Add-Ins dialog box.

5. In the Comments field, enter a description.

This information appears at the bottom of the Add-Ins dialog box when the add-in is selected.

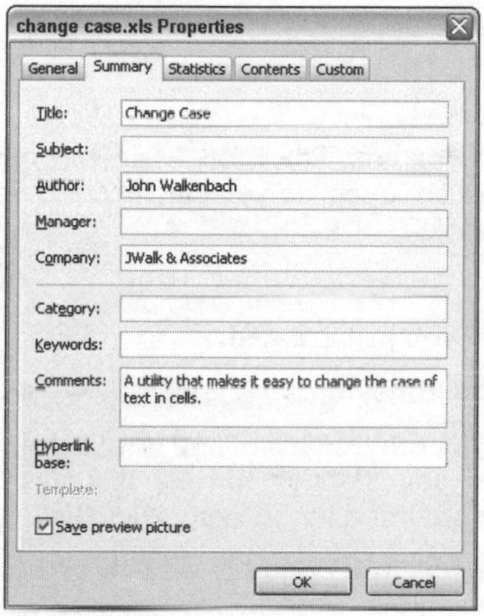

Figure 22-3:
Use the
Properties
dialog box
to enter
descriptive
information
about your
add-in.

Creating the add-in

At this point, you've tested the change case.xls file, and it's working correctly. The next step is to create the add-in:

1. Activate the VBE and select the change case.xls workbook in the Project window.

2. Choose Tools⇨*VBAProject* Properties and click the Protection tab.

3. Select the Lock Project for Viewing check box and enter a password (twice).

4. Click OK.

5. Save the workbook.

6. Reactivate Excel.

7. Activate the change case.xls workbook and choose File⇨Save As.

Excel displays its Save As dialog box.

8. In the Save as Type drop-down, select Microsoft Excel Add-In (*.xla).

9. Click Save.

A new add-in file (with an XLA extension) is created, and the original XLS version remains open.

Opening the add-in

To avoid confusion, close the XLS workbook before opening the add-in created from that workbook.

Open the add-in with these steps:

1. **Choose Tools⇨Add-Ins.**

   Excel displays the Add-Ins dialog box. The Tools⇨Add-Ins command is not available if no workbooks are open, so you may need to open a workbook or create a new workbook.

2. **Click the Browse button.**

3. **Locate and select the add-in you just created.**

4. **Click OK to close the Browse dialog box.**

   After you find your new add-in, the Add-Ins dialog box lists the add-in. As shown in Figure 22-4, the Add-Ins dialog box also displays the descriptive information you provided in the Properties dialog box.

5. **Click OK to close the dialog box and open the add-in.**

   The Tools menu displays the new menu item that executes the ChangeCase macro in the add-in.

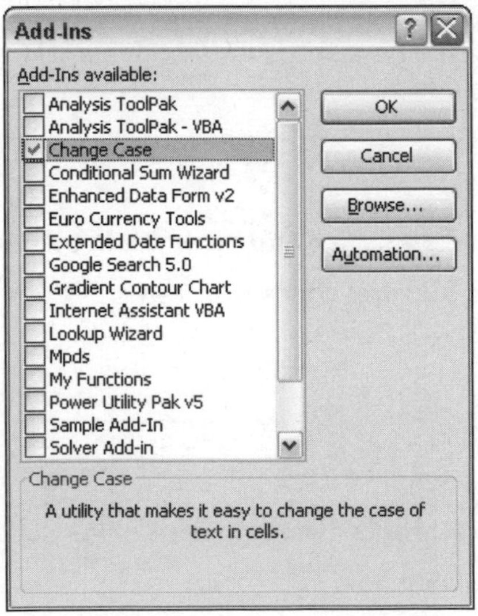

Figure 22-4:
The Add-Ins dialog box has the new add-in selected.

Distributing the add-in

You can distribute this add-in to other Excel users by simply giving them a copy of the XLA file; they don't need the XLS version. When they open the add-in, the new Change Case of Text command appears on the Tools menu. Because you locked the file with a password, your macro code cannot be viewed by others (unless they know the password).

Modifying the add-in

If you want to modify the add-in, you need to unlock it:

1. **Open your XLA file if it's not already open.**
2. **Activate the VBE.**
3. **Double-click the project's name in the Project window.**

   You are prompted for the password.

4. **Enter your password and click OK.**
5. **Make your changes to the code.**
6. **Save the file from the VBE by choosing File⇨Save.**

If you create an add-in that stores information in a worksheet, you must set the workbook's IsAddIn property to False to view the workbook. You do this in the Property window when the ThisWorkbook objects is selected; see Figure 22-5. After you've made your changes, make sure that you set the IsAddIn property back to True before you save the file.

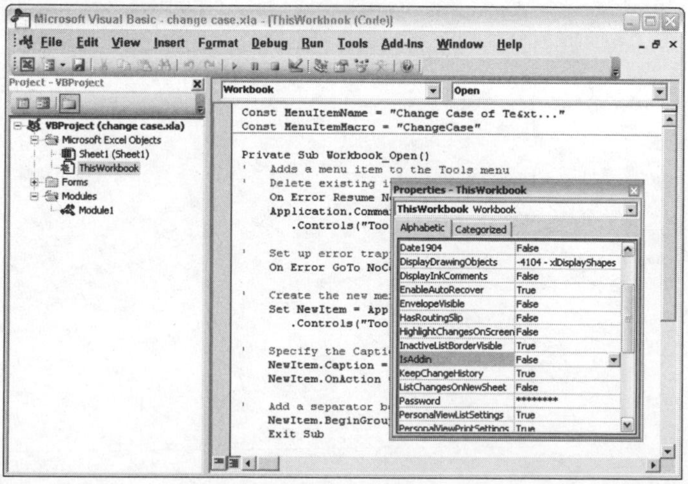

Figure 22-5:
Making an
add-in not
an add-in.

You now know how to work with add-ins and why you might want to create your own add-ins. One example in this chapter shows you the steps for creating an add-in that changes the case of text in selected cells. The best way to discover more about add-ins is by creating some.

Chapter 23

Interacting with Other Office Applications

*I*f you use Excel, you likely use other applications that comprise Microsoft Office. Just about everyone uses Word, and you're probably familiar with PowerPoint or Access.

In this chapter I present some simple examples that demonstrate how to use Excel VBA to interact with other Microsoft Office applications.

Starting Another Application from Excel

Starting another application from Excel is often useful. For example, you might want to launch another Microsoft Office application or even a DOS batch file from an Excel VBA macro.

Using the VBA Shell function

The VBA Shell function makes launching another program relatively easy. The following example starts the Windows Calculator program, which is named CALC.EXE:

```
      On Error Resume Next
      AppActivate "Calculator"
      If Err <> 0 Then
          Err = 0
          TaskID = Shell(Program, 1)
          If Err <> 0 Then MsgBox "Can't start " & Program
      End If
End Sub
```

This modified procedure uses an AppActivate statement to activate the application (Windows Calculator in this case) if it's already running. The argument for AppActivate is the Caption of the application's title bar. If the AppActivate statement generates an error, it means the Calculator isn't running. If it's not running, the routine starts the application using the Shell function.

Activating a Microsoft Office application

If the application that you want to start is one of several Microsoft applications, use the Application object's ActivateMicrosoftApp method. For example, the following procedure starts Word:

```
Sub StartWord()
    Application.ActivateMicrosoftApp xlMicrosoftWord
End Sub
```

If Word is already running when the preceding procedure is executed, it is activated. Other constants are available for this method:

- xlMicrosoftPowerPoint (PowerPoint)
- xlMicrosoftMail (Outlook)
- xlMicrosoftAccess (Access)
- xlMicrosoftFoxPro (FoxPro)
- xlMicrosoftProject (Project)
- xlMicrosoftSchedulePlus (SchedulePlus)

Using Automation in Excel

You can write an Excel macro to control other applications, such as Microsoft Word. More accurately, Excel macros control the most important component of Word: the so-called automation server. In such circumstances, Excel is called the *client application,* and Word is the *server application.*

```
Sub StartCalculator()
    Dim Program As String
    Dim TaskID As Double
    On Error Resume Next
    Program = "calc.exe"
    TaskID = Shell(Program, 1)
    If Err <> 0 Then
        MsgBox "Can't start " & Program
    End If
End Sub
```

Figure 23-1 shows the Windows calculator displayed as a result of running this procedure.

Figure 23-1:
The
Windows
Calculator
program.

The Shell function returns a task identification number for the application. You can use this number later to activate the task. The second argument for the Shell function determines how the application is displayed. (1 is the code for a normal-size window, with the focus.) Refer to the Help system for other argument values.

If the Shell function is unsuccessful, it generates an error. Therefore, this procedure uses an On Error statement to display a message if the executable file cannot be found or if some other error occurs.

But what if the Calculator program is already running? The StartCalculator procedure simply opens another instance of the program. In most cases, you want to activate the existing instance. The following modified code solves this problem:

```
Public TaskID

Sub StartCalculator2()
    Dim Program As String
    Dim TaskID As Double
    Program = "calc.exe"
```

The concept behind automation is quite appealing. A developer who needs to generate a chart, for example, can reach into another application's grab bag of objects, fetch a Chart object, and then manipulate its properties and use its methods. Automation, in a sense, blurs the boundaries between applications. For example, using automation, an end user might be working with an Access object inside Excel and not even realize it.

Some applications, such as Excel, can function as either a client application or a server application. Other applications can function only as client applications or only as server applications.

In the following sections, I demonstrate how to use VBA to access and manipulate the objects exposed by other applications. The examples use Microsoft Word, but the concepts apply to any application that exposes its objects for automation.

Getting Word's version number

The following example demonstrates how to create a Word object to provide access to the objects in Word's object model. This procedure creates the object, displays the version number, closes the Word application, and then destroys the object, freeing up the memory that it used:

```
Sub GetWordVersion()
    Dim WordApp As Object
    Set WordApp = CreateObject("Word.Application")
    MsgBox WordApp.Version
    WordApp.Quit
    Set WordApp = Nothing
End Sub
```

The Word object that's created in this procedure is invisible. If you want to see the object while it's being manipulated, set its Visible property to True, as follows:

```
WordApp.Visible = True
```

Most of the automation examples in this chapter use late binding as opposed to early binding. What's the difference? When you use *early binding,* you must establish a reference to a version-specific object library, using Tools⇨ References in the VBE. When you use *late binding,* setting that reference is not required. Both approaches have pros and cons.

Controlling Word from Excel

The example in Figure 23-2 demonstrates an automation session by using Word. The MakeMemos procedure creates three customized memos in Word and then saves each memo to a separate file. The information used to create the memos is stored in a worksheet.

Figure 23-2:
Word automatically generates three memos based on this Excel data.

	A	B	C	D	E
1	Region1	145	$134,555		
2	Region2	122	$127,883		Create Word Memos Using Data on This Worksheet
3	Region3	203	$288,323		
4					
5					
6			*Message:*		The monthly sales data for your region is listed below. This information was obtained from the central database. Please call if you have any questions.
7					
8					
9					
10					

make memos.xls — Sheet1

The code for the MakeMemos procedure is too lengthy to list here, but you can go to this book's Web site to check it out.

The MakeMemos procedure starts by creating an object called WordApp. The routine cycles through the three rows of data in Sheet1 and uses Word's properties and methods to create each memo and save it to disk. A range named Message (in cell E6) contains the text used in the memo. All of the action occurs behind the scenes: Word is not visible. Figure 23-3 shows a document created by the MakeMemos procedure.

Controlling Excel from Word

As you might expect, you can also control Excel from another application (such as another programming language or a Word VBA procedure). For example, you might want to perform some calculations in Excel and return the result to a Word document.

You can create any of the following Excel objects with the adjacent functions:

- ✔ **Application object:** CreateObject("Excel.Application")
- ✔ **Workbook object:** CreateObject("Excel.Sheet")
- ✔ **Chart object:** CreateObject("Excel.Chart")

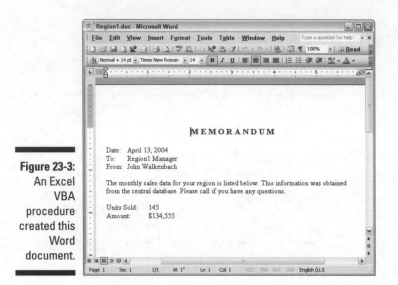

Figure 23-3:
An Excel
VBA
procedure
created this
Word
document.

The example described in this section is a Word macro that creates an Excel Workbook object (whose moniker is Excel.Sheet) from an existing workbook named projections.xls. The macro prompts the user for two values and then creates a data table and chart, which are stored in the Word document.

The initial workbook is shown in Figure 23-4. The MakeExcelChart procedure prompts the user for two values and inserts the values into the worksheet.

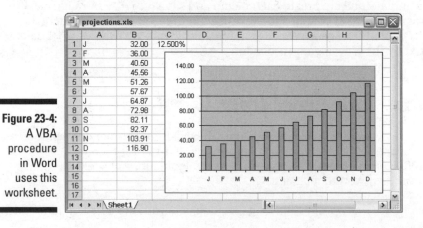

Figure 23-4:
A VBA
procedure
in Word
uses this
worksheet.

Recalculating the worksheet updates a chart. The data and the chart are then copied from the Excel object and pasted into a new document. The results are shown in Figure 23-5.

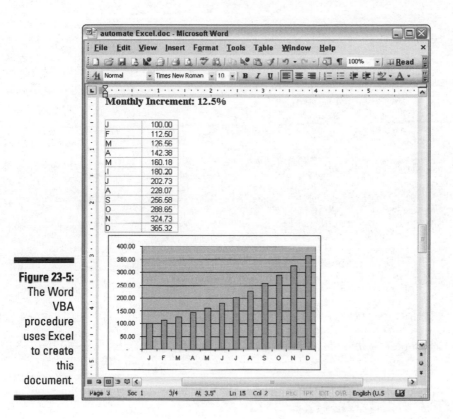

Figure 23-5:
The Word
VBA
procedure
uses Excel
to create
this
document.

The code for the MakeExcelChart procedure follows:

```
Sub MakeExcelChart()
    Dim XLSheet As Object
    Dim StartVal, PctChange
    Dim Wbook As String

'   Create a new document
    Documents.Add

'   Prompt for values
    StartVal = InputBox("Starting Value?")
    PctChange = InputBox("Percent Change?")

'   Create Sheet object
    Wbook = ThisDocument.Path & "\projections.xls"
    Set XLSheet = GetObject(Wbook, "Excel.Sheet").ActiveSheet

'   Put values in sheet
    XLSheet.Range("StartingValue") = StartVal
    XLSheet.Range("PctChange") = PctChange
    XLSheet.Calculate
```

```
'   Insert page heading
    Selection.Font.Size = 14
    Selection.Font.Bold = True
    Selection.TypeText "Monthly Increment: " & _
       Format(PctChange, "0.0%")
    Selection.TypeParagraph
    Selection.TypeParagraph

'   Copy data from sheet & paste to document
    XLSheet.Range("data").Copy
    Selection.Paste

'   Copy chart and paste to document
    XLSheet.ChartObjects(1).Copy
    Selection.PasteSpecial _
        Link:=False, _
        DataType:=wdPasteMetafilePicture, _
        Placement:=wdInLine, DisplayAsIcon:=False

'   Kill the object
    Set XLSheet = Nothing
End Sub
```

This example is available at the book's Web site.

Sending Personalized E-mail Using Outlook

The example in this section demonstrates automation with Microsoft Outlook. The code creates personalized e-mail messages by using data stored in an Excel worksheet.

Figure 23-6 shows a worksheet that contains data used in e-mail messages: name, e-mail address, and bonus amount. This procedure loops through the rows in the worksheet, retrieves the data, and creates an individualized message (stored in the Msg variable).

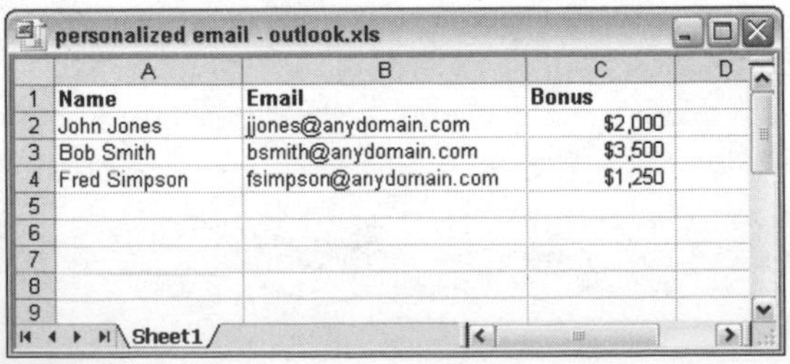

Figure 23-6:
This information is used in the Outlook Express e-mail messages.

	A	B	C	D
	personalized email - outlook.xls			
1	Name	Email	Bonus	
2	John Jones	jjones@anydomain.com	$2,000	
3	Bob Smith	bsmith@anydomain.com	$3,500	
4	Fred Simpson	fsimpson@anydomain.com	$1,250	
5				
6				
7				
8				
9				

Sheet1

```
Sub SendEmail()
  Dim OutlookApp As Object
  Dim MItem As Object
  Dim cell As Range
  Dim Subj As String
  Dim EmailAddr As String
  Dim Recipient As String
  Dim Bonus As String
  Dim Msg As String

  'Create Outlook object
  Set OutlookApp = CreateObject("Outlook.Application")

  'Loop through the rows
  For Each cell In _
    Columns("B").Cells.SpecialCells(xlCellTypeConstants)
    If cell.Value Like "*@*" Then
      'Get the data
      Subj = "Your Annual Bonus"
      Recipient = cell.Offset(0, -1).Value
      EmailAddr = cell.Value
      Bonus = Format(cell.Offset(0, 1).Value, "$0,000.")

      'Compose message
      Msg = "Dear " & Recipient & vbCrLf & vbCrLf
      Msg = Msg & "I am pleased to inform you that "
      Msg = Msg & "your annual bonus is "
      Msg = Msg & Bonus & vbCrLf & vbCrLf
      Msg = Msg & "William Rose" & vbCrLf
      Msg = Msg & "President"

      'Create Mail Item and send it
      Set MItem = OutlookApp.CreateItem(0)
      With MItem
        .To = EmailAddr
        .Subject = Subj
        .Body = Msg
        .Display
      End With
    End If
  Next
End Sub
```

This example uses the Display method, which simply displays the email messages. To actually send the messages, use the Send method instead.

Notice that two objects are involved: Outlook and MailItem. The Outlook object is created with this statement:

```
Set OutlookApp = CreateObject("Outlook.Application")
```

The MailItem object is created with this statement:

```
Set MItem = OutlookApp.CreateItem(0)
```

The code sets the To, Subject, and Body properties, and then uses the Send method to send each message. Figure 23-7 shows one of the e-mails created by Excel.

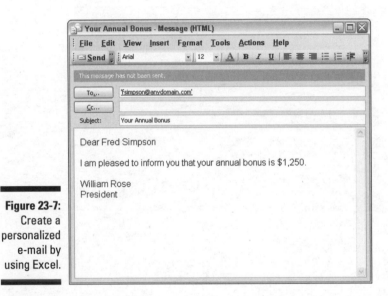

Figure 23-7:
Create a
personalized
e-mail by
using Excel.

This example is available on this book's Web site. To use this example you must have Microsoft Outlook installed.

Working with ADO

ActiveX Data Objects (ADO) is an object model that enables you to access data stored in a variety of database formats. This allows you to use a single object model for all your databases. In this section I present a simple example that uses ADO to retrieve data from an Access database.

ADO programming is a very complex topic. If you need to access external data in your Excel application, invest in one or more books that cover this topic in detail. This example is here so you can get a feel for how it works.

The following example retrieves data from an Access database named budget.mdb. This database contains one table named Budget, which has seven fields. This example retrieves the data in which the Item field contains the text "Lease" and the Division field contains the text "N. America." The qualifying data is stored in a Recordset object, and the data is then transferred to a worksheet (see Figure 23-8).

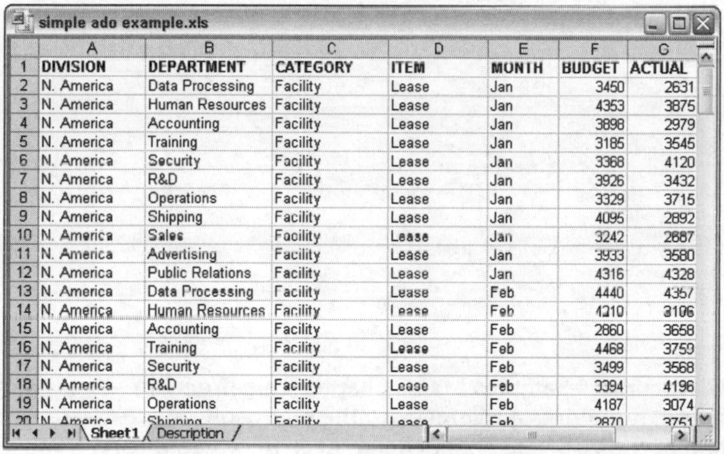

simple ado example.xls

	A	B	C	D	E	F	G
1	DIVISION	DEPARTMENT	CATEGORY	ITEM	MONTH	BUDGET	ACTUAL
2	N. America	Data Processing	Facility	Lease	Jan	3450	2631
3	N. America	Human Resources	Facility	Lease	Jan	4353	3875
4	N. America	Accounting	Facility	Lease	Jan	3898	2979
5	N. America	Training	Facility	Lease	Jan	3185	3545
6	N. America	Security	Facility	Lease	Jan	3368	4120
7	N. America	R&D	Facility	Lease	Jan	3926	3432
8	N. America	Operations	Facility	Lease	Jan	3329	3715
9	N. America	Shipping	Facility	Lease	Jan	4095	2892
10	N. America	Sales	Facility	Lease	Jan	3242	2687
11	N. America	Advertising	Facility	Lease	Jan	3933	3580
12	N. America	Public Relations	Facility	Lease	Jan	4316	4328
13	N. America	Data Processing	Facility	Lease	Feb	4440	4357
14	N. America	Human Resources	Facility	Lease	Feb	4210	3106
15	N. America	Accounting	Facility	Lease	Feb	2860	3658
16	N. America	Training	Facility	Lease	Feb	4468	3759
17	N. America	Security	Facility	Lease	Feb	3499	3568
18	N. America	R&D	Facility	Lease	Feb	3394	4196
19	N. America	Operations	Facility	Lease	Feb	4187	3074
20	N. America	Shipping	Facility	Lease	Feb	2870	3751

Sheet1 / Description

Figure 23-8: Retrieve data from an Access database.

```
Sub ADO_Demo()
'   This demo requires a reference to
'   the Microsoft ActiveX Data Objects 2.x Library

    Dim DBFullName As String
    Dim Cnct As String, Src As String
    Dim Connection As ADODB.Connection
    Dim Recordset As ADODB.Recordset
    Dim Col As Integer

    Cells.Clear

'   Database information
    DBFullName = ThisWorkbook.Path & "\budget.mdb"

'   Open the connection
    Set Connection = New ADODB.Connection
    Cnct = "Provider=Microsoft.Jet.OLEDB.4.0; "
    Cnct = Cnct & "Data Source=" & DBFullName & ";"
    Connection.Open ConnectionString:=Cnct
```

```
'    Create RecordSet
     Set Recordset = New ADODB.Recordset
     With Recordset
'        Filter
         Src = "SELECT * FROM Budget WHERE Item = 'Lease' "
         Src = Src & "and Division = 'N. America'"
         .Open Source:=Src, ActiveConnection:=Connection

'        Write the field names
         For Col = 0 To Recordset.Fields.Count - 1
            Range("A1").Offset(0, Col).Value = _
               Recordset.Fields(Col).Name
         Next

'        Write the recordset
         Range("A1").Offset(1, 0).CopyFromRecordset Recordset
     End With
     Set Recordset = Nothing
     Connection.Close
     Set Connection = Nothing
End Sub
```

Unlike the other examples in this chapter, this procedure uses early binding. Therefore, it requires a reference to the Microsoft ActiveX Data Objects 2.0 Library. In the VBE, use Tools⇨References to create this reference.

This example, along with the Access database, is available from this book's Web site.

Part VII
The Part of Tens

The 5th Wave   By Rich Tennant

"I'm sorry, but 'Arf', 'Bark', and 'Woof' are already registered domain names. How about 'Oink', 'Quack', or 'Moo'?"

In this part . . .

For reasons that are historical — as well as useful — all the books in the *For Dummies* series have chapters with lists in them. The next two chapters contain my own "ten" lists, which deal with frequently asked questions and other Excel resources.

Chapter 24

Ten VBA Questions (And Answers)

• •

In This Chapter

▶ Storing worksheet function procedures

▶ Limitation of the macro recorder

▶ Speeding up your VBA code

▶ Declaring variables explicitly

▶ Using the VBA line continuation character

• •

*1*n this chapter, I answer the questions most frequently asked about VBA.

The Top Ten Questions about VBA

I created a custom VBA function. When I try to use it in a formula, the formula displays #NAME?. What's wrong?

You probably have your function code in the wrong location. VBA code for worksheet functions must be in a standard VBA module — not in a module for a sheet or in ThisWorkbook.

Can I use the VBA macro recorder to record all of my macros?

No. Normally you use it only to record simple macros or as a starting point for a more complex macro. It cannot record macros that use variables, looping, or any other type of program flow constructs. In addition, you cannot record a Function procedure in the VBA macro recorder.

How can I prevent others from viewing my VBA code?

1. **In the VBE, choose Tools⇨VBA Project Properties.**

2. **In the dialog box, click the Protection tab and select Lock Project for Viewing.**

3. **Enter a password (twice) and click OK.**

Doing so prevents casual users from viewing your code, but it is certainly not 100 percent secure. Password-cracking utilities exist.

What's the VBA code for increasing the number of rows and columns in a worksheet?

No such code exists. The number of rows and columns is fixed and cannot be changed. No way.

When I refer to a worksheet in my VBA code, I get a "subscript out of range" error. I'm not using any subscripts. What gives?

This error occurs if you attempt to access an element in a collection that doesn't exist. For example, this statement generates the error if the active workbook doesn't contain a sheet named MySheet:

```
Set X = ActiveWorkbook.Sheets("MySheet")
```

Is there a VBA command that selects a range from the active cell to the last entry in a column or a row? (In other words, how can a macro accomplish the same thing as Ctrl+Shift+↓ or Ctrl+Shift+ →?)

Here's the VBA equivalent for Ctrl+Shift+↓:

```
Range(ActiveCell, ActiveCell.End(xlDown)).Select
```

For the other directions, use the constants xlToLeft, xlToRight, or xlUp instead of xlDown.

How can I make my VBA code run as fast as possible?

Here are a few tips:

- ✔ Make sure to declare all your variables as a specific data type. (Use Option Explicit in each module's Declarations section to force yourself to declare all variables.)

- ✔ If you reference an object (such as a range) more than once, create an object variable using the Set keyword.

- ✔ Use the With-End With construct whenever possible.

- ✔ If your macro writes data to a worksheet and you have lots of complex formulas, set the calculation mode to Manual while the macro runs.

- ✔ If your macro writes information to a worksheet, turn off screen updating by using Application.ScreenUpdating = False.

How can I display multiline messages in a message box?

The easiest way is to build your message in a string variable, using the vbNewLine constant to indicate where you want your line breaks to occur. The following is a quick example:

```
Msg = "You selected the following:" & vbNewLine
Msg = Msg & UserAns
MsgBox Msg
```

I've deleted all my macros, but Excel still asks me to enable macros when I open the workbook.

Empty modules in your workbook will cause this message. If you have empty module, remove them by right clicking and choosing Remove Module. Also, check the ThisWorkbook and Sheet modules to make sure these modules don't contain any macros.

Why can't I get the VBA line-continuation character (underscore) to work?

The line continuation sequence is actually two characters: a space followed by an underscore. Make sure to use both characters and press Enter after the underscore.

Chapter 25

(Almost) Ten Excel Resources

• •

This book is only an introduction to Excel VBA programming. If you hunger for more information, you can feed on the list of additional resources I've compiled here. You can discover new techniques, communicate with other Excel users, download useful files, ask questions, access the extensive Microsoft Knowledge Base, and lots more.

Several of these resources are online services or Internet resources, which tend to change frequently. The descriptions are accurate at the time I'm writing this, but I can't guarantee that this information will remain current.

The VBA Help System

I hope you've already discovered VBA's Help system. I find this reference source particularly useful for identifying objects, properties, and methods. It's readily available, it's free, and (for the most part) it's accurate. So use it.

Microsoft Product Support

Microsoft offers a wide variety of technical support options (some for free, others for a fee). To access Microsoft's support services (including the useful Knowledge Base), go here:

    http://support.microsoft.com

And don't forget about Microsoft's Office site, which has lots of material related to Excel:

    http://office.microsoft.com

Internet Newsgroups

Microsoft's newsgroups are perhaps the best place to go if you have a question. You can find hundreds of newsgroups devoted to Microsoft products — including a dozen or so newsgroups just for Excel. The best way to access these newsgroups is by using special newsreader software. (Microsoft Outlook Express is a good choice.) At msnews.microsoft.com, set your newsreader software to access the news server.

The more popular English-language, Excel-related newsgroups are listed here:

```
microsoft.public.excel.charting

microsoft.public.excel.misc

microsoft.public.excel.printing

microsoft.public.excel.programming

microsoft.public.excel.setup

microsoft.public.excel.worksheet.functions
```

If you prefer to access the newsgroups using your Web browser, you have two choices:

```
http://support.microsoft.com/newsgroups/

http://groups.google.com
```

Your question has probably already been answered. To search old newsgroup messages by keyword, point your Web browser to

```
http://groups.google.com
```

Internet Web Sites

Several Web sites contain Excel-related material. A good place to start your Web surfing is my very own site, which is named The Spreadsheet Page. After you get there, you can check out my material and then visit my links pages, which lead you to hundreds of other Excel-related sites. The URL for my site follows:

```
www.j-walk.com/ss/
```

Excel Blogs

You can find literally millions of blogs (short for *weblogs*) on the Web. A *blog* is basically a frequently updated diary. A few blogs are devoted exclusively to Excel. One of them is written by Dick Kusleika, who happens to be the technical editor for this book. You can read Dick's Daily Dose of Excel here:

```
www.dicks-blog.com/
```

Google

When I have a question about any topic (including Excel programming), my first line of attack is Google — currently the world's most popular search site.

```
www.google.com
```

Enter a few key search terms and see what Google finds. I get an answer about 90 percent of the time. If that fails, then I search the newsgroups (describe earlier) using this URL:

```
http://groups.google.com
```

Local User Groups

Many larger communities and universities have an Excel user group that meets periodically. If you can find a user group in your area, check it out. These groups are often an excellent source for contacts and sharing ideas.

My Other Book

Sorry, but I couldn't resist the opportunity for a blatant plug. To take VBA programming to the next level, check out my *Microsoft Excel 2003 Power Programming with VBA* (published by Wiley).

Index